Get the eBook FREE!

(PDF, ePub, Kindle, and liveBook all included)

We believe that once you buy a book from us, you should be able to read it in any format we have available. To get electronic versions of this book at no additional cost to you, purchase and then register this book at the Manning website.

Go to https://www.manning.com/freebook and follow the instructions to complete your pBook registration.

That's it!
Thanks from Manning!

Rust Servers, Services, and Apps

Rust Servers, Services, and Apps

PRABHU ESHWARLA

MANNING
SHELTER ISLAND

For online information and ordering of this and other Manning books, please visit
www.manning.com. The publisher offers discounts on this book when ordered in quantity.
For more information, please contact

Special Sales Department
Manning Publications Co.
20 Baldwin Road
PO Box 761
Shelter Island, NY 11964
Email: orders@manning.com

Manning Publications Co.
20 Baldwin Road
PO Box 761
Shelter Island, NY 11964

Development editor:	Elesha Hyde
Technical development editor:	Alain Couniot
Review editor:	Aleksandar Dragosavljevic
Production editor:	Keri Hales
Copy editor:	Andy Carroll
Proofreader:	Melody Dolab
Technical proofreader:	Jerry Kuch
Typesetter and cover designer:	Marija Tudor

ISBN 9781617298608
Printed in the United States of America

brief contents

contents

preface

Building high-performance network services remains a challenge with any programming language. Rust has several unique features that significantly lower the challenge threshold.

Indeed, Rust has been designed from the very beginning to be a language for highly concurrent and safe systems. Several programming languages (such as C, C++, Go, Java, JavaScript, and Python) are used to develop highly performant and reliable network services that can run on a single node or as part of a multi-node distributed system, either in on-premises data centers or in the cloud, but several points make Rust an attractive alternative:

- A small footprint (due to full control over memory and CPU usage)
- Security and reliability (due to memory and data-race safety, enforced by the compiler)
- Low latency (there is no garbage collector)
- Modern language features

This book teaches the various tools, techniques, and technologies that can be used to build efficient and reliable web services and applications using Rust. It also provides a hands-on introduction to network services and web applications in Rust, all the way from basic single-node, single-threaded servers built from standard library primitives to advanced multithreaded, asynchronous distributed servers, cutting across different layers of the protocol stack. You will learn about

- Networking primitives in the Rust standard library
- Basic HTTP services
- REST API servers backed by a relational database

- Distributed servers with P2P networking
- Highly concurrent asynchronous servers

This book is designed to teach you to develop web services and applications in Rust using a tutorial-like approach by taking a single example and progressively enhancing it over multiple iterations as you progress through the chapters. I hope you will find the book interesting and the approach practical enough to apply directly to your area of work.

acknowledgments

Writing a book of this nature in a fast-paced, deep-tech area is a significant commitment of time and effort.

I would first like to thank my family, who sacrificed a ton of time to allow me to complete this book. There aren't enough words to say how grateful I am to them.

I would like to thank the many people at Manning who have assisted in various ways to help me develop the book in a highly iterative and consultative manner. I want to thank Mike Stephens for giving me this opportunity, as well as the various development editors, in particular Elesha Hyde for her remarkable support, guidance, and patience in helping take the book to the finish line, tackling numerous challenges along the way. Many thanks also go to the production staff for creating this book in its final form. Last, but not least, my sincere gratitude to Alain Couniot, technical development editor, without whom this book simply would not have been completed. Thanks, Alain, for patiently and diligently reviewing the chapters, upgrading the code, and elevating the technical quality and relevance of the content for the readers. You rock!

Finally, I would also like to thank all the reviewers who provided valuable feedback on the manuscript: Adam Wendell, Alessandro Campeis, Alex Lucas, Bojan Djurkovic, Casey Burnett, Clifford Thurber, Dan Sheikh, David Paccoud, Gustavo Gomes, Hari Khalsa, Helmut Reiterer, Jerome Meyer, Josh Sandeman, Kent R. Spillner, Marcos Oliveira, Matthew Krasnick, Michal Rutka, Pethuru Raj Chelliah, Richard Vaughan, Slavomir Furman, Stephane Negri, Tim van Deurzen, Troi Eisler, Viacheslav Koryagin, William Wheeler, and Yves Dorfsman. Your suggestions were instrumental in making this book even better. My gratitude also goes to the MEAP readers who contributed on the liveBook forum with interesting questions and opinions and spotted the occasional typo.

about this book

This book is not a reference guide; rather, it is meant as an introduction and should serve as an inspiring guide to the breadth of network services that can be developed in Rust. It takes the form of a hands-on tutorial in order to maximize learning and retention.

Who should read this book

This book is designed primarily for backend software engineers involved or interested in server-side, web backend, and API development; distributed systems engineers who wish to explore Rust as an alternative to Go, Java, or C++; and software engineers working on low-latency servers and applications in areas such as machine learning, artificial intelligence, the Internet of Things, image/video/audio processing, and backends for real-time systems.

To get the most from this book, you should have both backend development experience and some familiarity with Rust. Specifically, as a backend developer, you should have proficiency in web service concepts including HTTP, JSON, database access with ORM, and API development in any high-level language (e.g., Java, JavaScript, Python, C#, Go, or Ruby). As an advanced beginner or intermediate-level Rust programmer, you should understand how to replicate and modify open source tutorials and repositories and be familiar with the following aspects of Rust:

- Rust primitives (data types), user-defined data structures (structs, enums), functions, expressions, and control loops (if, for, and while loops)
- Immutability, ownership, references, and borrowing
- Error handling with Result and option structures
- Basic functional constructs in Rust

- The Rust toolchain, including Cargo for build and dependency management and code formatting, documentation, and automated testing tools

Please see "Other online resources" later in this section for recommendations for refreshing or increasing your Rust knowledge.

How this book is organized: A road map

This book is organized as a series of practical projects, each dealing with a specific type of networking service that can be developed in Rust. You will learn by examining the code and by coding along. The relevant theory is explained along the way within the context of these projects. You will also be encouraged to try some suggested coding exercises.

This book contains 12 chapters divided among three parts. Part 1 sets the scene by introducing the basic concepts of a web application and laying down the foundations for the following sections. We will develop a web application backend of increasing sophistication, finally reaching a stage close to production readiness. Part 1 consists of the following chapters:

- Chapter 1 introduces key concepts, such as distributed architectures and web applications. It also introduces the application that we will develop in this book. Finally, it summarizes Rust's strengths and provides some hints as to when to use and not to use Rust.
- Chapter 2 is a warm-up chapter for the rest of the book. We will develop a few TCP-based components to get acquainted with Rust's capabilities in this domain.
- Chapter 3 shows how to build RESTful web services using Rust and some well-chosen crates among the rich ecosystem that already exists (and keeps growing). It also explains what application state is and how to manage it.
- Chapter 4 addresses the need to persist data in a database. We will use a simple but efficient crate that interacts with SQL databases.
- Chapter 5 tackles the important aspect of dealing with unforeseen circumstances upon invoking the web services we have developed so far.
- Chapter 6 shows how easy and safe it is to refactor code when developing with Rust as our web service API gets more powerful and sophisticated.

Part 2 deals with the other part of the web application, namely its frontend, with its graphical user interface (GUI). In this book, I have opted for a simple approach that relies on server-side rendering instead of sophisticated web frameworks that run in the browser. This part consists of three chapters:

- Chapter 7 introduces the chosen server-side rendering framework and shows how to prompt the user for input and how to deal with lists of items. It also shows how to interact with the backend web service developed in the previous part.

- Chapter 8 focuses on the templating engine used on the server side. It shows how to support user registration through a few forms.
- Chapter 9 addresses more advanced web application topics, such as user authentication, routing, and effectively using RESTful web services for maintaining data in a CRUD (create, read, update, delete) fashion.

Part 3 covers three advanced topics that are not directly related to the web service and web app we have built so far, but that are important for anyone interested in building complex Rust servers and preparing them for production deployment:

- Chapter 10 introduces asynchronous programming and how Rust supports this programming paradigm. Then, async programming is illustrated with a few simple examples.
- Chapter 11 shows the power of Rust for the development of peer-to-peer (P2P) applications using Rust and a few well-chosen crates.
- Chapter 12 demonstrates the preparation and packaging of our web application into a Docker image that can then be deployed in a variety of environments (from a local workstation to the cloud).

About the code

The source code for this book is available on GitHub: https://github.com/pesh war9/rust-servers-services-apps. This repository is structured by book chapter. Generally, the provided code for each chapter corresponds to the final stage of the code for the chapter. You are invited to code along, starting with the code in its state at the end of the previous chapter and letting it evolve incrementally as described in each chapter. In the case of a problem, the source code from GitHub should show you what went wrong or at least provide a good basis to resume your development.

Setting up the environment should be straightforward for anybody who has already developed a bit in Rust: all that is required is the standard Rust toolchain and a good IDE (integrated development environment), such as VS Code, with some Rust support extensions (the Rust Extension Pack is recommended; Rust Syntax and Rust Doc Viewer are nice additions too). To benefit the most from GitHub and version control, Git should also be installed, but this is not mandatory as you can also download the source code as a zip archive from GitHub.

This book contains many examples of source code both in numbered listings and in-line with normal text. In both cases, source code is formatted in a `fixed-width font` `like this` to separate it from ordinary text.

In many cases, the original source code has been reformatted; we've added line breaks and reworked indentation to accommodate the available page space in the book. In rare cases, even this was not enough, and listings include line-continuation markers (➥). Additionally, comments in the source code have often been removed from the listings when the code is described in the text. Code annotations accompany many of the listings, highlighting important concepts.

You can get executable snippets of code from the liveBook (online) version of this book at https://livebook.manning.com/book/rust-servers-services-and-apps. The complete code for the examples in the book is available for download from the Manning website at https://www.manning.com/books/rust-servers-services-and-apps and from GitHub at https://github.com/peshwar9/rust-servers-services-apps.

liveBook discussion forum

Purchase of *Rust Servers, Services, and Apps* includes free access to liveBook, Manning's online reading platform. Using liveBook's exclusive discussion features, you can attach comments to the book globally or to specific sections or paragraphs. It's a snap to make notes for yourself, ask and answer technical questions, and receive help from the author and other users. To access the forum, go to https://livebook.manning.com/book/rust -servers-services-and-apps/discussion. You can also learn more about Manning's forums and the rules of conduct at https://livebook.manning.com/discussion.

Manning's commitment to our readers is to provide a venue where a meaningful dialogue between individual readers and between readers and the author can take place. It is not a commitment to any specific amount of participation on the part of the author, whose contribution to the forum remains voluntary (and unpaid). We suggest you try asking the author some challenging questions lest his interest stray! The forum and the archives of previous discussions will be accessible from the publisher's website as long as the book is in print.

Other online resources

Rust as a programming language is supported through several excellent online resources, managed by the Rust creators, as well as a number of independent resources, such as on Medium. Here are some recommended resources:

- *The Rust Book*—The official guide from the developers of Rust (www.rust -lang.org/learn). This online book features a section on writing network servers, but it is very basic.
- *Rust by Example*—A companion to *The Rust Book* (https://doc.rust-lang.org/rust -by-example/index.html).
- *The Cargo Book*—Another book from the official Rust language site, devoted to the Cargo package manager (https://doc.rust-lang.org/cargo/index.html).
- The Rust Users Forum (https://users.rust-lang.org/)
- Medium Rust articles (https://medium.com/tag/rust)

about the author

PRABHU ESHWARLA is currently the CTO of a startup building a layer-1 blockchain, engineered using Rust. Prabhu became deeply interested in Rust as a programming language and has been actively learning and working on it since July 2019. He has previously held several software engineering and tech leadership roles at Hewlett Packard.

about the cover illustration

The figure on the cover of *Rust Servers, Services, and Apps* is "Homme Toungouse," or "Tungus Man," taken from a collection by Jacques Grasset de Saint-Sauveur, published in 1788. Each illustration is finely drawn and colored by hand.

In those days, it was easy to identify where people lived and what their trade or station in life was just by their dress. Manning celebrates the inventiveness and initiative of the computer business with book covers based on the rich diversity of regional culture centuries ago, brought back to life by pictures from collections such as this one.

Part 1

Web servers and services

Rust is a great programming language that is trending very positively nowadays. It was initially advertised as a systems programming language, along with other famous languages like C or Go(lang). Indeed, it is gradually finding its way into the Linux kernel: it is currently confined to drivers and modules, but its intrinsic qualities—mainly expressiveness, memory safety, and performance—will certainly open doors to more crucial parts of the operating system. At a slower pace, Rust is also making inroads into the still-confidential realm of WebAssembly (WASM), in the browser or in the serverless cloud.

Just like with Go, innovative developers have shown that Rust's applicability goes beyond systems programming and that it can be used, for example, to develop efficient web application backends supported by databases.

In this first part of the book, we will develop a simple yet representative web application using REST web services, backed by a relational database. We won't address the UI aspects yet; those will be handled in the second part of the book. In this part of the book, we will build the foundations for our web application, thinking big but starting small. We will then address increasingly specialized topics, such as database persistence, error handling, and API maintenance and refactoring.

After completing this part, you will be able to set up and develop robust application backends, complete with routing and error handling, using Rust and a handful of field-proven crates. You will then be ready to tackle part 2.

Why Rust for web applications?

This chapter covers

- An introduction to modern web applications
- Choosing Rust for web applications
- Visualizing the example application

Connected web applications that work over the internet form the backbone of modern businesses and human digital lives. As individuals, we use consumer-focused apps for social networking and communications, for e-commerce purchases, for travel bookings, to make payments and manage finances, for education, and to entertain ourselves, to name just a few. Likewise, business-focused applications are used across practically all functions and processes in an enterprise.

Today's web applications are mind-bogglingly complex distributed systems. Users of these applications interact through web or mobile frontend user interfaces. But users rarely see the complex environment of backend services and software infrastructure components that respond to the user requests made through an app's sleek user interfaces. Popular consumer apps have thousands of backend services and servers distributed in data centers around the globe. Each feature of an app may be executed on a different server, implemented with a different design choice, written in a different programming language, and located in a different geographical location. The seamless in-app user experience makes things look so easy. But developing modern web applications is *anything* but easy.

We use web applications every time we tweet, watch a movie on Netflix, listen to a song on Spotify, make a travel booking, order food, play an online game, hail a cab, or use any of numerous online services as part of our daily lives. Without distributed web applications, businesses and modern digital society would come to a grinding halt.

> **NOTE** Websites provide information about your business. Web applications provide services to your customers.

In this book, you will learn the concepts, techniques, and tools you'll need to use Rust to design and develop distributed web services and applications that communicate over standard internet protocols. Along the way, you will see core Rust concepts in action through practical working examples.

This book is for you if you are a web backend software engineer, full stack application developer, cloud or enterprise architect, CTO for a tech product, or simply a curious learner who is interested in building distributed web applications that are incredibly safe, efficient, highly performant, and that do not incur exorbitant costs to operate and maintain. By developing a working example through the course of this book, I will show you how to build web services and traditional web application frontends in pure Rust.

As you will notice throughout the chapters, Rust is a general-purpose language that efficiently supports the development of many different kinds of applications. This book presents a single application, but the techniques demonstrated are applicable to many other situations using the same or other crates (a library is called a *crate* in Rust terminology).

In this chapter, we will review the key characteristics of distributed web applications, understand how and where Rust shines, and outline the example application we will build together in this book.

1.1 *Introducing modern web applications*

We'll start by looking at the structure of modern, distributed web applications. Distributed systems have components that may be distributed across several different computing processors, communicate over a network, and concurrently execute workloads. Technically, your home computer resembles a networked distributed system (given modern multi-CPU and multi-core processors).

Popular types of distributed systems include

- Distributed networks such as telecommunication networks and the internet.
- Distributed client-server applications. (Most web-based applications fall into this category.)
- Distributed P2P applications such as BitTorrent and Tor.

- Real-time control systems such as air traffic and industrial control.
- Distributed server infrastructures such as cloud, grid, and other forms of scientific computing.

Distributed systems are broadly composed of three parts: distributed applications, a networking stack, and hardware and OS infrastructure.

Distributed applications can use a wide array of networking protocols to communicate internally between their components. However, HTTP is the overwhelming choice today for a web service or web application communicating with the outside world, due to its simplicity and universality.

Web applications are programs that use HTTP as the application-layer protocol and that provide functionality that is accessible to human users over standard internet browsers. When web applications are not monolithic but are composed of tens or hundreds of distributed application components that cooperate and communicate over a network, they are called *distributed* web applications. Examples of large-scale distributed web applications include social media applications such as Facebook and Twitter, e-commerce sites such as Amazon and eBay, sharing-economy apps like Uber and Airbnb, entertainment sites such as Netflix, and even user-friendly cloud provisioning applications from providers such as AWS, Google, and Azure.

Figure 1.1 is a representative logical view of a distributed systems stack for a modern web application. In the real world, such systems can be distributed over thousands of servers, but in the figure, you can see three servers connected through a networking stack. These servers may all be within a single data center or be distributed geographically in the cloud. Within each server, a layered view of the hardware and software components is shown.

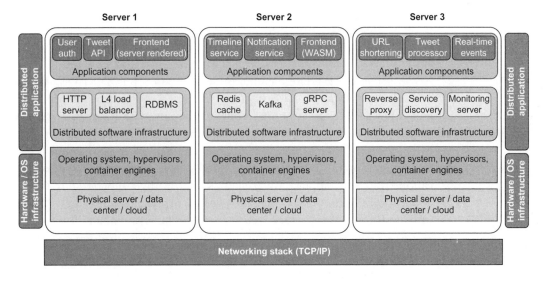

Figure 1.1   A simplified distributed systems stack for a social media application

- *Hardware and OS infrastructure components*—These are components such as physical servers (in a data center or cloud), operating system, and virtualization or container runtimes. Devices such as embedded controllers, sensors, and edge devices can also be classified in this layer (think of a futuristic case where tweets are sent to social media followers of a supermarket chain when stocks of RFID-labeled items are added to or removed from supermarket shelves).

- *Networking stack*—The networking stack comprises the four-layered Internet Protocol suite, which forms the communication backbone for the distributed system components, allowing them to communicate with each other across physical hardware. The four networking layers (ordered from lowest to highest level of abstraction) are

  - Network link/access layer
  - Internet layer
  - Transport layer
  - Application layer

  The first three layers are usually implemented at the hardware or OS level. For most distributed web applications, HTTP is the primary application layer protocol used. Popular API protocols such as REST, gRPC, and GraphQL use HTTP. For more details on the Internet Protocol suite, see the documentation at https://tools.ietf.org/id/draft-baker-ietf-core-04.html.

- *Distributed applications*—Distributed applications are a subset of distributed systems. Modern *n*-tier distributed applications are built as a combination of the following:

  - *Application frontends*—These can be mobile apps (running on iOS or Android) or web frontends running in an internet browser. These app frontends communicate with application backend services residing on remote servers (usually in a data center or a cloud platform). End users interact with application frontends.

  - *Application backends*—These contain the application business rules, database access logic, computation-heavy processes such as image or video processing, and other service integrations. They are deployed as individual processes (such as systemd processes on Unix/Linux) running on physical or virtual machines, or as microservices in container engines (such as Docker) managed by container orchestration environments (such as Kubernetes). Unlike application frontends, application backends expose their functionality through application programming interfaces (APIs). Application frontends interact with application backend services to complete tasks on behalf of users.

  - *Distributed software infrastructure*—This includes components that provide supporting services for application backends. Examples are protocol servers, databases, key/value stores, caching, messaging, load balancers and proxies, service discovery platforms, and other such infrastructure components used for communications, operations, and security and monitoring of distributed applications. Application backends interact with distributed software infrastructure for service discovery, communications, lifecycle support, security, monitoring, and so on.

Now that you've had an overview of distributed web applications, let's take a look at the benefits of using Rust to build them.

1.2 *Choosing Rust for web applications*

Rust can be used to build all three layers of distributed applications: frontends, backend services, and software infrastructure components. But each of these layers addresses a different set of concerns and characteristics. It is important to be aware of these while discussing the benefits of Rust.

For example, client frontends deal with aspects such as user interface design, user experience, tracking changes in application state and rendering updated views on screen, and constructing and updating the Document Object Model (DOM).

Backend services need well-designed APIs to reduce roundtrips, high throughput (measured in requests per second), short response times under varying loads, low and predictable latency for applications such as video streaming and online gaming, low memory and CPU footprints, service discovery, and availability.

The software infrastructure layer is concerned primarily with extremely low latencies, low-level control of network and other operating-system resources, frugal use of CPU and memory, efficient data structures and algorithms, built-in security, short start-up and shut-down times, and ergonomic APIs for application backend services.

As you can see, a single web application comprises components with at least three sets of characteristics and requirements. While each of these could be the topic of a book in itself, we will look at things more holistically and focus on a set of common characteristics that broadly benefit all three layers of a web application.

1.2.1 *Characteristics of web applications*

Web applications can be of different types:

- *Highly mission-critical applications* such as autonomous control of vehicles and smart grids, industrial automation, and high-speed trading applications in which successful trades depend on the ability to quickly and reliably respond to input events
- *High-volume transaction and messaging infrastructure* such as e-commerce platforms, social networks, and retail payment systems
- *Near real-time applications* such as online gaming servers, video or audio processing, video conferencing, and real-time collaboration tools

These applications have a common set of requirements:

- Should be safe, secure, and reliable
- Should be resource-efficient

- Must minimize latency
- Should support high concurrency

In addition, the following are nice-to-have requirements for such services:

- Should have quick startup and shutdown times
- Should be easy to maintain and refactor
- Must offer developer productivity

All these requirements can be addressed at the level of individual services and at the architectural level. For example, an individual service can achieve high concurrency by adopting multithreading or async I/O. Likewise, high concurrency can be achieved at an architectural level by adding several instances of a service behind a load balancer to process concurrent loads. When we talk about the benefits of Rust in this book, we are looking at the *individual service level* because architectural-level options are common to all programming languages.

1.2.2 *Benefits of Rust for web applications*

You've seen that modern web applications comprise web frontends, backends, and software infrastructure. The benefits of Rust for developing web frontends, either to replace or supplement portions of JavaScript code, are a hot topic nowadays. However, we will not discuss them in this book as this topic is large enough for a book of its own.

Here, we will focus primarily on the benefits of Rust for application backends and software infrastructure services. Rust meets all of the critical requirements that we identified in the previous section for such services. Let's see how.

RUST IS SAFE

When we talk about program safety, there are three distinct aspects to consider: *type safety*, *memory safety*, and *thread safety*.

Regarding *type safety*, Rust is a statically typed language. Type checking, which verifies and enforces type constraints, happens at compile time, so the types of variables have to be determined at compile time. If you do not specify a type for a variable, the compiler will try to infer it. If it is unable to do so, or if it sees conflicts, it will let you know and prevent you from proceeding. In this context, Rust is similar to Java, Scala, C, and C++. Type safety in Rust is very strongly enforced by the compiler, but with helpful error messages. This helps to eliminate an entire class of run-time errors.

Memory safety is, arguably, one of the most unique aspects of the Rust programming language. To do justice to this topic, let's analyze this in detail.

Mainstream programming languages can be classified into two groups based on how they provide memory management. The first group comprises languages with manual memory management, such as C and C++. The second group includes languages with a garbage collector, such as Java, C#, Python, Ruby, and Go.

Since developers are not perfect, manual memory management means accepting a degree of risk, and thus a lack of program correctness. So, for languages where low-level control of memory is not necessary and peak performance is not the primary goal, garbage collection has become a mainstream feature over the last 20 to 25 years. Garbage collection has made programs safer than manually managing memory, but it comes with limitations in terms of execution speed, the consumption of additional compute resources, and the possible stalling of program execution. Also, garbage collection only deals with memory, not other resources, such as network sockets and database handles.

Rust is the first popular language to propose an alternative—automatic memory management and memory safety without garbage collection. As you are probably aware, it achieves this through a unique *ownership model.* Rust enables developers to control the memory layout of their data structures and makes ownership explicit. Rust's ownership model of resource management is modeled around RAII (Resource Acquisition is Initialization)—a C++ programming concept—and smart pointers that enable safe memory usage.

In this model, each value declared in a Rust program is assigned an owner. Once a value is given away to another owner, it can no longer be used by the original owner. The value is automatically destroyed (memory is deallocated) when the owner of the value goes out of scope.

Rust can also grant temporary access to a value, another variable, or a function. This is called *borrowing.* The Rust compiler (specifically, the borrow checker) ensures that a reference to a value does not outlive the value being borrowed. To borrow a value, the & operator is used (called a *reference*). References are of two types: *immutable references,* &T, which allow sharing but not mutation, and *mutable references,* &mut T, which allow mutation but not sharing. Rust ensures that whenever there is a mutable borrow of an object, there are no other borrows of that object (either mutable or immutable). All this is enforced at compile time, leading to the elimination of entire classes of errors involving invalid memory access.

To summarize, you can program in Rust without fear of invalid memory access and without a garbage collector. Rust provides compile-time guarantees to prevent the following categories of memory-safety errors:

- Null pointer dereferences, where a program crashes because a pointer being dereferenced is null.
- Segmentation faults, where programs attempt to access a restricted area of memory.
- Dangling pointers, where a value associated with a pointer no longer exists.
- Buffer overflows, due to programs accessing elements before the start or beyond the end of an array. Rust iterators don't run out of bounds.

In Rust, memory safety and *thread safety* (which seem like two completely different concerns) are solved using the same foundational principle of ownership. For type safety, Rust, by default, ensures there is no undefined behavior due to data races. While some web development languages may offer similar guarantees, Rust goes one step further and prevents you from sharing objects that are not thread-safe between threads. Rust marks some data types as thread-safe and enforces these for you. Most other languages do not make this distinction between thread-safe and thread-unsafe data structures. The Rust compiler categorically prevents all types of data races, which makes multi-threaded programs much safer.

Here are a couple of references for a deeper dive into safety in Rust:

- `Send` and `Sync` traits: http://mng.bz/Bmzl
- Fearless concurrency with Rust: http://mng.bz/d1W1

In addition to what we've discussed, there are a few other features of Rust that improve the safety of programs:

- All variables in Rust are immutable by default, and explicit declaration is required before mutating any variable. This forces developers to think through how and where data gets modified and what the lifetime of each object is.
- Rust's ownership model handles not just memory management but the management of variables owning other resources, such as network sockets, database and file handles, and device descriptors.
- The lack of a garbage collector prevents nondeterministic behavior.
- `Match` clauses (which are equivalent to `Switch` statements in other languages) are exhaustive, which means that the compiler forces the developer to handle every possible variant in the `match` statement. This prevents developers from inadvertently missing out on handling certain code flow paths that might result in unexpected run-time behavior.
- The presence of algebraic data types makes it easier to represent the data model in a concise and verifiable manner.

Rust's statically typed system, ownership and borrowing model, lack of a garbage collector, immutable-by-default values, and exhaustive pattern matching, all of which are enforced by the compiler, provide Rust with an undeniable edge for developing safe applications.

RUST IS RESOURCE-EFFICIENT

System resources such as CPU, memory, and disk space have progressively become cheaper over the years. While this has proved to be very beneficial in the development and scaling of distributed applications, it also brings a few drawbacks. First, there is a general tendency among software teams to simply use more hardware to solve scalability challenges—more CPU, more memory, and more disk space. This is achieved either by adding more CPU, memory, and disk resources to the server (vertical scaling, a.k.a. *scaling up*) or by adding more machines to the network to share the load (horizontal scaling, a.k.a. *scaling out*).

One of the reasons why these approaches have become popular is the limitations of today's mainstream web development languages. High-level web-development languages such as JavaScript, Java, C#, Python, and Ruby do not allow fine-grained memory control to limit memory usage. Many programming languages do not utilize the multi-core architectures of modern CPUs well. Dynamic scripting languages do not make efficient memory allocations because the types of the variables are known only at run time, so optimizations are not possible, unlike with statically typed languages.

Rust offers the following innate features that enable the creation of resource-efficient services:

- Due to its ownership model of memory management, Rust makes it hard (if not impossible) to write code that leaks memory or other resources.
- Rust allows developers to tightly control memory layout for their programs.
- Rust does not have a garbage collector that consumes additional CPU and memory resources. Garbage-collection code generally runs in separate threads and consumes resources.
- Rust does not have a large, complex runtime. This gives developers tremendous flexibility in running Rust programs even on underpowered embedded systems and microcontrollers, like home appliances and industrial machines. Rust can run in bare metal without kernels.
- Rust discourages the deep copying of heap-allocated memory, and it provides various types of smart pointers to optimize the memory footprint of programs. The lack of a runtime in Rust makes it one of the few modern programming languages appropriate for extremely low-resource environments.

Rust combines the best of static typing, fine-grained memory control, efficient use of multi-core CPUs, and built-in asynchronous I/O semantics, all of which make it very resource-efficient in terms of CPU and memory utilization. All this translates to lower server costs and a lower operational burden for small and large applications alike.

RUST HAS LOW LATENCY

Latency for a round-trip network request and response depends both on *network latency* and *service latency*. *Network latency* is affected by many factors, such as transmission medium, propagation distance, router efficiency, and network bandwidth. *Service latency* depends on many factors, such as I/O delays in processing the request, whether there is a garbage collector that introduces non-deterministic delays, Hypervisor pauses, the amount of context switching (e.g., in multithreading), serialization and deserialization costs, etc.

From a purely programming language perspective, Rust provides low latency due to its low-level hardware control as a systems programming language. Rust does not have a garbage collector or runtime, and it has native support for non-blocking I/O, a good ecosystem of high-performance async (non-blocking) I/O libraries and runtimes, and zero-cost abstractions as a fundamental design principle of the language. Additionally, by default, Rust variables live on the stack, which is faster to manage.

Several different benchmarks have shown comparable performance between idiomatic Rust and idiomatic C++ for similar workloads, which is faster than the results for mainstream web development languages.

RUST ENABLES FEARLESS CONCURRENCY

We previously looked at Rust's concurrency features from the perspective of program safety. Now let's look at Rust's concurrency from the point of view of better multi-core CPU utilization, throughput, and performance for application and infrastructure services.

Rust is a concurrency-friendly language that enables developers to use the power of multi-core processors. Rust provides two types of concurrency: classic multithreading and asynchronous I/O:

- *Multithreading*—Rust's traditional multithreading support provides for both shared-memory and message-passing concurrency. Type-level guarantees are provided for the sharing of values. Threads can borrow values, assume ownership, and transition the scope of a value to a new thread. Rust also provides data-race safety, which prevents thread-blocking, improving performance. In order to improve memory efficiency and avoid the copying of data shared across threads, Rust provides *reference counting* as a mechanism to track the use of a variable by other processes or threads. The value is dropped when the count reaches zero, which provides for safe memory management. Additionally, mutexes are available in Rust for data synchronization across threads. References to immutable data need not use mutex.

- *Async I/O*—Async event-loop–based non-blocking I/O concurrency primitives are built into the Rust language with zero-cost futures and async-await. Non-blocking I/O ensures that code does not hang while waiting for data to be processed.

Further, Rust's rules of immutability provide for high levels of data concurrency.

RUST IS A PRODUCTIVE LANGUAGE

Even though Rust is first a systems-oriented programming language, it also adds the quality-of-life features of higher-level and functional programming languages. These are a few of the higher-level abstractions in Rust that make for a productive and delightful developer experience:

- Closures with anonymous functions
- Iterators
- Generics and macros
- Enums such as `Option` and `Result`
- Polymorphism through traits
- Dynamic dispatch through `Trait` objects

Rust not only allows developers to build efficient, safe, and performant software, it also optimizes for developer productivity with its expressiveness. It is not without reason that Rust has been the most-loved programming language in the Stack Overflow developer survey for five consecutive years: 2016–2020 (https://insights.stackoverflow.com/survey/2020).

NOTE For more insight into why senior developers love Rust, see the "Why the developers who use Rust love it so much" article on *The Overflow* blog: http://mng.bz/rWZj.

So far, you have seen how Rust offers a unique combination of memory safety, resource efficiency, low latency, high concurrency, and developer productivity. These impart to Rust the characteristics of the low-level control and speed of a system programming language, the developer productivity of higher-level languages, and a unique memory model without a garbage collector. Application backends and infrastructure services directly benefit from these characteristics, providing low-latency responses under high loads while being highly efficient in the use of system resources, such as multi-core CPUs and memory. Now let's take a look at some of the limitations of Rust.

1.2.3 *What does Rust not have?*

When it comes to programming languages, there is no one-size-fits-all option—no language can be claimed to be suitable for all use cases. Further, due to the nature of programming language design, what may be easy to do in one language can be difficult in another. In the interest of providing you with a complete view to decide whether to use Rust for the web, here are a few things you need to know:

- Rust has a steep learning curve. It is definitely a bigger leap for newcomers to programming or people coming from dynamic programming or scripting languages. The syntax can at times be difficult to read, even for experienced developers.
- Some things are harder to program in Rust compared to other languages, such as single and double linked lists. This is due to the way the language is designed.
- The Rust compiler is currently slower than those for many other compiled languages. However, compilation speed has improved over the last few years, and work is always underway to improve this.
- Rust's ecosystem of libraries and its community is still maturing compared to other mainstream languages.
- Rust developers are harder to find and hire at scale.
- The adoption of Rust in large companies and enterprises is still in its early days. Rust does not yet have a natural home to nurture it, such as Oracle for Java, Google for Golang, or Microsoft for C#.

You have now seen the benefits and drawbacks of using Rust to develop application backend services. In the next section, I will introduce the example application that we'll build in this book.

1.3 *Visualizing the example application*

In the following chapters, we will use Rust to build web servers, web services, and web applications, and we'll demonstrate concepts through a full-length example. Note that our goal is not to develop a *feature-complete* or *architecture-complete* distributed application, but to learn how to use Rust for the web domain.

This is important to keep in mind: we will only explore some paths—a very limited number of all possible paths—and we will totally disregard others that could be as promising and interesting. This is a deliberate choice to keep our discussion focused. For example, only REST web services will be developed, leaving SOAP services out completely. I fully realize how arbitrary this may seem.

This book will also not address some important aspects of modern software development, like continuous integration/continuous delivery (CI/CD). These are very important topics in today's practice, but there was nothing specific to Rust to be explained and we preferred not to address these aspects in the context of this book.

On the other hand, because containerization is a major trend nowadays, and because I deemed it interesting to show the deployment of a distributed application developed in Rust as containers, I will show how easy it is to deploy and run our example application using Docker and Docker Compose.

Similarly, in the final chapters of the book, we will take a short trip into the realm of peer-to-peer (P2P) networks, which are one of the most striking usages of async capabilities. This part of the book will, however, be slightly disconnected from the example application, as I didn't find a compelling use case for integrating P2P with it. Making use of P2P in our example application is therefore left as an exercise you can explore.

Let's now look at our example application.

1.3.1   *What will we build?*

In this book, we will build a digital storefront for tutors, called EzyTutors, where tutors can publish their course catalogs online. Tutors can be individuals or training businesses. The digital storefront will be a sales tool for tutors, not a marketplace.

EzyTutors—A digital storefront for tutors

Are you a tutor with a unique skill or knowledge that you'd like to monetize? Do you have the necessary time and resources to set up and manage your own website?

EzyTutors is just for you. Take your training business online in just a few minutes.

We've defined the product vision. Let's now talk about the scope, followed by the technical stack.

The storefront will allow tutors to register themselves and then sign in. They can create a course offering and associate it with a course category. A web page with their course list will be generated for each tutor, and they can then share it on social media with their network. There will also be a public website that will allow learners to search for courses, browse through courses by tutor, and view course details. Figure 1.2 shows the logical design of our example application.

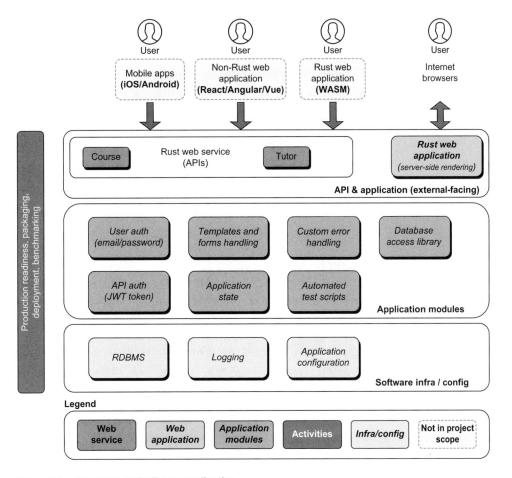

Figure 1.2 Our example EzyTutors application

Our technical stack will consist of a web service and a server-rendered web app written in pure Rust. There are several very popular approaches, like developing the GUI using a mature web framework such as React, Vue, or Angular, but to keep us focused on Rust, we won't use these approaches. There are many other good books on this topic.

The course data will be persisted in a relational database. We will use Actix Web for the web framework, SQLx for database connections, and Postgres for the database. Importantly, the design will be asynchronous all the way. Both Actix Web and SQLx support full asynchronous I/O, which is well suited for our web application workload, which is more I/O-heavy than computation-heavy.

We'll first build a web service that exposes RESTful APIs, connects to a database, and deals with errors and failures in an application-specific manner. We'll then simulate application lifecycle changes by enhancing the data model and adding additional functionality, which will require refactoring the code and database migration. This exercise will demonstrate one of the key strengths of Rust—the ability to fearlessly refactor the code (and reduce technical debt) with the aid of a strongly typed system and a strict but helpful compiler that has our back.

In addition to the web service, our example will demonstrate how to build a frontend in Rust; our chosen example will be a server-rendered client app. We'll use a template engine to render templates and forms for the server-rendered web application. It would also be possible to implement a WebAssembly-based in-browser app, but such an undertaking is out of the scope of this book.

Our web application can be developed and deployed on any platform that Rust supports: Linux, Windows, or macOS. This means that we will not use any external library that restricts the application to any specific computing platform. Our application will be capable of being deployed either in a traditional server-based deployment or in any cloud platform, either as a traditional binary or in a containerized environment (such as Docker or Kubernetes).

The chosen problem domain for our example application is a practical scenario, but it is not difficult to understand. This will allow us to focus on the core topic of the book—how to apply Rust to the web domain. As a bonus, we'll also strengthen our understanding of Rust by seeing concepts in action, such as traits, lifetimes, `Result` and `Option`, structs and enums, collections, smart pointers, derivable traits, associated functions and methods, modules and workspaces, unit testing, closures, and functional programming.

This book is about learning the foundations of web development in Rust. This book will not cover how to configure and deploy additional infrastructural components and tools, such as reverse proxy servers, load balancers, firewalls, TLS/SSL, monitoring servers, caching servers, DevOps tools, CDNs, etc., as these are not Rust-specific topics (though they are needed for large-scale production deployments).

In addition to building business functionality in Rust, our example application will demonstrate good development practices such as automated tests, code structuring for maintainability, separating configuration from code, generating documentation, and, of course, writing idiomatic Rust.

Are you ready for some practical Rust on the web?

1.3.2 *Technical guidelines for the example application*

This isn't a book about system architecture or software engineering theory. However, I would like to enumerate a few foundational guidelines I've adopted in the book that will help you better understand my rationale for the design choices in the code examples:

1 *Project structure*—We'll make heavy use of the Rust module system to separate various pieces of functionality and keep things organized. We'll use Cargo workspaces to group related projects together, which can include both binaries and libraries.

2 *Single responsibility principle*—Each logically separate piece of application functionality should be in its own module. For example, the handlers in the web tier should only deal with processing HTTP messages. The business and database-access logic should be in separate modules.

3 *Maintainability*—The following guidelines are related to the maintainability of code:

 – Variable and function names must be self-explanatory.
 – The formatting of code will be kept uniform using Rustfmt.
 – We will write automated test cases to detect and prevent regressions, as the code evolves iteratively.
 – Project structure and filenames must be intuitive to understand.

4 *Security*—In this book, we'll cover API authentication using JSON Web Tokens (JWT) and password-based user authentication. Infrastructure and network-level security will not be covered. However, it is important to remember that Rust inherently offers memory safety without a garbage collector and thread safety that prevents race conditions, thus preventing several classes of hard-to-find and hard-to-fix memory, concurrency, and security bugs.

5 *Application configuration*—Separating configuration from the application is a principle adopted for the example project.

6 *Use of external crates*—We will keep the use of external crates to a minimum. For example, custom error-handling functionality is built from scratch in this book, rather than using external crates that simplify and automate error handling. This is because taking shortcuts using external libraries sometimes impedes the learning process and deep understanding.

7 *Async I/O*—I made a deliberate choice to use libraries that support fully asynchronous I/O in the example application, both for network communications and for database access.

Now that we've covered the topics we'll discuss in the book, the goals of the example project, and the guidelines we'll use to steer our design choices, we can start digging into web servers and web services in our next chapter.

Summary

- Modern web applications are indispensable components of digital lives and businesses, but they are complex to build, deploy, and operate.
- Distributed web applications comprise application frontends, backend services, and distributed software infrastructure.
- Application backends and software infrastructure are composed of loosely coupled, cooperative network-oriented services. These have specific run-time characteristics to be satisfied, which affect the choice of tools and technologies used to build them.

- Rust is a highly suitable language for developing distributed web applications due to its safety, concurrency, low latency, and low hardware-resource footprint.
- This book is suitable for readers who are considering Rust for distributed web application development.
- We looked at the example application we will be building in this book and reviewed the key technical guidelines adopted for the code examples.

Writing a basic web server from scratch

2

This chapter covers
- Writing a TCP server in Rust
- Writing an HTTP server in Rust

In this chapter, you will delve deep into TCP and HTTP communications using Rust. These protocols are generally abstracted away for developers through the higher-level libraries and frameworks that are used to build web applications. So why is it important to discuss low-level protocols? This is a fair question.

Learning to work with TCP and HTTP is important because they form the foundation for most communications on the internet. Popular application communication protocols and techniques such as REST, gRPC, and WebSockets use HTTP and TCP for transport. Designing and building basic TCP and HTTP servers in Rust will give you the confidence to design, develop, and troubleshoot higher-level application backend services.

However, if you are eager to get started with the example application, you can move ahead to chapter 3 and come back to this chapter when you want to understand more.

In this chapter, you will learn the following:

- How to write a TCP client and server.
- How to build a library to convert between TCP raw byte streams and HTTP messages.
- How to build an HTTP server that can serve static web pages (a *web server*) as well as JSON data (a *web service*). You'll test the server with standard HTTP clients such as the cURL (command line) tool and a web browser.

Through this exercise, you will learn how Rust data types and traits can be used to model a real-world network protocol, and you'll strengthen your understanding of the fundamentals of Rust.

The chapter is structured in three sections. In the first section, we'll look at exactly what we're going to build in this chapter. In the second section, we'll develop a basic network server in Rust that can communicate over TCP/IP. In the third section, we'll build a web server that responds to GET requests for web pages and JSON data. We'll achieve all this using just the Rust standard library (no external crates). The HTTP server that we are going to build is not intended to be full-featured or production-ready, but it will serve our stated purpose.

Let's get started.

2.1   *The networking model*

We spoke about modern applications being constructed as a set of independent components and services, some belonging to the frontend, some to the backend, and some being part of the distributed software infrastructure. Whenever we have separate components, the question arises as to how these components talk to each other. How does the client (web browser or mobile app) talk to the backend service? How do the backend services talk to the software infrastructure, such as databases? This is where the *networking model* comes in.

A networking model describes how communication takes place between the sender of a message and its receiver. It addresses questions such as in what format the message should be sent and received, how the message should be broken up into bytes for physical data transmission, how errors should be handled if data packets do not arrive at the destination, and so on. The *OSI model* is the most popular networking model, and it is defined in terms of a comprehensive seven-layered framework. But for the purposes of internet communications, a simplified four-layer model called the *TCP/IP model* is often adequate to describe how communications take place over the internet between the client making a request and the server that processes that request.

> **NOTE** The TCP/IP model is described in Henrik Frystyk's 1994 article titled "The Internet Protocol Stack": www.w3.org/People/Frystyk/thesis/TcpIp .html.

The TCP/IP model (illustrated in figure 2.1) is a simplified set of standards and protocols for communications over the internet. It is organized into four abstract layers:

the network access layer, the network layer, the transport layer, and the application layer, with flexibility on networking protocols that can be used in each layer. The model is named after the two main protocols it is built on: Transmission Control Protocol (TCP) and Internet Protocol (IP). The main thing to note is that the four layers of the TCP/IP model complement each other in ensuring that a message is sent successfully from the sending process to the receiving process.

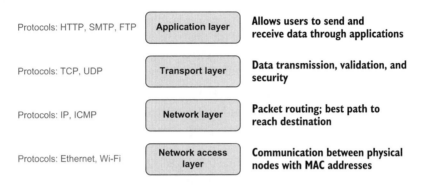

Figure 2.1   TCP/IP network model

Let's look at the role of each of these four layers of communications:

- *Application layer*—The application layer is the highest layer of abstraction. The semantics of the message are understood by this layer. For example, a web browser and web server communicate using HTTP, or an email client and email server communicate using SMTP (Simple Mail Transfer Protocol). There are other such protocols such as DNS (Domain Name Service) and FTP (File Transfer Protocol). All these are called *application-layer protocols* because they deal with specific user applications such as web browsing, emails, or file transfers. In this book, we will focus mainly on the HTTP protocol at the application layer.

- *Transport layer*—The transport layer provides reliable end-to-end communication. While the application layer deals with messages that have specific semantics (such as sending a GET request to get shipment details), the transport protocols deal with sending and receiving raw bytes. (Note that all application layer protocol messages eventually get converted into raw bytes for transmission by the transport layer.) TCP and UDP are the two main protocols used in this layer, with QUIC (Quick UDP Internet Connection) being a recent entrant. TCP is a connection-oriented protocol that allows data to be partitioned for transmission and reassembled in a reliable manner at the receiving end. UDP is a connectionless protocol, and it does not provide guarantees of delivery, unlike TCP. UDP is consequently faster and suitable for a certain class of applications, such as DNS lookups and voice or video applications. In this book, we will focus on the TCP protocol for the transport layer.

- *Network layer*—The network layer uses IP addresses and routers to locate and route packets of information to hosts across networks. While the transport layer is focused on sending and receiving raw bytes between two servers identified by their IP addresses and port numbers, the network layer determines the best path for sending data packets from source to destination. We do not need to work directly with the network layer—Rust's standard library provides the interface to work with TCP and sockets, and it handles the internals of network layer communications.
- *Network access layer*—The network access layer is the lowest layer of the TCP/IP network model. It is responsible for the transmission of data through a physical link between hosts, such as by using network cards. For our purposes, it does not matter what physical medium is used for network communications.

Now that you've had an overview of the TCP/IP networking model, it's time to learn how to use the TCP/IP protocol to send and receive messages in Rust.

2.2   *Writing a TCP server in Rust*

In this section, you will learn how to perform basic TCP/IP networking communications in Rust. It's fairly easy. We'll start by looking at how to use the TCP/IP constructs in the Rust standard library.

2.2.1   *Designing the TCP/IP communication flow*

The Rust standard library provides networking primitives through the `std::net` module; its documentation can be found here: https://doc.rust-lang.org/std/net/. This module supports basic TCP and UDP communications. Two specific data structures, `TcpListener` and `TcpStream`, contain the bulk of the methods needed to implement our scenario.

`TcpListener` is used to create a TCP socket server that binds to a specific port. A client can send a message to a socket server at the specified socket address (a combination of the machine's IP address and a port number). Multiple TCP socket servers may be running on a machine, and when there is an incoming network connection on the network card, the operating system routes the message to the right TCP socket server using the port number.

The following example code creates a socket server:

```
use std::net::TcpListener;

let listener = TcpListener::bind("127.0.0.1:3000")
```

After binding to a port, the socket server should start to listen for the next incoming connection. This is achieved as follows:

```
listener.accept()
```

For listening continually (in a loop) for incoming connections, the following method is used:

```
listener.incoming()
```

The `listener.incoming()` method returns an iterator over the connections received on this listener. Each connection represents a stream of bytes of type `TcpStream`. Data can be transmitted or received on this `TcpStream` object. Note that reading and writing to `TcpStream` is done in raw bytes, as shown in the following snippet (error handling is excluded for simplicity):

```
for stream in listener.incoming() {
    //Read from stream into a bytes buffer
    stream.read(&mut [0;1024]);
    // construct a message and write to stream
    let message = "Hello".as_bytes();
    stream.write(message)
}
```

In the preceding code, we have constructed a *bytes buffer* (called a *byte slice* in Rust) for reading from a stream. For writing to a stream, we have constructed a *string slice* and converted it to a byte slice using the `as_bytes()` method.

So far, we've seen the server side of a TCP socket server. On the client side, a connection can be established with the TCP socket server:

```
let stream = TcpStream.connect("172.217.167.142:80")
```

To recap, connection management functions are available from the `TcpListener` struct of the `std::net` module. To read and write on a connection, the `TcpStream` struct is used.

Let's now apply this knowledge to write a working TCP client and server.

2.2.2 Writing the TCP server and client

Let's first set up a project structure. For Rust projects, a *workspace* is a container project that holds other projects. The benefit of the workspace structure is that it enables us to manage multiple projects as one unit. It also helps us to store all related projects seamlessly within a single Git repo.

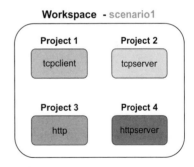

As shown in figure 2.2, we will create a workspace project called `scenario1`. Under this workspace, we will create four new Rust projects using Cargo, the Rust project build and dependencies tool. The four projects are `tcpclient`, `tcpserver`, `http`, and `httpserver`.

Figure 2.2 Cargo workspace structure for scenario 1

To start a new Cargo project, we can use the following command:

```
cargo new scenario1 && cd scenario1
```

The scenario1 directory can also be referred to as the workspace root. Under the scenario1 directory, we'll create the following four new Rust projects:

- `tcpserver` will be the binary project for TCP server code.
- `tcpclient` will be the binary project for TCP client code.

- httpserver will be the binary project for HTTP server code.
- http will be the library project for HTTP protocol functionality.

You can use the following commands to create the projects:

```
cargo new tcpserver
cargo new tcpclient
cargo new httpserver
cargo new --lib http
```

Now that the projects are created, we have to declare the scenario1 project as a work-space and specify its relationship with the four subprojects. Add the following.

Listing 2.1   scenario1/Cargo.toml

```
[workspace]
members = [
    "tcpserver","tcpclient", "http", "httpserver",
]
```

We will write the code for the TCP server and client in two iterations:

1 We will write the TCP server and client to do a sanity check that a connection is being established from client to server.
2 We will send a text from client to server and have the server echo it back.

Following along with the code

Many of the code snippets shown in this chapter (and throughout the book) include code annotations to describe the code. If you are copying and pasting code (from any chapter in this book) into your code editor, ensure you remove the code annotations (or the program will not compile). Also, the pasted code may sometimes be mis-aligned, so in case of compilation errors, manual verification may be needed to compare the pasted code with the code snippets in the chapter.

ITERATION 1

In the tcpserver folder, modify src/main.rs as follows.

Listing 2.2   First iteration of TCP server (tcpserver/src/main.rs)

```
use std::net::TcpListener;

fn main() {
    let connection_listener = TcpListener::bind(
    "127.0.0.1:3000").unwrap();
    println!("Running on port 3000");
    for stream in connection_listener.incoming() {
        let _stream = stream.unwrap();
        println!("Connection established");
    }
}
```

Initialize a socket server to bind to IP address 127.0.0.1 (localhost) and port 3000.

The socket server waits (listens) for incoming connections.

When a new connection comes in, it is of type Result<TcpStream,Error>, which, when unwrapped, returns a TcpStream if successful, or, in the case of a connection error, exits the program with a panic.

From the root folder of the workspace (scenario1), run the following command:

```
cargo run -p tcpserver
```
◁─┐ **The -p argument specifies which package
in the workspace you want to run.**

The server will start, and the message "Running on port 3000" will be printed to the terminal. We now have a working TCP server listening on port 3000 on localhost.

Let's next write a TCP client to establish a connection with the TCP server.

Listing 2.3   tcpclient/src/main.rs

```
use std::net::TcpStream;

fn main() {
    let _stream = TcpStream::connect("localhost:3000").unwrap();
}
```
**The TCP client initiates a connection to a
remote server running on localhost:3000.**

In a new terminal, from the root folder of the workspace, run the following command:

```
cargo run -p tcpclient
```

You will see the message "Connection established" printed to the terminal where the TCP server is running, as follows:

```
Running on port 3000
Connection established
```

We now have a TCP server running on port 3000, and we have a TCP client that can establish a connection to it. It's time to try sending a message from our client and make sure the server can echo it back.

ITERATION 2

Modify the tcpserver/src/main.rs file as follows.

Listing 2.4   Completing the TCP server

```
use std::io::{Read, Write};
use std::net::TcpListener;
fn main() {
    let connection_listener = TcpListener::bind("127.0.0.1:3000").unwrap();
    println!("Running on port 3000");
    for stream in connection_listener.incoming() {
        let mut stream = stream.unwrap();
        println!("Connection established");
        let mut buffer = [0; 1024];
        stream.read(&mut buffer).unwrap();
        stream.write(&mut buffer).unwrap();
    }
}
```
**TcpStream implements Read and Write traits, so include the
std::io module to bring the Read and Write traits into scope.**

**Make the stream mutable so
you can read and write to it.**

**Read from the
incoming stream.**

**Echo back whatever is received to
the client on the same connection.**

In listing 2.4, we are echoing back to the client whatever we receive from it. Run the TCP server with `cargo run -p tcpserver` from the workspace root directory.

Read and Write traits

Traits in Rust define shared behavior. They are similar to *interfaces* in other languages, with some differences. The Rust standard library (std) defines several traits that are implemented by data types within std. These traits can also be implemented by user-defined data types such as structs and enums. Read and Write are two such traits defined in the Rust standard library.

The Read trait allows for reading bytes from a source. Examples of sources that implement the Read trait include File, Stdin (standard input), and TcpStream. Implementers of the Read trait are required to implement one method: read(). This allows us to use the same read() method to read from a File, Stdin, TcpStream, or any other type that implements the Read trait.

Similarly, the Write trait represents objects that are byte-oriented sinks. Implementers of the Write trait implement two methods: write () and flush (). Examples of types that implement the Write trait include File, Stderr, Stdout, and TcpStream. This trait allows us to write to a File, standard output, standard error, or TcpStream using the write() method.

The next step is to modify the TCP client to send a message to the server and then print what is received back from the server. Modify the file tcpclient/src/main.rs as follows.

Listing 2.5   Completing the TCP client

```
use std::io::{Read, Write};
use std::net::TcpStream;
use std::str;

fn main() {
    let mut stream = TcpStream::connect("localhost:3000").unwrap();
    stream.write("Hello".as_bytes()).unwrap();
    let mut buffer = [0; 5];
    stream.read(&mut buffer).unwrap();
    println!(
        "Got response from server:{:?}",
        str::from_utf8(&buffer).unwrap()
    );
}
```

Annotations:
- **Write a "Hello" message to the TCP server connection.**
- **Read the bytes received from server.**
- **Print out what is received from the server. The server sends raw bytes, and we have to convert them into UTF-8 str type to print them to the terminal.**

Run the TCP client with `cargo run -p tcpclient` from the workspace root. Make sure that the TCP server is also running in another terminal window.

You will see the following message printed to the terminal window of the TCP client:

```
Got response from server:"Hello"
```

Congratulations. You have written a TCP server and a TCP client that can communicate with each other.

The `Result` type and `unwrap()` method

In Rust, it is idiomatic for a function or method that can fail to return a `Result<T,E>` type. This means the `Result` type wraps another data type, `T`, in the case of success, or it wraps an `Error` type in the case of failure, which is then returned to the calling function. The calling function in turn inspects the `Result` type and unwraps it to receive either the value of type `T` or type `Error` for further processing.

In the examples so far, we have made use of the `unwrap()` method in several places to retrieve the value embedded within the `Result` object by the standard library methods. The `unwrap()` method returns the value of type `T` if the operation is successful, or it panics in case of error. In a real-world application, this is not the right approach, as the `Result` type in Rust is for recoverable failures, while a panic is used for unrecoverable failures. However, we have used it here because using `unwrap()` simplifies our code for learning purposes. We will cover proper error handling in later chapters.

In this section, you have learned how to implement TCP communications in Rust. You have also seen that TCP is a low-level protocol that only deals in byte streams. It does not have any understanding of the semantics of the messages and data being exchanged. For writing web applications, semantic messages are easier to deal with than raw byte streams, so we need to work with a higher-level application protocol, such as HTTP, rather than TCP. We will look at this in the next section.

2.3 Writing an HTTP server in Rust

In this section, we'll build a web server in Rust that can communicate with HTTP messages.

Rust does not have built-in support for HTTP. There is no `std::http` module that we can work with. Even though third-party HTTP crates are available, we'll write one from scratch. As we do so, you will learn how to use Rust to develop lower-level libraries and servers that modern web applications in turn rely upon.

Let's first visualize the features of the web server that we are going to build. The communication flow between the client and the various modules of the web server is depicted in figure 2.3.

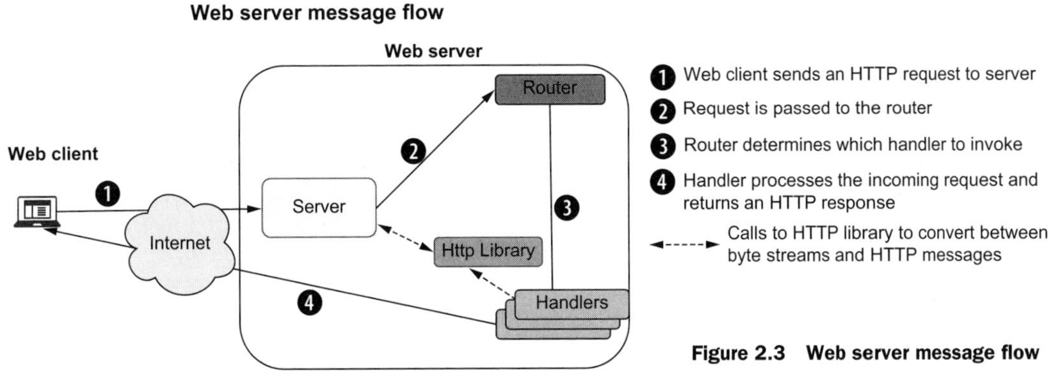

Web server message flow

1. Web client sends an HTTP request to server
2. Request is passed to the router
3. Router determines which handler to invoke
4. Handler processes the incoming request and returns an HTTP response

- - - ▶ Calls to HTTP library to convert between byte streams and HTTP messages

Figure 2.3 Web server message flow

Our web server will have four components: a server, router, handler, and HTTP library. Each of these components has a specific purpose, in line with the *single responsibility principle* (SRP). The *server* listens for incoming TCP byte streams. The *HTTP library* interprets the byte stream and converts it to an HTTP request (message). The *router* accepts an HTTP request and determines which handler to invoke. The *handler* processes the HTTP request and constructs an HTTP response. The HTTP response message is converted back to a byte stream using the HTTP library, and the byte stream is then sent back to the client.

Figure 2.4 shows another view of the HTTP client/server communications, this time depicting how the HTTP messages flow through the TCP/IP protocol stack. The TCP/IP communications are handled at the operating system level on both the client and server sides, and the web application developer only works with HTTP messages.

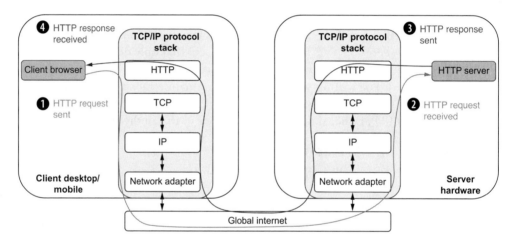

Figure 2.4   HTTP communications with a protocol stack

We'll build the code in the following sequence:

1 Build the `http` library.
2 Write the `main()` function for the project.
3 Write the `server` module.
4 Write the `router` module.
5 Write the `handler` module.

For convenience, figure 2.5 summarizes the code design, showing the key modules, structs, and methods for the `http` library and `httpserver` project. There are two main components in the figure:

- `http`—A library containing the types `HttpRequest` and `HttpResponse`. It implements the logic for converting between HTTP requests and responses and corresponding Rust data structures.

- `httpserver`—The main web server, which incorporates a `main()` function, a socket server, and a handler and router, manages the coordination among them. It serves as both a web server (serving HTML) and a web service (serving JSON).

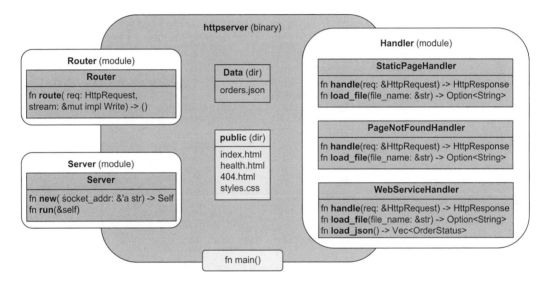

Figure 2.5   Design overview of the web server

Shall we get started?

2.3.1   *Parsing HTTP request messages*

In this section, we will build an HTTP library. The library will contain data structures and methods to do the following:

- Interpret an incoming byte stream and convert it into an HTTP request message
- Construct an HTTP response message and convert it into a byte stream for transmitting over the wire

We have already created a library called `http` under the `scenario1` workspace. The code for the HTTP library will be placed under the http/src folder.

In http/src/lib.rs, add the following code:

```
pub mod httprequest;
```

This tells the compiler that we are creating a new publicly accessible module called `httprequest` in the `http` library. You can also delete the test script that was automatically generated by Cargo from this file. We'll write test cases later.

Next, we'll create two new files, httprequest.rs and httpresponse.rs, under http/src to contain the functionality for dealing with HTTP requests and responses respectively.

We will start by designing the Rust data structures to hold an HTTP request. When a byte stream comes in over a TCP connection, we will parse it and convert it into strongly typed Rust data structures for further processing. Our HTTP server program can then work with these Rust data structures, rather than with the TCP streams.

Table 2.1 summarizes the Rust data structures needed to represent an incoming HTTP request.

Table 2.1   The data structures for incoming HTTP requests

Data structure name	Rust data type	Description
HttpRequest	struct	Represents an HTTP request
Method	enum	Specifies the allowed values (variants) for HTTP methods
Version	enum	Specifies the allowed values for HTTP Versions

We'll implement a few traits on these data structures to impart some behavior. Table 2.2 describes the traits we will implement on the three data structures.

Table 2.2   Traits implemented by the data structures for HTTP requests

Rust trait implemented	Description
From<&str>	Enables the conversion of incoming string slices to the HttpRequest data structure
Debug	Used to print debug messages
PartialEq	Used to compare values as part of parsing and automated test scripts

Let's now convert this design into code.

THE METHOD ENUM

The code for the `Method` enum is shown in the following snippet. We use an `enum` data structure as we only want to allow predefined values for the HTTP method in our implementation. We will only support two HTTP methods in this implementation: GET and POST requests. We'll also add a third type, `Uninitialized`, to be used during the initialization of data structures in the running program.

Add the following code to http/src/httprequest.rs:

```
#[derive(Debug, PartialEq)]
pub enum Method {
    Get,
    Post,
    Uninitialized,
}
```

The trait implementation for `Method` is shown next (also to be added to httprequest.rs):

```
impl From<&str> for Method {
    fn from(s: &str) -> Method {
        match s {
            "GET" => Method::Get,
            "POST" => Method::Post,
            _ => Method::Uninitialized,
        }
    }
}
```

Implementing the `from` method in the `From` trait enables us to read the `method` string from the HTTP request line and convert it into the `Method::Get` or `Method::Post` variant. To understand the benefit of implementing this trait and to test if this method works, let's write some test code. Throughout this book, I have deliberately limited the testing to unit tests so we can focus on Rust-specific aspects of the code.

Add the following test to http/src/httprequest.rs:

```
#[cfg(test)]
mod tests {
    use super::*;
    #[test]
    fn test_method_into() {
        let m: Method = "GET".into();
        assert_eq!(m, Method::Get);
    }
}
```

From the workspace root, run the following command:

```
cargo test -p http
```

You will notice a message similar to the following, stating that the test has passed.

```
running 1 test
test httprequest::tests::test_method_into ... ok

test result: ok. 1 passed; 0 failed; 0 ignored; 0 measured; 0 filtered out
```

The "GET" in the test is converted into the Method::Get variant using just the .into() syntax. This is the benefit of implementing the From trait—it makes for clean, readable code.

Let's now look at the code for the Version enum.

THE VERSION ENUM

The definition of the Version enum is shown next. We will support two HTTP versions for illustration, though we will only be working with HTTP/1.1 for our examples. There is also a third type, Uninitialized, to be used as the default initial value.

Add the following code to http/src/httprequest.rs:

```
#[derive(Debug, PartialEq)]
pub enum Version {
    V1_1,
    V2_0,
    Uninitialized,
}
```

The trait implementation for Version is similar to that for the Method enum (also to be added to httprequest.rs):

```
impl From<&str> for Version {
    fn from(s: &str) -> Version {
        match s {
            "HTTP/1.1" => Version::V1_1,
            _ => Version::Uninitialized,
        }
    }
}
```

Implementing the from method in the From trait enables us to read the HTTP protocol version from the incoming HTTP request and convert it into a Version variant.

Let's test if this method works. Add the following code to http/src/httprequest.rs, inside the previously added mod tests block (after the test_method_into() function), and run the test from the workspace root with cargo test -p http:

```
#[test]
    fn test_version_into() {
        let m: Version = "HTTP/1.1".into();
        assert_eq!(m, Version::V1_1);
    }
```

You will see the following message on your terminal:

```
running 2 tests
test httprequest::tests::test_method_into ... ok
test httprequest::tests::test_version_into ... ok

test result: ok. 2 passed; 0 failed; 0 ignored; 0 measured; 0 filtered out
```

Both the tests now pass. The string "HTTP/1.1" is converted into the Version::V1_1 variant using just the .into() syntax—this is again the benefit of implementing the From trait.

THE HTTPREQUEST STRUCT

The HttpRequest struct in the following listing represents the complete HTTP request. Add this code to the beginning of the http/src/httprequest.rs file.

Listing 2.6 Data structures for the HTTP request

```rust
use std::collections::HashMap;

#[derive(Debug, PartialEq)]
pub enum Resource {
    Path(String),
}

#[derive(Debug)]
pub struct HttpRequest {
    pub method: Method,
    pub version: Version,
    pub resource: Resource,
    pub headers: HashMap<String, String>,
    pub msg_body: String,
}
```

The From<&str> trait implementation for the HttpRequest struct is at the core of our exercise. This enables us to convert the incoming request into a Rust HTTP Request data structure that is convenient to process further.

Figure 2.6 shows the structure of a typical HTTP request, consisting of a request line, a set of one or more header lines followed by a blank line, and then an optional message body. We'll have to parse all these lines and convert them into our Http-Request type. That is going to be the job of the from() function as part of the From <&str> trait implementation.

The core logic for the From<&str> trait implementation is listed here:

1 Read each line in the incoming HTTP request. Each line is delimited by CRLF (\r\n).

2 Evaluate each line as follows:

– If the line is a request line (we will look for the keyword HTTP because all request lines contain the HTTP keyword and a version number), we extract the method, path, and HTTP version from the line.

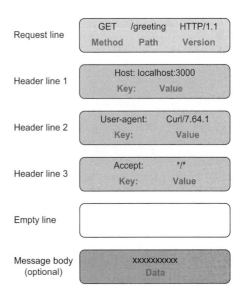

Figure 2.6 Structure of an HTTP request

- If the line is a header line (identified by the separator :), we extract `key` and `value` for the header item and add them to the list of headers for the request. Note that there can be multiple header lines in an HTTP request. To keep things simple, we'll make the assumption that the `key` and `value` must be composed of printable ASCII characters (i.e., characters with values between 33 and 126 in base 10, except for the colon).
- If a line is empty (`\n\r`), we treat it as a separator line. No action is needed in this case.
- If the message body is present, we scan and store it as a `String`.

First, let's look at the skeleton of the code. Don't type this in yet—this is just to show you the structure of the code:

```
impl From<String> for HttpRequest {
    fn from(req: String) -> Self {}
}
fn process_req_line(s: &str) -> (Method, Resource, Version) {}
fn process_header_line(s: &str) -> (String, String) {}
```

We have a `from()` method that we should implement for the `From` trait. There are also two supporting functions for parsing the request line and header lines respectively.

Let's first look at the `from()` method. Add this code to httprequest.rs.

> ### Listing 2.7   Parsing incoming HTTP requests: the `from()` method

```
impl From<String> for HttpRequest {
    fn from(req: String) -> Self {
        let mut parsed_method = Method::Uninitialized;
        let mut parsed_version = Version::V1_1;
        let mut parsed_resource = Resource::Path("".to_string());
        let mut parsed_headers = HashMap::new();
        let mut parsed_msg_body = "";

        // Read each line in the incoming HTTP request
        for line in req.lines() {
            // If the line read is request line, call function
            ➥process_req_line()
            if line.contains("HTTP") {
                let (method, resource, version) = process_req_line(line);
                parsed_method = method;
                parsed_version = version;
                parsed_resource = resource;
            // If the line read is header line, call function
            ➥process_header_line()
            } else if line.contains(":") {
                let (key, value) = process_header_line(line);
                parsed_headers.insert(key, value);
            // If it is blank line, do nothing
            } else if line.len() == 0 {
            // If none of these, treat it as message body
            } else {
```

```
                parsed_msg_body = line;
            }
        }
        // Parse the incoming HTTP request into HttpRequest struct
        HttpRequest {
            method: parsed_method,
            version: parsed_version,
            resource: parsed_resource,
            headers: parsed_headers,
            msg_body: parsed_msg_body.to_string(),
        }
    }
}
```

Based on the logic described earlier, we are trying to detect the various types of lines in the incoming HTTP `Request`, and then we construct an `HttpRequest` struct with the parsed values.

Now let's look at the two supporting methods. The following listing shows the code for processing the request line of the incoming request. Add it to httprequest.rs after the `impl From<String> for HttpRequest {}` block.

```
fn process_req_line(s: &str) -> (Method, Resource, Version) {
    // Parse the request line into individual chunks split by whitespaces.
    let mut words = s.split_whitespace();
    // Extract the HTTP method from first part of the request line
    let method = words.next().unwrap();
    // Extract the resource (URI/URL) from second part of the request line
    let resource = words.next().unwrap();
    // Extract the HTTP version from third part of the request line
    let version = words.next().unwrap();

    (
        method.into(),
        Resource::Path(resource.to_string()),
        version.into(),
    )
}
```

The next listing shows the code for parsing the header line. Add it to httprequest.rs after the `process_req_line()` function.

```
fn process_header_line(s: &str) -> (String, String) {
    // Parse the header line into words split by separator (':')
    let mut header_items = s.split(":");
    let mut key = String::from("");
    let mut value = String::from("");
    // Extract the key part of the header
    if let Some(k) = header_items.next() {
```

```
        key = k.to_string();
    }
    // Extract the value part of the header
    if let Some(v) = header_items.next() {
        value = v.to_string()
    }

    (key, value)
}
```

This completes the code for the `From` trait implementation for the `HttpRequest`
struct.

Let's write a unit test for the HTTP request parsing logic in http/src/httpre-
quest.rs, inside `mod tests` (the tests module). Recall that we've already written the
`test_method_into()` and `test_version_into()` functions in the `tests` module. At
this point, the `tests` module in the httprequest.rs file should look like the following
snippet:

```
#[cfg(test)]
mod tests {
    use super::*;
    #[test]
    fn test_method_into() {
        let m: Method = "GET".into();
        assert_eq!(m, Method::Get);
    }
    #[test]
    fn test_version_into() {
        let m: Version = "HTTP/1.1".into();
        assert_eq!(m, Version::V1_1);
    }
}
```

Now we'll add the following test function to the same `tests` module after the
`test_version_into()` function.

Listing 2.10   Test scripts for parsing HTTP requests

```
#[test]                                                          Simulate an incoming
    fn test_read_http() {                                           HTTP request.
        let s: String = String::from("GET /greeting HTTP/1.1\r\nHost:
        ➥ localhost:3000\r\nUser-Agent: curl/7.64.1\r\nAccept:
        ➥ */*\r\n\r\n");                                   ◄─────
        let mut headers_expected = HashMap::new();
        headers_expected.insert("Host".into(), " localhost".into());
        headers_expected.insert("Accept".into(), " */*".into());
        headers_expected.insert("User-Agent".into(), " curl/7.64.1".into());
        let req: HttpRequest = s.into();          ◄────
        assert_eq!(Method::Get, req.method);
        assert_eq!(Version::V1_1, req.version);   ◄────┐
```

Construct an expected headers list. (points to `let mut headers_expected = HashMap::new();`)

Verify that the method is parsed correctly. (points to `assert_eq!(Method::Get, req.method);`)

Parse the entire incoming multiline HTTP request into the HttpRequest struct. (points to `let req: HttpRequest = s.into();`)

Verify that the HTTP version is parsed correctly. (points to `assert_eq!(Version::V1_1, req.version);`)

```
        assert_eq!(Resource::Path("/greeting".to_string()), req.resource);   ◁┐
        assert_eq!(headers_expected, req.headers);   ◁┐
}
```

Verify that the headers are parsed correctly.

Verify that the path (resource URI) is parsed correctly.

Now run the test with `cargo test -p http` from the workspace root folder. You should see the following message indicating that all three tests have passed:

```
running 3 tests
test httprequest::tests::test_method_into ... ok
test httprequest::tests::test_version_into ... ok
test httprequest::tests::test_read_http ... ok

test result: ok. 3 passed; 0 failed; 0 ignored; 0 measured; 0 filtered out
```

We have now completed the code for HTTP request processing. This library can parse an incoming HTTP GET or POST message and convert it into a Rust data struct. Let's now write the code to process HTTP responses.

2.3.2 *Constructing HTTP response messages*

Let's define an `HttpResponse` struct, which will represent the HTTP Response message within our program. We will also write a method to convert this struct (serialize it) into a well-formed HTTP message that can be understood by an HTTP client (such as a web browser).

Figure 2.7 shows the structure of a typical HTTP response. This will help us define our struct.

If you didn't already do so, create a http/src/httpresponse.rs file. Add `httpresponse` to the module exports section of http/lib.rs so that it looks like this:

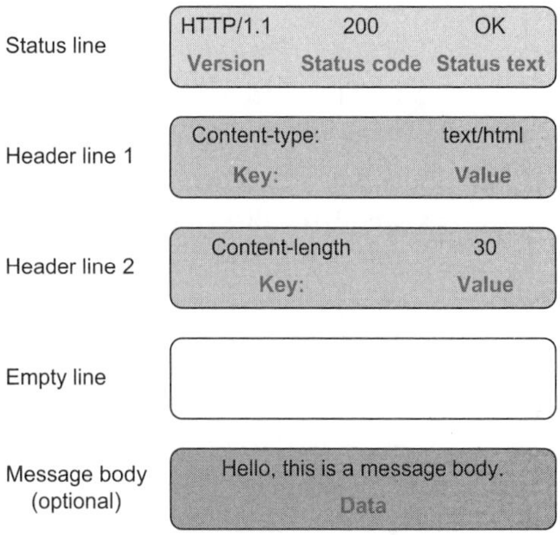

	HTTP/1.1	200	OK
Status line	Version	Status code	Status text

	Content-type:		text/html
Header line 1	Key:		Value

	Content-length		30
Header line 2	Key:		Value

Empty line

	Hello, this is a message body.
Message body (optional)	Data

Figure 2.7   Structure of an HTTP response

```
pub mod httprequest;
pub mod httpresponse;
```

Add the following code to http/src/httpresponse.rs.

Listing 2.11   Structure of the HTTP response

```
use std::collections::HashMap;
use std::io::{Result, Write};

#[derive(Debug, PartialEq, Clone)]
pub struct HttpResponse<'a> {
```

```
    version: &'a str,
    status_code: &'a str,
    status_text: &'a str,
    headers: Option<HashMap<&'a str, &'a str>>,
    body: Option<String>,
}
```

The `HttpResponse` struct contains a protocol version, status code, status description, a list of optional headers, and an optional body. Note the use of the lifetime annotation `'a` for all the member fields that are of reference types.

> ## Lifetimes in Rust
> In Rust, every reference has a lifetime, which is the scope for which the reference is valid. Lifetimes are an important feature in Rust, aimed at preventing dangling pointers and use-after-free errors, which are common in languages with manually managed memory (such as C/C++). The Rust compiler either infers (if not specified) or uses (if specified) the lifetime annotation of a reference to verify that a reference does not outlive the underlying value it points to.

Also note the use of the `#[derive]` annotation for the `Debug`, `PartialEq`, and `Clone` traits. These are called *derivable* traits because we are asking the compiler to derive the implementation of these traits for our `HttpResponse` struct. By implementing these traits, our struct acquires the ability to be printed out for debugging purposes, to have its member values compared with other values, and to have itself cloned.

We will implement the following methods for the `HttpResponse` struct:

- *A* `Default` *trait implementation*—Earlier we auto-derived a few traits using the `#[derive]` annotation. We'll now manually implement the `Default` trait. This will let us specify default values for the struct members.
- *A* `new()` *method*—This method will create a new struct with default values for its members.
- *A* `send_response()` *method*—This method will serialize the contents of the `HttpResponse` struct into a valid HTTP response message for on-the-wire transmission, and it will send the raw bytes over the TCP connection.
- *Getter methods*—We'll also implement a set of getter methods for `version`, `status_code`, `status_text`, `headers`, and `body`, which are the member fields of the `HttpResponse` struct.
- *A* `From` *trait implementation*—Lastly, we will implement the `From` trait, which will help us convert the `HttpResponse` struct into a `String` type representing a valid HTTP response message.

Let's add the code for all of these to http/src/httpresponse.rs.

IMPLEMENTING THE DEFAULT TRAIT
We'll start with the `Default` trait implementation for the `HttpResponse` struct.

Listing 2.12   The `Default` trait implementation for the HTTP response

```
impl<'a> Default for HttpResponse<'a> {
    fn default() -> Self {
        Self {
            version: "HTTP/1.1".into(),
            status_code: "200".into(),
            status_text: "OK".into(),
            headers: None,
            body: None,
        }
    }
}
```

Implementing a `Default` trait allows us to create a new struct with default values as follows:

```
let mut response: HttpResponse<'a> = HttpResponse::default();
```

IMPLEMENTING THE NEW() METHOD

The `new()` method accepts a few parameters, sets the defaults for the others, and returns an `HttpResponse` struct. Add the following code under the `impl` block of the `HttpResponse` struct. As this struct has a reference type for one of its members, the `impl` block declaration also has to specify a lifetime parameter (shown here as `'a`).

Listing 2.13   The `new()` method for `HttpResponse` (httpresponse.rs)

```
impl<'a> HttpResponse<'a> {
    pub fn new(
        status_code: &'a str,
        headers: Option<HashMap<&'a str, &'a str>>,
        body: Option<String>,
    ) -> HttpResponse<'a> {
        let mut response: HttpResponse<'a> = HttpResponse::default();
        if status_code != "200" {
            response.status_code = status_code.into();
        };
        response.headers = match &headers {
            Some(_h) => headers,
            None => {
                let mut h = HashMap::new();
                h.insert("Content-Type", "text/html");
                Some(h)
            }
        };
        response.status_text = match response.status_code {
            "200" => "OK".into(),
            "400" => "Bad Request".into(),
            "404" => "Not Found".into(),
            "500" => "Internal Server Error".into(),
            _ => "Not Found".into(),
        };
        response.body = body;
```

```
        response
    }
}
```

The `new()` method starts by constructing a struct with default parameters. The values passed as parameters are then evaluated and incorporated into the struct.

IMPLEMENTING THE SEND_RESPONSE() METHOD

The `send_response()` method is used to convert the `HttpResponse` struct into a `String` and transmit it over the TCP connection. This can be added within the `impl` block in httpresponse.rs, after the `new()` method:

```
impl<'a> HttpResponse<'a> {
    // new() method not shown here
    pub fn send_response(&self, write_stream: &mut impl Write) ->
    ➥Result<()> {
        let res = self.clone();
        let response_string: String = String::from(res);
        let _ = write!(write_stream, "{}", response_string);
        Ok(())
    }
}
```

This method accepts a TCP stream (that implements a `Write` trait) as input, and it writes the well-formed HTTP response message to the stream.

IMPLEMENTING GETTER METHODS FOR THE HTTPRESPONSE STRUCT

Let's write getter methods for each of the members of the struct. We need these to construct the HTML response message in httpresponse.rs.

Listing 2.14   Getter methods for `HttpResponse`

```
impl<'a> HttpResponse<'a> {
    fn version(&self) -> &str {
        self.version
    }
    fn status_code(&self) -> &str {
        self.status_code
    }
    fn status_text(&self) -> &str {
        self.status_text
    }
    fn headers(&self) -> String {
        let map: HashMap<&str, &str> = self.headers.clone().unwrap();
        let mut header_string: String = "".into();
        for (k, v) in map.iter() {
            header_string = format!("{}{}:{}\r\n", header_string, k, v);
        }
        header_string
    }
    pub fn body(&self) -> &str {
        match &self.body {
            Some(b) => b.as_str(),
```

```
            None => "",
        }
    }
}
```

The getter methods allow us to convert the data members into string types.

IMPLEMENTING THE FROM TRAIT

Lastly, let's implement the `from` method in the `From` trait, which will be used to convert (serialize) the `HttpResponse` struct into an HTTP response message string, in httpresponse.rs.

Listing 2.15   Code to serialize a Rust struct into an HTTP response message

```
impl<'a> From<HttpResponse<'a>> for String {
    fn from(res: HttpResponse) -> String {
        let res1 = res.clone();
        format!(
            "{} {} {}\r\n{}Content-Length: {}\r\n\r\n{}",
            &res1.version(),
            &res1.status_code(),
            &res1.status_text(),
            &res1.headers(),
            &res.body.unwrap().len(),
            &res1.body()
        )
    }
}
```

Note the use of `\r\n` in the `format` string. This inserts a newline character. Recall that the HTTP response message consists of the following sequence: status line, headers, blank line, and optional message body.

Let's write a few unit tests. In a moment, we'll create a test module block like the following and add each test to this block. Don't type this in yet—this is just to show you the structure of the test code:

```
#[cfg(test)]
mod tests {
    use super::*;
    // Add unit tests here. Each test needs to have a  #[test] annotation
}
```

We'll first check that the `HttpResponse` struct was constructed for the message with a status code of 200 (Success). Add the following to httpresponse.rs toward the end of the file.

Listing 2.16   Test script for an HTTP success (200) message

```
#[cfg(test)]
mod tests {
    use super::*;
```

```
#[test]
    fn test_response_struct_creation_200() {
        let response_actual = HttpResponse::new(
            "200",
            None,
            Some("Item was shipped on 21st Dec 2020".into()),
        );
        let response_expected = HttpResponse {
            version: "HTTP/1.1",
            status_code: "200",
            status_text: "OK",
            headers: {
                let mut h = HashMap::new();
                h.insert("Content-Type", "text/html");
                Some(h)
            },
            body: Some("Item was shipped on 21st Dec 2020".into()),
        };
        assert_eq!(response_actual, response_expected);
    }
}
```

Next, we'll test for a 404 (page not found) HTTP message. Add the following test case within the mod tests {} block, after the test_response_struct_creation_200() test function.

Listing 2.17   Test script for a 404 message

```
#[test]
    fn test_response_struct_creation_404() {
        let response_actual = HttpResponse::new(
            "404",
            None,
            Some("Item was shipped on 21st Dec 2020".into()),
        );
        let response_expected = HttpResponse {
            version: "HTTP/1.1",
            status_code: "404",
            status_text: "Not Found",
            headers: {
                let mut h = HashMap::new();
                h.insert("Content-Type", "text/html");
                Some(h)
            },
            body: Some("Item was shipped on 21st Dec 2020".into()),
        };
        assert_eq!(response_actual, response_expected);
    }
```

Lastly, we'll check if the HttpResponse struct is being serialized into an on-the-wire HTTP response message in the right format. Add the following test within the mod tests {} block, after the test_response_struct_creation_404() test function.

Listing 2.18 Test script to check for a well-formed HTTP response message

```
#[test]
    fn test_http_response_creation() {
        let response_expected = HttpResponse {
            version: "HTTP/1.1",
            status_code: "404",
            status_text: "Not Found",
            headers: {
                let mut h = HashMap::new();
                h.insert("Content-Type", "text/html");
                Some(h)
            },
            body: Some("Item was shipped on 21st Dec 2020".into()),
        };
        let http_string: String = response_expected.into();
        let response_actual = "HTTP/1.1 404 Not Found\r\nContent-Type:
    ➥text/html\r\nContent-Length: 33\r\n\r\nItem was
    ➥shipped on 21st Dec 2020";
        assert_eq!(http_string, response_actual);
    }
```

Let's run the tests now. Run the following command from the workspace root:

```
cargo test -p http
```

You should see the following message showing that six tests have passed in the `http` module. Note that this includes tests for both the HTTP request and HTTP response modules:

```
running 6 tests
test httprequest::tests::test_method_into ... ok
test httprequest::tests::test_version_into ... ok
test httpresponse::tests::test_http_response_creation ... ok
test httpresponse::tests::test_response_struct_creation_200 ... ok
test httprequest::tests::test_read_http ... ok
test httpresponse::tests::test_response_struct_creation_404 ... ok

test result: ok. 6 passed; 0 failed; 0 ignored; 0 measured; 0 filtered out
```

If the test fails, check for any typos or misalignment in the code (if you copied and pasted it). In particular, recheck the following string literal (which is quite long and prone to mistakes):

```
"HTTP/1.1 404 Not Found\r\nContent-Type:text/html\r\nContent-Length:
➥33\r\n\r\nItem was shipped on 21st Dec 2020";
```

If you are still having trouble executing the tests, refer back to the Git repo. This completes the code for the `http` library. Recall the design of the HTTP server, shown again in figure 2.8.

We've written the `http` library. Now we need to write the `main()` function, server, router, and handler. We will have to switch from the `http` project to the `httpserver` project directory to write this code.

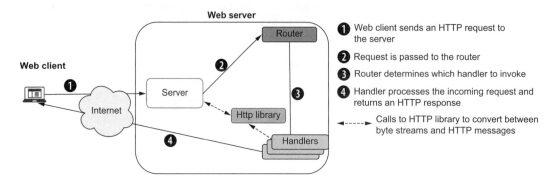

Figure 2.8   Web server message flow

To refer to the `http` library from the `httpserver` project, add the following code to the Cargo.toml file of the latter:

```
[dependencies]
http = {path = "../http"}
```

2.3.3   *Writing the main() function and server module*

Let's take a top-down approach. We'll start with the `main()` function in httpserver/ src/main.rs.

Listing 2.19   The `main()` function

```
mod handler;
mod server;
mod router;
use server::Server;
fn main() {
    // Start a server
    let server = Server::new("localhost:3000");
    //Run the server
    server.run();
}
```

The `main` function imports three modules: `handler`, `server`, and `router`. Now we need to create these three files—handler.rs, server.rs, and router.rs—under httpserver/src. We'll write the code for the `server` module in httpserver/src/server.rs.

Listing 2.20   The `server` module

```
use super::router::Router;
use http::httprequest::HttpRequest;
use std::io::prelude::*;
use std::net::TcpListener;
use std::str;
```

```
pub struct Server<'a> {
    socket_addr: &'a str,
}
impl<'a> Server<'a> {
    pub fn new(socket_addr: &'a str) -> Self {
        Server { socket_addr }
    }
    pub fn run(&self) {
        // Start a server listening on socket address
        let connection_listener = TcpListener::bind(
        ➥self.socket_addr).unwrap();
        println!("Running on {}", self.socket_addr);
        // Listen to incoming connections in a loop
        for stream in connection_listener.incoming() {
            let mut stream = stream.unwrap();
            println!("Connection established");
            let mut read_buffer = [0; 90];
            stream.read(&mut read_buffer).unwrap();
            // Convert HTTP request to Rust data structure
            let req: HttpRequest = String::from_utf8(
            ➥read_buffer.to_vec()).unwrap().into();
            // Route request to appropriate handler
            Router::route(req, &mut stream);
        }
    }
}
```

The server module has two methods. The new() method accepts a socket address (host and port) and returns a Server instance. The run() method performs the following:

- Binds on the socket
- Listens to incoming connections
- Reads a byte stream on a valid connection
- Converts the stream into an HttpRequest struct instance
- Passes the request to Router for further processing

2.3.4 *Writing the router and handler modules*

The router module inspects the incoming HTTP request and determines which handler to route the request to for processing. Add the following code to httpserver/src/router.rs.

Listing 2.21   The router module

```
use super::handler::{Handler, PageNotFoundHandler, StaticPageHandler,➥
WebServiceHandler};
use http::{httprequest, httprequest::HttpRequest,➥
httpresponse::HttpResponse};
use std::io::prelude::*;
pub struct Router;
impl Router {
    pub fn route(req: HttpRequest, stream: &mut impl Write) -> () {
```

```
        match req.method {
            // If GET request
            httprequest::Method::Get => match &req.resource {
                httprequest::Resource::Path(s) => {
                    // Parse the URI
                    let route: Vec<&str> = s.split("/").collect();
                    match route[1] {
                        // if the route begins with /api, invoke Web service
                        "api" => {
                            let resp: HttpResponse =
                            ➥WebServiceHandler::handle(&req);
                            let _ = resp.send_response(stream);
                        }
                         // Else, invoke static page handler
                        _ => {
                            let resp: HttpResponse =
                            ➥StaticPageHandler::handle(&req);
                            let _ = resp.send_response(stream);
                        }
                    }
                }
            },
            // If method is not GET request, return 404 page
            _ => {
                let resp: HttpResponse = PageNotFoundHandler::handle(&req);
                let _ = resp.send_response(stream);
            }
        }
    }
}
```

The `router` checks if the incoming method is a GET request. If so, it performs checks
in the following order:

1 If the GET request route begins with /api, it routes the request to the Web-
   ServiceHandler.
2 If the GET request is for any other resource, it assumes the request is for a static
   page and routes the request to the StaticPageHandler.
3 If it is not a GET request, it sends back a 404 error page.

For the handler modules, let's add a couple of external crates to handle JSON serialization and deserialization: serde and serde_json. The Cargo.toml file for the httpserver project will look like this:

```
[dependencies]
http = {path = "../http"}
serde = {version = "1.0.117",features = ["derive"]}
serde_json = "1.0.59"
```

Let's start with module imports. Add the following code to httpserver/src/handler.rs:

```
use http::{httprequest::HttpRequest, httpresponse::HttpResponse};
use serde::{Deserialize, Serialize};
```

```
use std::collections::HashMap;
use std::env;
use std::fs;
```

Now let's define a trait called `Handler` as follows.

Listing 2.22   Defining the `Handler` trait

```
pub trait Handler {
    fn handle(req: &HttpRequest) -> HttpResponse;
    fn load_file(file_name: &str) -> Option<String> {
        let default_path = format!("{}/public", env!("CARGO_MANIFEST_DIR"));
        let public_path = env::var("PUBLIC_PATH").unwrap_or(default_path);
        let full_path = format!("{}/{}", public_path, file_name);

        let contents = fs::read_to_string(full_path);
        contents.ok()
    }
}
```

Note that the `Handler` trait contains two methods:

- `handle()`—This method has to be implemented for any other user data type to implement the trait.
- `load_file()`—This method loads a file (non-JSON) from the public directory in the httpserver root folder. The implementation is already provided as part of the trait definition.

We'll now define the following data structures:

- `StaticPageHandler`—To serve static web pages
- `WebServiceHandler`—To serve JSON data
- `PageNotFoundHandler`—To serve a 404 page
- `OrderStatus`—To load data read from a JSON file

Add the following code to httpserver/src/handler.rs.

Listing 2.23   Data structures for the handler

```
#[derive(Serialize, Deserialize)]
pub struct OrderStatus {
    order_id: i32,
    order_date: String,
    order_status: String,
}

pub struct StaticPageHandler;

pub struct PageNotFoundHandler;

pub struct WebServiceHandler;
```

Now let's implement the `Handler` trait for the three handler structs. We'll start with the `PageNotFoundHandler`:

```
impl Handler for PageNotFoundHandler {
    fn handle(_req: &HttpRequest) -> HttpResponse {
        HttpResponse::new("404", None, Self::load_file("404.html"))
    }
}
```

If the `handle` method on the `PageNotFoundHandler` struct is invoked, it will return a new `HttpResponse` struct instance with a status code of 404 and a body containing some HTML loaded from the 404.html file.

Next is the code for the `StaticPageHandler`.

Listing 2.24   A handler to serve static web pages

```
impl Handler for StaticPageHandler {
    fn handle(req: &HttpRequest) -> HttpResponse {
        // Get the path of static page resource being requested
        let http::httprequest::Resource::Path(s) = &req.resource;

        // Parse the URI
        let route: Vec<&str> = s.split("/").collect();
        match route[1] {
            "" => HttpResponse::new("200", None,
            ➥Self::load_file("index.html")),
            "health" => HttpResponse::new("200", None,
            ➥Self::load_file("health.html")),
            path => match Self::load_file(path) {
                Some(contents) => {
                    let mut map: HashMap<&str, &str> = HashMap::new();
                    if path.ends_with(".css") {
                        map.insert("Content-Type", "text/css");
                    } else if path.ends_with(".js") {
                        map.insert("Content-Type", "text/javascript");
                    } else {
                        map.insert("Content-Type", "text/html");
                    }
                    HttpResponse::new("200", Some(map), Some(contents))
                }
                None => HttpResponse::new("404", None,
                ➥Self::load_file("404.html")),
            },
        }
    }
}
```

If the `handle()` method is called on the `StaticPageHandler`, the following processing is performed:

- If the incoming request is for `localhost:3000/`, the contents from the index.html file are loaded, and a new `HttpResponse` struct is constructed.

- If the incoming request is for `localhost:3000/health`, the contents from the health.html file are loaded, and a new `HttpResponse` struct is constructed.
- If the incoming request is for any other file, the method tries to locate that file in the httpserver/public folder. If the file is not found, it sends back a 404 error page. If the file is found, the contents are loaded and embedded within an `HttpResponse` struct. Note that the `Content-Type` header in the HTTP response message is set according to the type of file.

Let's now look at the last part of the code: `WebServiceHandler`.

Listing 2.25 A handler to serve JSON data

```
impl WebServiceHandler {                              Define a load_json() method to
    fn load_json() -> Vec<OrderStatus> {    ⟵──      load the orders.json file from disk.
        let default_path = format!("{}/data", env!("CARGO_MANIFEST_DIR"));
        let data_path = env::var("DATA_PATH").unwrap_or(default_path);
        let full_path = format!("{}/{}", data_path, "orders.json");
        let json_contents = fs::read_to_string(full_path);
        let orders: Vec<OrderStatus> =
            serde_json::from_str(json_contents.unwrap().as_str()).unwrap();
        orders
    }
}
// Implement the Handler trait
impl Handler for WebServiceHandler {
    fn handle(req: &HttpRequest) -> HttpResponse {
        let http::httprequest::Resource::Path(s) = &req.resource;

        // Parse the URI
        let route: Vec<&str> = s.split("/").collect();
        // if route if /api/shipping/orders, return json
        match route[2] {
            "shipping" if route.len() > 2 && route[3] == "orders" => {
                let body = Some(serde_json::to_string(
                    ⟿&Self::load_json()).unwrap());
                let mut headers: HashMap<&str, &str> = HashMap::new();
                headers.insert("Content-Type", "application/json");
                HttpResponse::new("200", Some(headers), body)
            }
            _ => HttpResponse::new("404", None, Self::load_file("404.html")),
        }
    }
}
```

If the `handle()` method is called on the `WebServiceHandler` struct, the following processing is done:

- If the GET request is for `localhost:3000/api/shipping/orders`, the JSON file with orders is loaded, and this is serialized into JSON, which is returned as part of the body of the response.
- If it is any other route, a 404 error page is returned.

We're done with the code. We now have to create the HTML and JSON files to test the web server.

2.3.5   *Testing the web server*

In this section, we'll first create the test web pages and JSON data. We'll then test the web server for various scenarios and analyze the results.

Create two subfolders, data and public, under the httpserver root folder. In the public folder, create four files: index.html, health.html, 404.html, and styles.css. In the data folder, create an orders.json file.

Example contents for these files are shown in the following listings. You can alter them according to your preference.

Listing 2.26   The index web page (httpserver/public/index.html)

```
<!DOCTYPE html>
<html lang="en">
  <head>
    <meta charset="utf-8" />
    <link rel="stylesheet" href="styles.css">
    <title>Index!</title>
  </head>
  <body>
    <h1>Hello, welcome to home page</h1>
    <p>This is the index page for the web site</p>
  </body>
</html>
```

Listing 2.27   The style sheet for formatting the page (httpserver/public/styles.css)

```
h1 {
  color: red;
  margin-left: 25px;
}
```

Listing 2.28   The health web page (httpserver/public/health.html)

```
<!DOCTYPE html>
<html lang="en">
  <head>
    <meta charset="utf-8" />
    <title>Health!</title>
  </head>
  <body>
    <h1>Hello welcome to health page!</h1>
    <p>This site is perfectly fine</p>
  </body>
</html>
```

Listing 2.29   Page-not-found file (httpserver/public/404.html)

```html
<!DOCTYPE html>
  <html lang="en">
<head>
<meta charset="utf-8" /> <title>Not Found!</title>
   </head>
   <body>
     <h1>404 Error</h1>
     <p>Sorry the requested page does not exist</p>
   </body>
</html>
```

Listing 2.30   The JSON data file for orders (httpserver/data/orders.json)

```json
[
    {
        "order_id": 1,
        "order_date": "21 Jan 2020",
        "order_status": "Delivered"
    },
    {
        "order_id": 2,
        "order_date": "2 Feb 2020",
        "order_status": "Pending"
    }
]
```

We're ready to run the web server now. Run it from the workspace root as follows:

```
cargo run -p httpserver
```

Then, from a browser window or using the curl tool, test the following URLs:

```
localhost:3000/
localhost:3000/health
localhost:3000/api/shipping/orders
localhost:3000/invalid-path
```

If you invoke these commands on a browser, for the first URL, you should see the heading in red font. Go to the network tab in the Chrome browser (or to equivalent developer tools on other browsers) and view the files downloaded by the browser. You'll see that in addition to the index.html file, the styles.css file was also automatically downloaded by the browser, which results in the styling being applied to the index page. If you inspect further, you'll see that the Content-Type of text/css has been sent for the css file, and text/html has been set for the HTML file, all from our web server to the browser.

Likewise, if you inspect the response content-type sent for the /api/shipping/orders path, you will see application/json received by the browser as part of the response headers.

In this section, we have written an HTTP server and a library of HTTP messages that can serve static pages and JSON data. While the former capability is associated with the term *web server*, the latter is where we start to see web service capabilities. Our `httpserver` project functions as both a static web server as well as a web service serving JSON data. Of course, a regular web service would serve more methods than just `GET` requests, but this exercise was intended to demonstrate how you can use Rust to build such a web server and web service from scratch, without using any web frameworks or external HTTP libraries.

I hope you enjoyed following along with the code and got to a working server. If you had any difficulties, you can refer to the code repository for chapter 2: https://git.manning.com/agileauthor/eshwarla/-/tree/master/code.

You now have the foundational knowledge to understand how Rust can be used to develop a low-level HTTP library and web server, as well as the beginnings of a web service. In the next chapter, we will dive right into developing web services using a production-ready web framework that is written in Rust.

Summary

- The TCP/IP model is a simplified set of standards and protocols for communication over the internet. It is organized into four abstract layers: the network access layer, internet layer, transport layer, and application layer. TCP is the transport-layer protocol over which other application-level protocols, such as HTTP, operate. We built a server and client that exchanged data using the TCP protocol.

- TCP is a stream-oriented protocol where data is exchanged as a continuous stream of bytes.

- We built a basic TCP server and client using the Rust standard library. TCP does not understand the semantics of messages, such as HTTP. Our TCP client and server simply exchanged a stream of bytes without any understanding of the data transmitted.

- HTTP is an application-layer protocol and is the foundation for most web services. In most cases, HTTP uses TCP as the transport protocol.

- We built an HTTP library to parse incoming HTTP requests and construct HTTP responses. The HTTP requests and responses were modeled using Rust structs and enums.

- We built an HTTP server that serves two types of content: static web pages (with associated files, such as stylesheets) and JSON data.

- Our web server can accept requests and send responses to standard HTTP clients, such as browsers and the curl tool.

- We added additional behavior to our custom structs by implementing several traits. Some of them were auto-derived using Rust annotations, and others were hand-coded. We also made use of lifetime annotations to specify the lifetimes of references within structs.

Building a RESTful web service

This chapter covers

- Getting started with Actix
- Writing a RESTful web service

In this chapter, we will build our first real web service. It will expose a set of APIs over HTTP, and it will use the *representational state transfer* (REST) architectural style.

We'll build the web service using Actix (https://actix.rs), a lightweight web framework written in Rust, which is also one of the most mature in terms of code activity, adoption, and ecosystem. We will warm up by writing some introductory code in Actix so you can learn its foundational concepts and structure. Later in this chapter, we will design and build a set of REST APIs using a thread-safe in-memory data store.

The complete code for this chapter can be found at https://git.manning.com/agileauthor/eshwarla/-/tree/master/code.

3.1 Getting started with Actix

In this book, we are going to build a digital storefront aimed at tutors. We'll call our digital platform *EzyTutors* because we want tutors to be able to easily publish their training catalogs online, which can in turn trigger the interest of learners and generate sales.

To kickstart this journey, we'll build a set of simple APIs that allow tutors to create courses and learners to retrieve courses.

This introduction to Actix is organized into two parts. In the first subsection, we will build a basic async HTTP server using Actix that demonstrates a simple health-check API. This will help you understand the foundational concepts of Actix. In the second subsection, we will design and build REST APIs for the tutor web service. We will rely on an in-memory data store (rather than a database) and use test-driven development. Along the way, you will be introduced to key Actix concepts such as *routes, handlers, HTTP requests, parameters,* and *HTTP responses.*

Let's write some code, shall we?

Why Actix?

This book is about developing high-performance web services and applications in Rust. The web frameworks I considered while writing this book were Actix, Rocket, Warp, and Tide. Warp and Tide are relatively new, whereas Actix and Rocket lead the pack in terms of adoption and level of activity. I chose Actix over Rocket because Rocket does not yet have native async support, and async support is a key factor in improving performance in I/O-heavy workloads (such as web service APIs) at scale.

3.1.1   *Writing the first REST API*

In this section, we'll write an Actix server that can respond to an HTTP request.

A note about the project structure

There are many ways to organize the code that you will be building over the course of this book.

The first option is to create a workspace project (similar to the one we created in chapter 2) and create separate projects under the workspace, one per chapter.

The second option is to create a separate cargo binary project for each chapter. The grouping options for deployment can be determined at a later time.

Either approach is fine, but in this book, we'll adopt the first approach to keep things organized. We'll create a workspace project, `ezytutors`, which will hold the other projects.

First, we'll create a new project with this command:

```
cargo new ezytutors && cd ezytutors
```

This will create a *binary* Cargo project.

Let's convert this into a workspace project. Under this workspace, we'll store the web service and applications that we will build in future chapters. Add the following to Cargo.toml:

```
[workspace]
members = ["tutor-nodb"]
```

`tutor-nodb` is the name of the web service we will create in this chapter. Create another Cargo project as follows:

```
cargo new tutor-nodb && cd tutor-nodb
```

This will create a binary Rust project called `tutor-nodb` under the `ezytutors` workspace. For convenience, we will refer to this as the "tutor web service" henceforth. The root folder of this Cargo project contains an src subfolder and a Cargo.toml file.

Add the following dependencies in Cargo.toml in the tutor web service:

```
[dependencies]
actix-web = "4.2.1"
actix-rt = "2.7.0"
```

You can use this version of actix-web or whichever later version is available at the time you are reading this.

The async runtime for Actix. Rust requires an external runtime engine for executing async code.

Add the following binary declaration to the same Cargo.toml file to specify the name of the binary file:

```
[[bin]]
name = "basic-server"
```

Let's now create a source file called basic-server.rs under the tutor-nodb/src/bin folder. This will contain the `main()` function, which is the entry point for the binary.

There are four basic steps involved in creating and starting a basic HTTP server in Actix:

1 Configure the routes, which are paths to various resources in a web server. For our example, we will configure a /health route to perform health checks on the server.

2 Configure a handler. The handler is the function that processes requests for a route. We will define a health-check handler to service the /health route.

3 Construct a web application, and register the routes and handlers with the application.

4 Construct an HTTP server linked to the web application, and run the server.

These four steps are highlighted in listing 3.1 with annotations. Add that code to src/bin/basic-server.rs. Don't worry if you don't understand all the steps and code—just type it in for now, and it will be explained in detail later.

> **NOTE** I highly recommend that you type in the code line by line, rather than copying and pasting it into your editor. This will provide you with a better return on your learning time, as you will be practicing rather than just reading.

Listing 3.1   Writing a basic Actix web server

```
// Module imports
use actix_web::{web, App, HttpResponse, HttpServer, Responder};
use std::io;
                                    For HTTP GET requests coming in on the /health route, the Actix
// Configure route          ◁──┘   web server will route the request to health_check_handler().
pub fn general_routes(cfg: &mut web::ServiceConfig) {
    cfg.route("/health", web::get().to(health_check_handler));
}
                                    The handler constructs an HTTP
//Configure handler         ◁──┘   response with a greeting.
pub async fn health_check_handler() -> impl Responder {
    HttpResponse::Ok().json("Hello. EzyTutors is alive and kicking")
}

// Instantiate and run the HTTP server
#[actix_rt::main]
async fn main() -> io::Result<()> {                Construct an Actix web application instance,
    // Construct app and configure routes  ◁──┘   and register the configured routes.
    let app = move || App::new().configure(general_routes);

    // Start HTTP server                                         ◁──┐ Initialize a web server,
    HttpServer::new(app).bind("127.0.0.1:3000")?.run().await         load the application,
}                                                                    bind it to a socket,
                                                                     and run the server.
```

You can run the server in one of two ways. If you are in the ezytutors workspace folder root, run the following command:

```
cargo run -p tutor-nodb --bin basic-server
```

The -p flag tells Cargo to build and run the binary for the tutor-nodb project within the workspace.

Alternatively, you can run the command from within the tutor-nodb folder as follows:

```
cargo run --bin basic-server
```

In a web browser, visit the following URL:

```
localhost:3000/health
```

You will see the following printed:

```
Hello, EzyTutors is alive and kicking
```

Congratulations! You have built your first REST API in Actix.

3.1.2   *Understanding Actix concepts*

In the previous section, we wrote a basic Actix web server (an Actix HTTP server). The server was configured to run a web application with a single route, /health, that returns the health status of the web application service. Figure 3.1 shows the components of Actix that we used in the code.

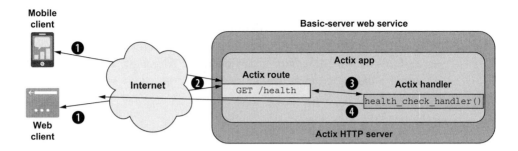

1 HTTP GET request for a health check is sent from a web or mobile browser to the Actix server.

2 The Actix HTTP server directs the request to the /health route in the Actix application.

3 The /health route directs the request to the health_check_handler().

4 The health_check_handler() returns a response to the web or mobile browser.

Figure 3.1 Components of the Actix web server

Here is the sequence of steps shown in the figure:

1 When you typed localhost:3000/health in your browser, an HTTP GET request message was constructed by the browser and sent to the Actix basic-server listening at the localhost:3000 port.

2 The Actix basic-server inspected the GET request and determined the route in the message to be /health. The server then routed the request to the web application (app) that had the /health route defined.

3 The web application in turn determined the handler for the route /health to be health_check_handler(), and it routed the message to that handler.

4 The health_check_handler() handler constructed an HTTP response with a text message and sent it back to the browser.

You will have noticed the terms *HTTP server*, *web application*, *route*, and *handler* used prominently. These are key concepts within Actix for building web services. Recall that we also used the terms *server*, *route*, and *handler* in chapter 2. Conceptually, these are similar, but let's look at them in more detail in the context of Actix:

- *HTTP (web) server*—An HTTP server is responsible for serving HTTP requests. It understands and implements the HTTP protocol. By default, the HTTP server starts a number of threads (called *workers*) to process incoming requests.

  An Actix HTTP server is built around the concept of web applications, and it requires one for initialization. It constructs one application instance per OS thread.

- *App*—An app, or Actix web application, is a grouping of the set of routes it can handle.

- *Routes and handlers*—A route in Actix tells the Actix web server how to process an incoming request. A route is defined in terms of a *route path*, an *HTTP method*, and a *handler* function. Said differently, a request handler is registered with an application's *route* on a *path* for a particular *HTTP method*. The structure of an Actix route is illustrated in figure 3.2.

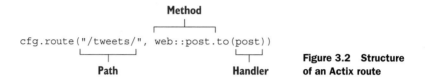

Figure 3.2   Structure of an Actix route

> **Actix concurrency**
>
> Actix supports two levels of concurrency.
>
> It supports *asynchronous I/O*, wherein a given OS-native thread performs other tasks while waiting on I/O (such as listening for network connections).
>
> It also supports *multithreading for parallelism*, and by default, it starts a number of OS-native threads (called *workers*) equal to the number of logical CPUs in the system.

This is the route we implemented earlier for the health check:

```
cfg.route(
    "/health",          ⟵  Path
    web::get()              ⟵  HTTP method      Request handler
    .to(health_check_handler));                  method
```

The preceding route specifies that if an HTTP GET request arrives for the path /health, the request should be routed to the request handler method health_check_handler().

A request handler is an asynchronous method that accepts zero or more parameters and returns an HTTP response. The following is a request handler that we implemented in the previous example:

```
pub async fn health_check_handler() -> impl Responder {
    HttpResponse::Ok().json("Hello, EzyTutors is alive and kicking")
}
```

In this code, health_check_handler() is a function that implements the Responder trait. Types that implement the Responder trait acquire the capability to send HTTP responses. Note that this handler does not accept any input parameters, but it is possible to send data along with HTTP requests from the client, and that data will be made available to handlers. You'll see such an example in the next section.

More about Actix Web

Actix Web (often referred to as just Actix) is a modern, Rust-based, lightweight and fast web framework. Actix Web has consistently featured among the best web frameworks in TechEmpower performance benchmarks (www.techempower.com/benchmarks/).

Actix Web is among the most mature Rust web frameworks and supports features such as those listed here:

- Support for HTTP/1.x and HTTP/2.
- Support for request and response preprocessing.
- Middleware can be configured for features such as CORS, session management, logging, and authentication.
- It supports asynchronous I/O. This provides the ability for the Actix server to perform other activities while waiting on network I/O.
- Content compression.
- Can connect to multiple databases.
- Provides an additional layer of testing utilities (over the Rust testing framework) to support testing of HTTP requests and responses.
- Supports static web page hosting and server-rendered templates.

More technical details about the Actix Web framework can be found here: https://docs.rs/crate/actix-web/2.0.0.

Using a framework like Actix Web significantly speeds up the prototyping and development of web APIs in Rust, as it takes care of the low-level details of dealing with HTTP protocols and messages. It also provides several utility functions and features to make web application development easier.

While Actix Web has an extensive feature set, we'll only be able to cover a subset of the features in this book, such as HTTP methods that provide CRUD (create, read, update, delete) functionality for resources, persistence with databases, error handling, state management, JWT authentication, and configuring middleware.

In this section, we built a basic Actix web service exposing a health-check API, and we reviewed key features of the Actix framework. In the next section, we will build the web service for the EzyTutors social network.

3.2 *Building web APIs with REST*

This section will take you through the typical steps in developing a RESTful web service with Actix.

A web service is a network-oriented service, which means it communicates through messages over a network. Web services use HTTP as the primary protocol for exchanging messages. Several architectural styles can be used to develop web services, such as SOAP/XML, REST/HTTP, and gRPC/HTTP. In this chapter, we will use the REST architectural style.

REST APIs

REST stands for *representational state transfer*. It is a term used to visualize web services as a network of resources, each having its own state. Users trigger operations such as GET, PUT, POST, and DELETE on resources identified by URIs (for example, https://www.google.com/search?q=weather%20berlin can be used to get the current weather for Berlin).

Resources are application entities such as users, shipments, courses, etc. Operations on resources, such as POST and PUT, can result in *state changes* in the resources. The latest state is returned to the client making the request.

The REST architecture defines a set of properties (called *constraints*) that a web service must adopt:

- *Client-server architecture*—This architecture allows for the separation of concerns. The client and server are decoupled and can evolve independently.
- *Statelessness*—This means there is no client context stored on the server between consecutive requests from the same client.
- *Layered system*—This approach allows for the presence of intermediaries, such as load balancers and proxies between the client and the server.
- *Cacheability*—This supports the caching of server responses by clients to improve performance.
- *Uniform interface*—This defines uniform ways to address and manipulate resources and to standardize messages.
- *Well-defined state changes*—State changes are clearly defined. For example, GET requests do not result in state changes, but POST, PUT, and DELETE messages do.

Note that REST is not a formal standard but an architectural style. As a result, there may be variations in the way RESTful services are implemented.

A web service that exposes APIs using the REST architectural style is called a *RESTful web service*. We'll build a RESTful web service in this section for our EzyTutors digital storefront. I've chosen the RESTful style for the APIs because they are intuitive, widely used, and suited for external-facing APIs (as opposed to gRPC, which is more suited to APIs between internal services).

The core functionality of our web service in this chapter will be to allow a new course to be posted, a course list for a tutor to be retrieved, and details for an individual course to be retrieved. Our initial data model will contain just one resource: course.

But before we get to the data model, let's finalize the structure of the project and code and also determine how we'll store this data in memory in a way that is safely accessible across multiple Actix worker threads.

3.2.1   *Defining the project scope and structure*

We will build three RESTful APIs for the tutor web service. These APIs will be registered on an Actix web application, which in turn will be deployed on the Actix HttpServer.

The APIs will be designed to be invoked from a web frontend or mobile application. We'll test the GET API requests using a standard browser and the POST requests using curl, a command-line HTTP client (you can alternatively use a tool like Postman, if you prefer).

We'll use an in-memory data structure to store the courses instead of a database. This is just for simplicity. A relational database will be added in the next chapter.

Figure 3.3 shows the various components of the web service that we'll build and how the HTTP requests from web and mobile clients are handled by the web service. Recall figure 3.1 illustrating the basic server, which was similar.

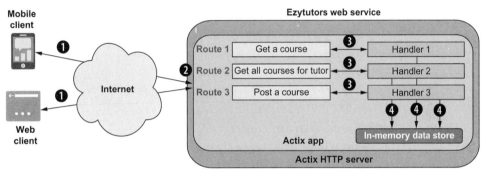

❶ The web service API request is sent from web and mobile clients to the Actix HTTP server.

❷ The Actix HTTP server directs the request to the respective route in the Actix application.

❸ Each route directs the request to the corresponding handler.

❹ Each handler stores and retrieves data from the in-memory data store and sends HTTP responses back to web and mobile clients.

Figure 3.3 Components of the web service

These are the steps in the request and response message flow:

1. The HTTP requests are constructed by web or mobile clients and sent to the domain address and port number where the Actix web server is listening.
2. The Actix web server routes the request to the Actix web app.
3. The Actix web app has been configured with the routes for the three APIs. It inspects the route configuration, determines the right handler for the specified route, and forwards the request to the handler function.
4. The request handlers parse the request parameters, read or write to the in-memory data store, and return an HTTP response. Any errors in processing are also returned as HTTP responses with the appropriate status codes.

That, in brief, is how a request-response flow works in Actix Web. These are the APIs we will build:

- POST /courses—Create a new course and save it in the web service.

- GET /courses/tutor_id—Get a list of courses offered by a tutor.
- GET /courses/tutor_id/course_id—Get course details.

Now that we have reviewed the scope of the project, let's look at how the code will be organized:

- bin/tutor-service.rs—Contains the main() function
- models.rs—Contains the data model for the web service
- state.rs—Application state is defined here
- routes.rs—Contains the route definitions
- handlers.rs—Contains handler functions that respond to HTTP requests
- Cargo.toml—Configuration file and dependencies specification for the project

Figure 3.4 shows the code structure.

In this section, we will organize the project repository so that two different binaries can be built, each with different code. This is something that Rust's Cargo tool enables us to do easily.

First, update Cargo.toml to look like the following listing.

Figure 3.4   Project structure of the EzyTutors web service

Listing 3.2   Configuration for the basic Actix web server

```
[package]
name = "tutor-nodb"
version = "0.1.0"
authors = ["peshwar9"]
edition = "2018"
default-run="tutor-service"

[[bin]]
name = "basic-server"

[[bin]]
name = "tutor-service"

[dependencies]
#Actix web framework and run-time
actix-web = "3.0.0"
actix-rt = "1.1.1"
```

You will notice that we've defined two binaries for this project. The first one is basic-server, which we built in the previous section. The second one is tutor-service, which we will build now.

We also have two dependencies to include: the `actix-web` framework and the `actix-rt` runtime.

Note also that under the `[package]` tag, we've added a `default-run` parameter with the value `tutor_service`. This tells Cargo that the `tutor_service` binary should be built unless otherwise specified. This allows us to build and run the tutor service with `cargo run -p tutor-nodb`, rather than `cargo run -p tutor-nodb --bin tutor-service`.

Finally, create a new file, tutor-nodb/src/bin/tutor-service.rs. This will contain the code for the web service in this section.

We've now covered the project scope and structure. Let's turn our attention to another topic—how we will store the data in the web service. I've already said we won't use a database in this chapter; we'll store the data in memory. This is fine for a single-threaded server, like the one we built in the last chapter, but Actix is a multithreaded server. Each thread (Actix worker) runs a separate instance of the application. How can we make sure that two threads are not trying to mutate the same data in-memory simultaneously?

Rust has features such as `Arc` and `Mutex` that we can use to address this problem. But where in the web service should we define the shared data, and how can we make it available to the handlers, which is where the processing will take place? The Actix Web framework gives us an elegant way to address this. Actix allows us to define application state of any custom type and to access it using a built-in extractor. We'll take a closer look at this in the next section.

3.2.2 Defining and managing application state

The term *application state* can be used in different contexts to mean different things. W3C defines application state as how an application is: its configuration, attributes, condition, or information content (www.w3.org/2001/tag/doc/state.html). State changes happen in an application component when triggered by an event. More specifically, in the context of applications that provide a RESTful web API to manage resources over a URI (such as the one we're discussing in this chapter), application state is closely related to the state of the resources that are part of the application. In this chapter, we are specifically dealing with `course` as the only resource. So, it can be said that the state of our application changes as courses are added or removed for a tutor. In most real-world applications, the state of resources is persisted to a data store. However, in our case, we will be storing the application state in memory.

An Actix web server by default spawns a number of threads on startup (this is configurable). Each thread runs an instance of the web application and can process incoming requests independently. However, by design, there is no built-in sharing of data across Actix threads. You may wonder why we would want to share data across threads. Take the example of a database connection pool. It makes sense for multiple threads to use a common connection pool to handle database connections. Such data can be modeled in Actix as application state. This state is injected by the Actix framework into the request handlers such that handlers can access state as parameters in their method signatures. All routes within an Actix app can share application state.

In the tutor web service, we want to store a list of courses in memory as application state. We'd like this state to be made available to all the handlers and shared safely across different threads.

Before we get to the courses, let's try a simpler example to learn how we can define and use application state with Actix. Let's define a simple application state type with two elements:

- A string *data type (representing a static string response to a health-check request)*—This string value will be shared immutable state, accessible from all threads—the values cannot be modified after they are initially defined.
- An integer *data type (representing the number of times a user has visited a particular route)*—This numeric value will be shared mutable state—the value can be mutated from every thread. However, before a value can be modified, the thread has to acquire control over the data. This is achieved by defining the numeric value with the protection of Mutex, a mechanism provided in the Rust standard library for safe cross-thread communications.

Here is what we need to do for our first iteration of the tutor service:

1 Define application state for the health-check API in src/state.rs.
2 Update the main function (of the Actix server) to initialize and register application state in src/bin/tutor-service.rs.
3 Define the route for the health-check route in src/routes.rs.
4 Construct an HTTP response in src/handlers.rs using this application state.

DEFINING THE APPLICATION STATE

Add the following code to define application state in tutor-nodb/src/state.rs:

```
use std::sync::Mutex;

pub struct AppState {
    pub health_check_response: String,        Shared immutable state
    pub visit_count: Mutex<u32>,              Shared mutable state
}
```

INITIALIZING AND REGISTERING THE APPLICATION STATE

Add the following code in tutor-nodb/src/bin/tutor-service.rs.

Listing 3.3   Building an Actix web server with application state

```
use actix_web::{web, App, HttpServer};
use std::io;
use std::sync::Mutex;

#[path = "../handlers.rs"]
mod handlers;
#[path = "../routes.rs"]
mod routes;
#[path = "../state.rs"]
mod state;
```

```
use routes::*;
use state::AppState;

#[actix_rt::main]
async fn main() -> io::Result<()> {
  let shared_data = web::Data::new(AppState {          ◁——  Initialize the
                                                             application state.
    health_check_response: "I'm good. You've already asked me ".to_string(),
    visit_count: Mutex::new(0),
  });                                       Define the web
  let app = move || {          ◁——         application.
      App::new()
          .app_data(shared_data.clone())    ◁——  Register the application state
                                                  with the web application.
          .configure(general_routes)  ◁——
  };                                        Configure routes for
                                            the web application.

  HttpServer::new(app).bind("127.0.0.1:3000")?.run().await     ◁——
}
                                    Initialize the Actix web server with the web
                                    application, listen on port 3000, and run the server.
```

DEFINING THE ROUTE

Let's define the health-check route in tutor-nodb/src/routes.rs:

```
use super::handlers::*;
use actix_web::web;

pub fn general_routes(cfg: &mut web::ServiceConfig) {
    cfg.route("/health", web::get().to(health_check_handler));
}
```

UPDATING THE HEALTH-CHECK HANDLER TO USE APPLICATION STATE

Add the following code for the health-check handler in tutor-nodb/src/handlers.rs.

> **Listing 3.4 Health-check handler using application state**

Data members of the application state struct (AppState) can be directly accessed using standard dot notation.

Application state registered with the Actix web application is made available to all handler functions as an extractor object of type web::Data<T>, where T is the type of the custom application state that developers have defined.

```
use super::state::AppState;
use actix_web::{web, HttpResponse};

pub async fn health_check_handler(app_state: web::Data<AppState>) ->
➥HttpResponse {                                             ◁——
    let health_check_response = &app_state.health_check_response;
    let mut visit_count = app_state.visit_count.lock().unwrap();     ◁——
    let response = format!("{} {} times", health_check_response,
    ➥visit_count);       ◁——
    *visit_count += 1;
    HttpResponse::Ok().json(&response)
}
```

Update the value of the field representing shared mutable state. Since the lock on this data has already been acquired, the value of the field can be updated safely. The lock on the data is automatically released when the handler function finishes execution.

Construct a response string to send back to the browser client.

A field representing shared mutable state (visit_count) has to be locked first before accessing to prevent multiple threads from updating the value of the field simultaneously.

To recap, we have done the following:

- Defined app state in src/state.rs
- Registered app state with the web application in src/bin/tutor-service.rs
- Defined the route in src/routes.rs
- Wrote a health-check handler function to read and update application state in src/handlers.rs

From the root directory of the tutor web service (ezytutors/tutor-nodb), run the following command:

```
cargo run
```

Note that we previously specified the default binary in Cargo.toml as follows:

```
default-run="tutor-service"
```

Otherwise, we would have had to specify the following command to run the tutor-service binary, because there are two binaries defined in this project.

```
cargo run --bin tutor-service
```

Go to a browser, and type in the following:

```
localhost:3000/health
```

Every time you refresh the browser window, you will find that the visit count has been incremented. You'll see a message similar to this:

```
I'm good. You've already asked me  2 times
```

We've now seen how to define and use application state. This is quite a useful feature for sharing data and injecting dependencies across an application in a safe manner. We'll use this feature more in the coming chapters.

3.2.3 *Defining the data model*

Before we develop the individual APIs for the tutor web service, let's first take care of two things:

- Defining the data model for the web service
- Defining the in-memory data store

These are prerequisites for building APIs.

DEFINING THE DATA MODEL FOR COURSES

Let's define a Rust data structure to represent a course. A course in our web application will have the following attributes:

- *Tutor ID*—Denotes the tutor who offers the course.
- *Course ID*—This is a unique identifier for the course. In our system, a course ID will be unique to a tutor.
- *Course name*—This is the name of the course offered by the tutor.

- *Posted time*—A timestamp indicating when the course was recorded by the web service.

To create a new course, the user of the API has to specify the `tutor_id` and `course_name`. The `course_id` and `posted_time` will be generated by the web service.

I have kept the data model simple in order to keep our focus on the objective of the chapter. To record `posted_time`, we will use a third-party crate called `chrono`.

For serializing and deserializing Rust data structures to and from on-the-wire format, for transmission in HTTP messages, we will use another third-party crate, `serde`.

Let's first update the Cargo.toml file in the ezytutors/tutor-nodb folder to add the two external crates, `chrono` and `serde`:

```
[dependencies]
//actix dependencies not shown here

# Data serialization library
serde = { version = "1.0.110", features = ["derive"] }
# Other utilities
chrono = {version = "0.4.11", features = ["serde"]}
```

Add the following code to tutor-nodb/src/models.rs.

Listing 3.5   Data model for courses

The #derive annotation derives the implementations for four traits: Deserialize, Serialize, Debug, and Clone. The first two are part of the serde crate and help to convert Rust data structs to and from on-the-wire formats. Implementing the Debug trait will help us print the Course struct values for debug purposes. The Clone trait helps address the Rust ownership rules during processing.

```
use actix_web::web;
use chrono::NaiveDateTime;
use serde::{Deserialize, Serialize};

#[derive(Deserialize, Serialize, Debug, Clone)]
pub struct Course {
    pub tutor_id: i32,
    pub course_id: Option<i32>,
    pub course_name: String,
    pub posted_time: Option<NaiveDateTime>,
}
impl From<web::Json<Course>> for Course {
    fn from(course: web::Json<Course>) -> Self {
        Course {
            tutor_id: course.tutor_id,
            course_id: course.course_id,
            course_name: course.course_name.clone(),
            posted_time: course.posted_time,
        }
    }
}
```

NativeDateTime is a chrono data type for storing timestamp information.

This function will convert data from incoming HTTP requests to Rust structs.

In this listing, you will notice that `course_id` and `posted_time` have been declared to be of type `Option<i32>` and `Option<NaiveDateTime>` respectively. This means that these two fields can either hold a valid value of type `i32` and `chrono::NaiveDateTime` respectively, or they can both hold a value of None if no value is assigned to these fields.

Further, toward the end of listing 3.5, you will notice a From trait implementation. This is a trait implementation that contains a function to convert web::Json<Course> to the Course data type. What exactly does this mean?

We saw earlier that application state registered with the Actix web server is made available to handlers using the web::Data<T> extractor. Likewise, data from an incoming request body is made available to handler functions through the web::Json<T> extractor. When a POST request is sent from a web client with the tutor_id and course_name as a data payload, these fields are automatically extracted from the web::Json<T> Actix object and converted to the Course Rust type by this method. This is the purpose of the From trait implementation in listing 3.5.

Derivable traits

Traits in Rust are like *interfaces* in other languages. They are used to define shared behavior. Data types implementing a trait share common behavior that is defined in the trait. For example, we could define a trait called RemoveCourse as follows:

```
trait RemoveCourse {
    fn remove(self, course_id) -> Self;
}
struct TrainingInstitute;
struct IndividualTutor;

impl RemoveCourse for IndividualTutor {
    // An individual tutor's request is enough to remove a course.
}
impl RemoveCourse for TrainingInstitute {
    // There may be additional approvals needed to remove a course
    offering for business customers
}
```

Assuming we have two types of tutors—training institutes (business customers) and individual tutors—both types can implement the RemoveCourse trait. This means they will share the common behavior that courses offered by both types can be removed from our web service. However, the details of the processing needed for removing a course may vary because business customers may require multiple levels of approvals before the decision to remove a course is taken. This is an example of a custom trait.

The Rust standard library defines several traits, which are implemented by the types within Rust. Interestingly, these traits can be implemented by custom structs defined at the application level. For example, Debug is a trait defined in the Rust standard library to print out the value of a Rust data type for debugging. A custom struct (defined by the application) can also choose to implement this trait to print out the values of the custom type for debugging.

Such trait implementations can be auto-derived by the Rust compiler when we specify the #[derive()] annotation above the type definition—these are called *derivable traits.* Examples of derivable traits in Rust include `Eq`, `PartialEq`, `Clone`, `Copy`, and `Debug`.

Note that such trait implementations can also be manually implemented if complex behavior is desired.

ADDING COURSE COLLECTION TO APPLICATION STATE

We have defined the data model for `course`, but how will we store courses as they are added? We do not want to use a relational database or a similar persistent data store just yet. Let's start with a simpler option.

We saw earlier that Actix provides a feature to share application state across multiple threads of execution. Why not use this feature for our in-memory data store?

Earlier we defined an `AppState` struct in tutor-nodb/src/state.rs to keep track of visit counts. Let's enhance that struct to also store the course collection:

```
use super::models::Course;
use std::sync::Mutex;
pub struct AppState {
    pub health_check_response: String,
    pub visit_count: Mutex<u32>,
    pub courses: Mutex<Vec<Course>>,    <--| Courses are stored in application
}                                            state as a Vec collection
                                             protected by a Mutex.
```

Since we have altered the definition of application state, we should reflect this in the `main()` function. In tutor-nodb/src/bin/tutor-service.rs, make sure that all the module imports are correctly declared.

Listing 3.6 Module imports for the `main()` function

```
use actix_web::{web, App, HttpServer};
use std::io;
use std::sync::Mutex;

#[path = "../handlers.rs"]
mod handlers;
#[path = "../models.rs"]
mod models;
#[path = "../routes.rs"]
mod routes;
#[path = "../state.rs"]
mod state;
use routes::*;
use state::AppState;
```

Then, in the `main()` function, initialize the `courses` collection with an empty vector collection in `AppState`:

```
async fn main() -> io::Result<()> {
  let shared_data = web::Data::new(AppState {
```

```
    health_check_response: "I'm good. You've already asked me ".to_string(),
    visit_count: Mutex::new(0),
    courses: Mutex::new(vec![]),            ◁──┐  The courses field is initialized with
    });                                         │  a Mutex-protected empty vector.
// other code
}
```

We haven't written any new APIs yet, but we have done the following:

- Added a data model module
- Updated the `main()` function
- Changed the application state struct to include a course collection
- Updated routes and handlers
- Updated Cargo.toml

Let's ensure that nothing is broken. Build and run the code with the following command from within the tutor-nodb folder:

```
cargo run
```

You should be able to test it with the following URL from the web browser:

```
curl localhost:3000/health
```

Things should work as before. If you are able to view the health page with a message containing a visitor count, you can proceed. If not, review the code in each of the files for oversights or typos. If you still cannot get it to work, refer to the completed code within the code repository.

We're now ready to write the code for the three course-related APIs in the coming sections. For writing the APIs, we'll define a uniform set of steps that we can follow (like a template). We will execute these steps to write each API. By the end of this chapter, these steps should be ingrained in you:

1. Define the route configuration.
2. Write the handler function.
3. Write automated test scripts.
4. Build the service, and test the API.

The route configuration for all new routes will be added in tutor-nodb/src/routes.rs, and the handler function will be added in tutor-nodb/src/handlers.rs. The automated test scripts will also be added to tutor-nodb/src/handlers.rs for our project.

3.2.4   *Posting a course*

Let's now implement a REST API for posting a new course. We'll follow the set of steps we defined toward the end of the previous section.

STEP 1: DEFINE THE ROUTE CONFIGURATION

Let's add the following route to tutor-nodb/src/routes.rs after the `general_routes` block:

```
pub fn course_routes(cfg: &mut web::ServiceConfig) {
    cfg
    .service(web::scope("/courses")
    .route("/", web::post().to(new_course)));
}
```

The `service(web::scope("/courses"))` expression creates a new resource scope called `courses`, under which all APIs related to courses can be added.

A *scope* is a set of resources with a common root path. A set of routes can be registered under a scope, and application state can be shared among routes within the same scope. For example, we can create two separate scope declarations, one for `courses` and one for `tutors`, and access routes registered under them as follows:

```
localhost:3000/courses/1   // retrieve details for course with id 1
localhost:3000/tutors/1    // retrieve details for tutor with id 1
```

These are only examples for illustration—don't test them now, as we have not yet defined these routes. What we have defined so far is one route under `courses` that matches an incoming POST request with the path `/courses/` and routes it to a handler called `new_course`.

Let's look at how we could invoke the route after implementing the API. The following command could be used to post a new course:

```
curl -X POST localhost:3000/courses/ -H "Content-Type: application/json"
➥-d '{"tutor_id":1, "course_name":"Hello , my first course  !"}'
```

Note that this command will not work yet—we have to do two things before it will. First, we have to register this new route group with the web application that is initialized in the `main()` function. Second, we have to define the `new_course` handler method.

Modify the `main()` function in tutor-nodb/src/bin/tutor-service.rs so that it looks like this:

```
let app = move || {
        App::new()
            .app_data(shared_data.clone())
            .configure(general_routes)
            .configure(course_routes)       Register the new course_routes
    };                                      group with the application.
```

We've now completed the route configuration, but the code won't compile yet. Let's write the handler function to post a new course.

STEP 2: WRITE THE HANDLER FUNCTION

Recall that an Actix handler function processes an incoming HTTP request using the data payload and URL parameters sent with the request, and it sends back an HTTP response. Let's write the handler for processing a POST request for a new course. Once the new course is created by the handler, it is stored as part of the `AppState` struct, which is then automatically made available to the other handlers in the application.

Add the following code to tutor-nodb/src/handlers.rs.

Listing 3.7   Handler function for posting a new course

```
// previous imports not shown here
use super::models::Course;
use chrono::Utc;

pub async fn new_course(
    new_course: web::Json<Course>,
    app_state: web::Data<AppState>,
) -> HttpResponse {
    println!("Received new course");
    let course_count_for_user = app_state
        .courses
        .lock()
        .unwrap()
        .clone()
        .into_iter()
        .filter(|course| course.tutor_id == new_course.tutor_id)
        .count();
    let new_course = Course {
        tutor_id: new_course.tutor_id,
        course_id: Some(course_count_for_user + 1),
        course_name: new_course.course_name.clone(),
        posted_time: Some(Utc::now().naive_utc()),
    };
    app_state.courses.lock().unwrap().push(new_course);
    HttpResponse::Ok().json("Added course")
}
```

The handler function takes two parameters: data payload from HTTP request and application state.

Since the course collection is protected by a Mutex, we have to lock it first to access the data.

Convert the course collection (stored within AppState) into an iterator so that we can iterate through each element in the collection for processing.

Review each element in the collection, and filter only for the courses corresponding to the tutor_id (received as part of the HTTP request).

The number of elements in the filtered list is retrieved. This is used to generate the ID for the next course.

Create a new course instance.

Add the new course instance to the course collection that is part of the application state (AppState).

Send back an HTTP response to the web client.

To recap, this handler function does the following:

- Gets write access to the course collection stored in the application state (AppState)
- Extracts the data payload from the incoming request
- Generates a new course ID by calculating the number of existing courses for the tutor and incrementing by 1
- Creates a new course instance
- Adds the new course instance to the course collection in AppState

Let's write the test scripts for this function, which we can use for automated testing.

STEP 3: WRITE AUTOMATED TEST SCRIPTS

Actix Web provides utilities for automated testing, over and above what Rust provides. To write tests for Actix services, we first must start with the basic Rust testing utilities—placing tests within the tests module and annotating it for the compiler. In addition, Actix provides an #[actix_rt::test] annotation for async test functions, to instruct the Actix runtime to execute these tests.

Let's create a test script for posting a new course. To do this, we'll need to construct the course details to be posted, and we'll need to initialize the application state. Add this code in tutor-nodb/src/handlers.rs toward the end of the source file.

Listing 3.8 Test script for posting a new course

> The #[cfg(test)] annotation on the tests module tells Rust to compile and run the tests only when the Cargo test command is run, and not for the cargo build or cargo run commands.

```
#[cfg(test)]
mod tests {
    use super::*;
    use actix_web::http::StatusCode;
    use std::sync::Mutex;

    #[actix_rt::test]
    async fn post_course_test() {
        let course = web::Json(Course {
            tutor_id: 1,
            course_name: "Hello, this is test course".into(),
            course_id: None,
            posted_time: None,
        });
        let app_state: web::Data<AppState> = web::Data::new(AppState {
            health_check_response: "".to_string(),
            visit_count: Mutex::new(0),
            courses: Mutex::new(vec![]),
        });
        let resp = new_course(course, app_state).await;
        assert_eq!(resp.status(), StatusCode::OK);
    }
}
```

Import all handler declarations from the parent module (which hosts the tests module).

Tests in Rust are written within the tests module.

Normal Rust tests are annotated with #[test], but since this is an asynchronous test function, we have to alert the async runtime of Actix Web to execute this async test function.

Construct a web::Json<T> object representing the request data payload (the new course data from the tutor).

Construct a web::Data<T> object representing the application state.

Verify whether the HTTP status response code (returned from the handler) indicates success.

Invoke the handler function with application state and a simulated request data payload.

Run this test from the tutor-nodb folder with the following command:

```
cargo test
```

You should see the test successfully executed with a message that looks similar to this:

```
running 1 test
test handlers::tests::post_course_test ... ok

test result: ok. 1 passed; 0 failed; 0 ignored; 0 measured; 0 filtered out
```

STEP 4: BUILD THE SERVICE, AND TEST THE API

Build and run the server from the tutor-no-db folder with this command:

```
cargo run
```

From a command line, run the following curl command (or use a GUI tool like Postman):

```
curl -X POST localhost:3000/courses/ -H "Content-Type: application/json"
-d '{"tutor_id":1, "course_name":"Hello , my first course  !"}'
```

You should see the message "Added course" returned from server. You've now built an API for posting a new course. Next, let's retrieve all existing courses for a tutor.

3.2.5   Getting all the courses for a tutor

Now we'll implement the handler function to retrieve all courses for a tutor. You know the drill—there are four steps to follow.

STEP 1: DEFINE THE ROUTE CONFIGURATION

Since we have the foundation of our code established, things should be quicker from now on.

Let's add a new route in src/routes.rs:

```
pub fn course_routes(cfg: &mut web::ServiceConfig) {
    cfg.service(
        web::scope("/courses")
            .route("/", web::post().to(new_course))
            .route("/{tutor_id}", web::get().to(get_courses_for_tutor)),
    );
}
```

Add a new route for getting courses for a tutor (represented by the tutor_id variable).

STEP 2: WRITE THE HANDLER FUNCTION

The handler function does the following:

1 Retrieves courses from `AppState`
2 Filters courses corresponding to the `tutor_id` requested
3 Returns the list

The following code should be entered in src/handlers.rs.

Listing 3.9   Handler function to get all courses for a tutor

```
pub async fn get_courses_for_tutor(
    app_state: web::Data<AppState>,
    params: web::Path<(i32)>,
) -> HttpResponse {
    let tutor_id: i32 = params.0;

    let filtered_courses = app_state
        .courses
        .lock()
        .unwrap()
        .clone()
        .into_iter()
        .filter(|course| course.tutor_id == tutor_id)
        .collect::<Vec<Course>>();

    if filtered_courses.len() > 0 {
        HttpResponse::Ok().json(filtered_courses)
    } else {
        HttpResponse::Ok().json("No courses found for tutor".to_string())
    }
}
```

Filter for courses corresponding to the tutor requested by the web client.

If courses are found for the tutor, return a success response with the course list.

If courses are not found for the tutor, send an error message.

STEP 3: WRITE AUTOMATED TEST SCRIPTS

In this test script, we will invoke the `get_courses_for_tutor` handler function. This function takes two arguments: application state and a URL path parameter (denoting the tutor ID). For example, if the user types the following in the browser, it means they want to see a list of all courses with a `tutor_id` of 1:

```
localhost:3000/courses/1
```

Recall that this maps to the route definition in src/routes.rs, shown here for reference:

```
.route("/{tutor_id}", web::get().to(get_courses_for_tutor))
```

The Actix framework automatically passes the application state and the URL path parameter to the handler function, `get_courses_for_tutor`, in the normal course of execution. However, for testing purposes, we have to manually simulate the function arguments by constructing an application state object and URL path parameter. You will see these steps annotated in the next listing.

Enter the following test script in the `tests` module in src/handlers.rs.

Listing 3.10 Test script for retrieving courses for a tutor

```
#[actix_rt::test]                                                     Construct
async fn get_all_courses_success() {                               the app state.
    let app_state: web::Data<AppState> = web::Data::new(AppState {  ◁
        health_check_response: "".to_string(),
        visit_count: Mutex::new(0),
        courses: Mutex::new(vec![]),
    });                                                          Simulate a request
    let tutor_id: web::Path<(i32)> = web::Path::from((1));  ◁┘  parameter.
    let resp = get_courses_for_tutor(app_state, tutor_id).await;  ◁  Invoke the
    assert_eq!(resp.status(), StatusCode::OK);  ◁┐  Check the    handler.
}                                                └  response.
```

STEP 4: BUILD THE SERVICE, AND TEST THE API

Build and run the server from the tutor-nodb folder with this command:

```
cargo run
```

Post a few courses from the command line as shown here (or use a GUI tool like Postman):

```
curl -X POST localhost:3000/courses/ -H "Content-Type: application/json"
➥-d '{"tutor_id":1, "course_name":"Hello , my first course  !"}'
curl -X POST localhost:3000/courses/ -H "Content-Type: application/json"
➥-d '{"tutor_id":1, "course_name":"Hello , my second course  !"}'
curl -X POST localhost:3000/courses/ -H "Content-Type: application/json"
➥-d '{"tutor_id":1, "course_name":"Hello , my third course  !"}'
```

From a web browser, go to the following URL:

```
localhost:3000/courses/1
```

You should see the courses displayed as follows:

```
[{"tutor_id":1,"course_id":1,"course_name":"Hello , my first course  !",
"posted_time":"2020-09-05T06:26:51.866230"},{"tutor_id":1,"course_id":2,
"course_name":"Hello , my second course  !","posted_time":
"2020-09-05T06:27:22.284195"},{"tutor_id":1,"course_id":3,
"course_name":"Hello , my third course  !",
"posted_time":"2020-09-05T06:57:03.850014"}]
```

Try posting more courses and verify the results. Our web service is now capable of retrieving a course list for a tutor.

3.2.6   *Getting the details of a single course*

Now we'll implement a handler function to search for and retrieve details for a specific course. Let's again go through our four-step process.

STEP 1: DEFINE THE ROUTE CONFIGURATION

Add the following new route in src/routes.rs:

```
pub fn course_routes(cfg: &mut web::ServiceConfig) {
  cfg.service(
    web::scope("/courses")
      .route("/", web::post().to(new_course))
      .route("/{tutor_id}", web::get().to(get_courses_for_tutor))
      .route("/{tutor_id}/{course_id}", web::get().to(get_course_detail)),  ◁──┐
  );                                                                            │
}                                                            Add a new route │
                                                        to get course details. │
```

STEP 2: WRITE THE HANDLER FUNCTION

The handler function is similar to the previous API (which retrieved all courses for a tutor), except for the additional step of filtering on the course ID.

> **Listing 3.11   Handler function to retrieve details for a single course**

```
pub async fn get_course_detail(
    app_state: web::Data<AppState>,
    params: web::Path<(i32, i32)>,
) -> HttpResponse {
    let (tutor_id, course_id) = params.0;
    let selected_course = app_state
        .courses
        .lock()                                    Retrieve the course corresponding
        .unwrap()                                  to the tutor_id and course_id sent
        .clone()                                        as request parameters.
        .into_iter()
        .find(|x| x.tutor_id == tutor_id && x.course_id == Some(
          course_id))                                   ◁──
        .ok_or("Course not found");   ◁──┐  Convert Option<T> to Result<T,E>. If
                                          │  Option<T> evaluates to Some(val), it returns
    if let Ok(course) = selected_course { │  Ok(val). If None is found, it returns Err(err).
        HttpResponse::Ok().json(course)
    } else {
```

```
        HttpResponse::Ok().json("Course not found".to_string())
    }
}
```

STEP 3: WRITE AUTOMATED TEST SCRIPTS

In this test script, we will invoke the `get_course_detail` handler function. This function takes two arguments: application state and URL path parameters. For example, suppose the user types the following in the browser:

```
localhost:3000/courses/1/1
```

This means the user wants to see details for the course with a user ID of `1` (the first parameter in URL path) and a course ID of `1` (the second parameter in the URL path).

Recall that this `/1/1` portion of the URL maps to the route definition in src/routes.rs, shown here for reference:

```
.route("/{tutor_id}/{course_id}", web::get().to(get_course_detail)),
```

The Actix framework automatically passes the application state and the URL path parameters to the `get_course_detail` handler function in the normal course of execution. But for testing purposes, we have to manually simulate the function arguments by constructing an application state object and URL path parameters. You will see these steps annotated in the next listing.

Add the following test function to the `tests` module within src/handlers.rs.

Listing 3.12 Test case to retrieve course details

```
#[actix_rt::test]
    async fn get_one_course_success() {
        let app_state: web::Data<AppState> = web::Data::new(AppState {      ◁──┐
            health_check_response: "".to_string(),                    Construct the
            visit_count: Mutex::new(0),                               app state.
            courses: Mutex::new(vec![]),
        });
        let params: web::Path<(i32, i32)> = web::Path::from((1, 1));        ◁──┐
        let resp = get_course_detail(app_state, params).await;
        assert_eq!(resp.status(), StatusCode::OK);
    }
```

Invoke the handler. → `let resp = get_course_detail(app_state, params).await;`

Check the response. → `assert_eq!(resp.status(), StatusCode::OK);`

Construct an object of type web::Path with two parameters. This is to simulate a user typing localhost:3000/courses/1/1 in a web browser.

STEP 4: BUILD THE SERVER, AND TEST THE API

Build and run the server from the tutor-nodb folder with the following command:

```
cargo run
```

Post two new courses from the command line:

```
curl -X POST localhost:3000/courses/ -H "Content-Type: application/json"
➥-d '{"tutor_id":1, "course_name":"Hello , my first course  !"}'
curl -X POST localhost:3000/courses/ -H "Content-Type: application/json"
➥-d '{"tutor_id":1, "course_name":"Hello , my second course  !"}'
```

From a web browser, go to the following URL:

```
localhost:3000/courses/1/1
```

You should see the course details displayed for tutor_id = 1 and course_id = 1, as shown here:

```
{"tutor_id":1,"course_id":1,"course_name":"Hello , my first course  !",
➥"posted_time":"2020-09-05T06:26:51.866230"}
```

You can add more courses and check that the correct details are displayed for the other course IDs. Our web service is now capable of retrieving the details for a single course.

Note that the tests shown in this chapter are only intended to demonstrate how to write test scripts for various types of APIs with different types of data payloads and URL parameters sent from the web client. Real-world tests would be more exhaustive, covering various success and failure scenarios.

In this chapter, you've built a set of RESTful APIs for a tutor web application from scratch, starting with data models, routes, application state, and request handlers. You also wrote automated test cases using Actix Web's built-in test execution support for web applications.

Congratulations—you have built your first web service in Rust! What you have learned in this chapter, namely, implementing RESTful web services, can be reused in a large variety of applications. This is the beauty of REST: its principles are simple and stable and can be reused in many situations.

In the next chapter, we will continue to develop the code built here, adding a persistence layer for the web service using a relational database.

Summary

- Actix is a modern, lightweight web framework written in Rust. It provides an async HTTP server that offers safe concurrency and high performance.
- The key components of Actix Web that we used in this chapter are HttpServer, App, routes, handlers, request extractors, HttpResponse, and application state. These are the core components needed to build RESTful APIs in Rust using Actix.
- A web service is a combination of one or more APIs, accessible over HTTP at a particular domain address and port. APIs can be built using different architectural styles. REST is a popular and intuitive architectural style used to build APIs, and it aligns well with the HTTP protocol standards.
- Each RESTful API is configured as a route in Actix. A route is a combination of a path that identifies a resource, an HTTP method, and a handler function.
- A RESTful API call sent from a web or mobile client is received over HTTP by the Actix HttpServer listening on a specific port. The request is passed on to the Actix web application registered with it. One or more routes are registered with the Actix web application, which routes the incoming request to a handler function (based on the request path and HTTP method).

- Actix provides two types of concurrency: multithreading and async I/O. This enables the development of high performance web services.
- The Actix HTTP server uses multithreading concurrency by starting multiple worker threads on startup, equal to the number of logical CPUs in the system. Each thread runs a separate instance of the Actix web application.
- In addition to multithreading, Actix uses async I/O, which is another type of concurrency mechanism. This enables an Actix web application to perform other tasks while waiting on I/O on a single thread. Actix has its own Async runtime that is based on `Tokio`, a popular production-ready async library in Rust.
- Actix allows the web application to define custom application state, and it provides a mechanism for safely accessing this state from each handler function. Since each application instance of Actix runs in a separate thread, Actix provides a safe mechanism for accessing and mutating this shared state without conflicts or data races.
- At a minimum, a RESTful API implementation in Actix requires a route configuration and a handler function to be added.
- Actix also provides utilities for writing automated test cases.

Performing database operations

This chapter covers

- Writing our first async connection to a database
- Setting up the web service and writing unit tests
- Creating and querying records in the database

In the previous chapter, we built a web service that uses an *in-memory data store*. In this chapter, we'll enhance that web service, replacing the in-memory data store with a *relational database*.

Our enhanced web service will expose the same set of APIs as before, but we will now have a proper database to persist the data to disk—we do not want our data to get lost every time we restart the web service. As there are many parts involved, we will develop this database-backed web service iteratively over three iterations of code:

- In the first iteration, you'll learn how to connect asynchronously to a Postgres database, using a database connection pool, from a vanilla Rust program.
- In the second iteration, we'll set up the project structure for the Actix-based web service and write unit tests.
- In the third iteration, we'll write the actual handler functions to create database records and query the results.

At the end of each iteration, we will have a working version of the code that can be inspected, run, and tested independently.

4.1   Setting up the project structure

The final code structure for this chapter is shown in figure 4.1.

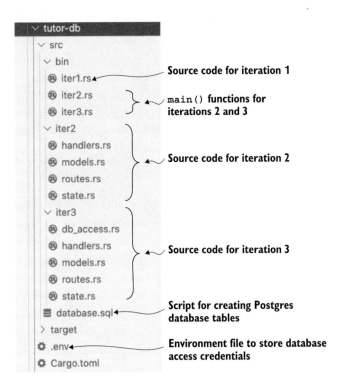

Figure 4.1   Project structure for chapter 4

With these goals in mind, let's get started. Go to the root of the `ezytutors` workspace root (which we created in the previous chapter), and execute the following two steps:

1   Add the following code to Cargo.toml. Note that `tutor-nodb` was the project we created in the previous chapter:

```
[workspace]
members = ["tutor-nodb", "tutor-db"]
```

2   Create a new Cargo project, `tutor-db`:

```
cargo new tutor-db
cd tutor-db
```

Note that all subsequent command-line statements in this chapter will need to be run from this project root folder (ezytutors/tutor-db). To make that easier, let's set an environment variable for the project root:

```
export PROJECT_ROOT=.
```

> **NOTE** The dot at the end of the export statement represents the current directory. Alternatively, you can replace it with a suitable fully qualified path name.

Environment variables

In this chapter, we will use the following environment variables:

- `PROJECT_ROOT`—Represents the home directory of the project. For this chapter, it is the tutor-db root directory, which also contains the Cargo.toml file for the project.
- `DATABASE_USER`—Represents the database username that has read/write access rights to the database (which we will create later in this chapter).

Please ensure you either set these variables manually in your shell session or add them to your shell profile script (e.g., `.bash_profile`).

The complete code for this chapter can be found at https://github.com/peshwar9/rust-servers-services-apps/tree/master/chapter4/.

Software versions

This chapter has been tested with the following versions of software on Ubuntu 22.04 (LTS) x64:

- rustc 1.59.0
- actix-web 4.2.1
- actix-rt 2.7.0
- sqlx 0.6.2

If you have any difficulty in compiling or building the program, you can adjust your development environment to develop and test with these versions.

4.2 *Writing our first async connection to database (iteration 1)*

In this section, we'll write a simple Rust program to connect to the Postgres database and query the database. All the code in this section will reside in just one file: tutor-db/src/bin/iter1.rs.

4.2.1 *Selecting the database and connection library*

In this chapter, we'll use PostgreSQL (I will refer to it as simply *Postgres* henceforth) as our relational database. Postgres is a popular open source relational database that is known for its scalability, reliability, feature set, and ability to handle large, complicated data workloads.

To connect to Postgres, we'll use the Rust `sqlx` crate. This crate requires us to write queries as raw SQL statements, and it performs compile-time checking of the query, provides a built-in connection pool, and returns an asynchronous connection to Postgres. Compile-time checking is very useful for detecting and preventing runtime errors.

Having an asynchronous connection from our web service to the database means that our tutor web service will be free to perform other tasks while waiting on a response from the database. If we were to use a synchronous (blocking) connection to the database (such as with the Diesel ORM), the web service would have to wait until the database operation was completed.

> **Why use `sqlx`?**
>
> Using asynchronous database connections can improve transaction throughput and the performance response time of the web service under heavy loads, all other things being equal. Hence the use of `sqlx`.
>
> The primary alternative to `sqlx` is to use Diesel, a pure-Rust object-relational mapper (ORM) solution. For those who are used to ORMs from other programming languages and web frameworks, Diesel may be a preferred option. But at the time of writing, Diesel does not yet support asynchronous connections to databases. Given that the Actix framework is asynchronous, the programming model is simpler if we use a library such as `sqlx` to make async connections to the database too.

Let's start with setting up the database.

4.2.2 Setting up the database and connecting with an async pool

In this section, we'll complete the prerequisites needed to get started with databases. These are the steps:

1 Add the `sqlx` dependency to Cargo.toml.
2 Install Postgres, and verify the installation.
3 Create a new database, and set up access credentials.
4 Define the database model in Rust, and create a table in the database.
5 Write Rust code to connect to the database and perform a query.

For step 5, we won't use the Actix web server—we'll write a vanilla Rust program instead. Our primary goal in this section is to eliminate database setup and configuration issues, learn to use `sqlx` to connect to databases, and do a sanity test for database connectivity. By the end of this section, you will have learned to query the Postgres database using `sqlx` and display query results on your terminal.

Let's look at each step in detail.

STEP 1: ADD SQLX DEPENDENCIES TO CARGO.TOML

As discussed earlier, we'll use the `sqlx` async client to communicate with a Postgres database. Add the following dependencies in the `Cargo.toml` file of the `tutor-db` project (located in $PROJECT_ROOT):

```
[dependencies]
#Actix web framework and run-time
actix-web = "4.1.0"
actix-rt = "2.7.0"
#Environment variable access libraries
dotenv = "0.15.0"

#Postgres access library
sqlx = {version = "0.6.2", default_features = false, features =
➥["postgres","runtime-tokio-native-tls", "macros","chrono"]}

# Data serialization library
serde = { version = "1.0.144", features = ["derive"] }

# Other utils
chrono = {version = "0.4.22", features = ["serde"]}

# Openssl for build (if openssl is not already installed on the dev server)
openssl = { version = "0.10.41", features = ["vendored"] }
```

Async runtime for Actix

Used to load environment variables into memory

The sqlx crate will be used for asynchronous connections to the Postgres database.

serde is used for serialization/deserialization.

chrono is used for date-time related functions.

Needed to build the binary

STEP 2: INSTALL POSTGRES AND VERIFY INSTALLATION

If you already have Postgres installed, you can move on to the next step. Otherwise, please refer to the appendix, which covers the steps involved in installing Postgres.

STEP 3: CREATE A NEW DATABASE AND ACCESS CREDENTIALS

Switch over to the Postgres account on your development machine or server. If you are on Linux, you can use the following command:

```
sudo -i -u postgres
```

You can now access a Postgres prompt (shell) with the following command:

```
psql
```

This will log you into the PostgreSQL prompt, and you can interact with the Postgres database. You should now be able to see the following prompt (let's call it the *psql shell prompt*):

```
postgres=#
```

Now that we are at the psql shell prompt, we can create a new database and a new user and associate the user with the database.

First, let's create a database called `ezytutors` with the following command:

```
postgres=# create database ezytutors;
```

Next, create a new user, `truuser`, with the password `mypassword` as shown (replace the username and password with your own):

```
postgres=# create user truuser with password 'mypassword';
```

Grant access privileges for the newly created user to the `ezytutors` database:

```
postgres=# grant all privileges on database ezytutors to truuser;
```

You can now quit the Postgres shell prompt with the following command:

```
postgres=# \q
```

Exit from the Postgres user account:

```
exit
```

You should now be in the prompt for the original user you used to log into the Linux server (or development machine).

Now let's ensure you are able to log into the `postgres` database using the new user and password. Let's first set an environment variable for the database user as follows (replace the value of `DATABASE_USER` with the user name you created in the previous step):

```
export DATABASE_USER=truuser
```

On the command line, you can use the following command to log in to the `ezytutors` database with the user name you created. The `--password` flag prompts for password entry:

```
psql -U $DATABASE_USER -d ezytutors --password
```

Type the password at the prompt, and you should be logged into a psql shell with the following prompt:

```
ezytutors=>
```

At this prompt, type the following to list the databases:

```
\list
```

You'll see the `ezytutors` database listed, similar to this:

```
List of databases
   Name    |  Owner   | Encoding | Collate  |  Ctype  |    Access privileges
-----------+----------+----------+----------+---------+---------------------
 ezytutors | postgres | UTF8     | C.UTF-8  | C.UTF-8 | =Tc/postgres        +
           |          |          |          |         | postgres=CTc/postgres+
           |          |          |          |         | truuser=CTc/postgres
```

If you've reached this far, great! If not, consult the Postgres installation and setup instructions for your development environment at www.postgresql.org/docs/12/app -psql.html.

NOTE You can also perform the preceding steps from a GUI admin interface, should you choose to install a GUI tool, such as cPanel (from a cloud provider) or pgAdmin (which is available to download for free).

STEP 4: DEFINE THE RUST DATABASE MODEL, AND CREATE A TABLE

We're now ready to define our database model in our Rust program and create the database table. There are a couple of ways to do this:

- Use plain database SQL scripts, which are independent of a database access library such as `sqlx`.
- Use the `sqlx` CLI.

We will use the first approach for this chapter because the `sqlx` CLI is in early beta at the time of writing. Depending on when you are reading this, a stable release of the `sqlx` CLI may be available.

Create a database.sql file under the src folder of the project root, and enter the following script:

```
/* Drop table if it already exists*/
drop table if exists ezy_course_c4;
/* Create a table. */
/* Note: Don't put a comma after last field */
create table ezy_course_c4
(
    course_id serial primary key,
    tutor_id INT not null,
    course_name varchar(140) not null,
    posted_time TIMESTAMP default now()
);

/* Load seed data for testing */
insert into ezy_course_c4
    (course_id,tutor_id, course_name,posted_time)
values(1, 1, 'First course', '2020-12-17 05:40:00');
insert into ezy_course_c4
    (course_id, tutor_id, course_name,posted_time)
values(2, 1, 'Second course', '2020-12-18 05:45:00');
```

Here we are creating a table with the name `ezy_course_c4`. The `c4` suffix is to indicate that this table definition is from chapter 4, as this will allow us to evolve the table definition in a future chapter.

Run the script with the following command from your terminal command prompt. Enter a password if prompted:

```
psql -U $DATABASE_USER -d ezytutors < $PROJECT_ROOT/src/database.sql
```

This script creates a table called `ezy_course_c4` within the `ezytutors` database, and it loads seed data for testing.

From the SQL shell or admin GUI, run the following SQL statement, and verify that the records are displayed from the `ezy_course_c4` table in the `ezytutors` database.

```
psql -U $DATABASE_USER -d ezytutors --password
select * from ezy_course_c4;
```

You should see results similar to these:

```
course_id | tutor_id |  course_name  |     posted_time
-----------+----------+---------------+---------------------
        1 |        1 | First course  | 2020-12-17 05:40:00
        2 |        1 | Second course | 2020-12-18 05:45:00
(2 rows)
```

STEP 5: WRITE CODE TO CONNECT TO THE DATABASE AND QUERY THE TABLE

We're now ready to write the Rust code to connect to the database! In src/bin/
iter1.rs, under the project root, add the following code:

```
use dotenv::dotenv;
use std::env;
use std::io;
use sqlx::postgres::PgPool;         ┌─  Define the data structure
use chrono::NaiveDateTime;          │   to represent a course.
#[derive(Debug)]              ◄─────┘
pub struct Course {
    pub course_id: i32,
    pub tutor_id: i32,
    pub course_name: String,              Used to run an asynchronous
    pub posted_time: Option<NaiveDateTime>,   Actix web server, and to connect
}                                         to the database using sqlx
#[actix_rt::main]             ◄─────────────
async fn main() -> io::Result<()> {   ┌─  Load the environment
    dotenv().ok();              ◄─────┘   variables into memory.
    let database_url = env::var("DATABASE_URL").expect(
    ➥"DATABASE_URL is not set in .env file");
    let db_pool = PgPool::connect(&database_url).await.unwrap();   ◄──
    let course_rows = sqlx::query!(
        r#"select course_id, tutor_id, course_name, posted_time from
        ➥ezy_course_c4 where course_id = $1"#,
        1
    )
    .fetch_all(&db_pool)
    .await
    .unwrap();
    let mut courses_list = vec![];
    for course_row in course_rows {
        courses_list.push(Course {
            course_id: course_row.course_id,
            tutor_id: course_row.tutor_id,
            course_name: course_row.course_name,
            posted_time: Some(chrono::NaiveDateTime::from(
            ➥course_row.posted_time.unwrap())),
        })
    }
    println!("Courses = {:?}", courses_list);
    Ok(())
}
```

Define the query to be executed.

Fetch all rows from the table, passing the reference to the database connection pool.

Create a database connection pool with sqlx. This helps to manage the number of database connections efficiently across multiple threads spawned by the Actix Web framework.

Retrieve the value of the DATABASE_URL environment variable. This value should be set either using a shell prompt or in an .env file.

Create an .env file in the project root directory, and make the following entry:

```
DATABASE_URL=postgres://<my-user>:<mypassword>@127.0.0.1:5432/ezytutors
```

Replace `<my-user>` and `<mypassword>` with the user name and password you used while setting up the database. `5432` refers to the default port where the Postgres server runs, and `ezytutors` is the name of the database we wish to connect to.

Run the code with the following command:

```
cargo run --bin iter1
```

Note that by using the `--bin` flag, we are telling Cargo to run the `main()` function located in iter1.rs from the $PROJECT_ROOT/src/bin directory.

You should see the query results displayed to your terminal as shown here:

```
Courses = [Course { course_id: 1, tutor_id: 1, course_name: "First course",
⮑posted_time: 2020-12-17T05:40:00 }]
```

Great! We are now able to connect to the database from a Rust program using the `sqlx` crate.

Running the program from the workspace root instead of the project root

You can also choose to run the program from the workspace root (the ezytutors directory) instead of the project root (the tutordb directory). To do so, you need to add an additional flag to the `cargo run` command as shown here:

```
cargo run --bin iter1 -p tutordb
```

Since the ezytutors workspace contains many projects, we need to tell the Cargo which project to execute. This is done by using the `-p` flag along with the project name (`tutordb`).

Note also that if you choose to do this, the .env file containing the database access credentials should be located within the workspace root as opposed to the project root.

In this chapter, I will follow the convention of executing the program from the project root.

4.3   Setting up the web service and writing unit tests (iteration 2)

Now that we know how to connect to a Postgres database using `sqlx`, let's get back to writing our database-backed web service. By the end of this section, you will have a code structure for the web service that includes routes, a database model, application state, a `main()` function, unit test scripts for the three APIs, and skeletal code for the handler functions.

This section serves as an interim checkpoint. You will be able to compile the web service and ensure there are no compilation errors before proceeding any further. However, the web service won't do anything useful until we write the handler functions in the next section.

These are the steps we'll perform in this section:

1 Set up dependencies and routes.
2 Set up the application state and the data model.
3 Set up the connection pool using dependency injection.
4 Write unit tests.

4.3.1 Setting up the dependencies and routes

Create a folder called iter2 under $PROJECT_ROOT/src. The code for this section will be organized as follows:

- *src/bin/iter2.rs*—Contains the main() function
- *src/iter2/routes.rs*—Contains routes
- *src/iter2/handlers.rs*—Contains handler functions
- *src/iter2/models.rs*—Contains the data structure to represent a course and utility methods
- *src/iter2/state.rs*—Application state containing the dependencies injected into each thread of the application's execution

Basically, the main() function will be in the iter.rs file under the src/bin folder of the project root, and the rest of the files will be placed in the src/iter2 folder.

We'll reuse the same set of routes defined in the previous chapter. The code to be placed in the $PROJECT_ROOT/src/iter2/routes.rs file is shown in the next listing.

> **Listing 4.1   Routes for the tutor web service**

```
use super::handlers::*;
use actix_web::web;

pub fn general_routes(cfg: &mut web::ServiceConfig) {
    cfg.route("/health", web::get().to(health_check_handler));
}

pub fn course_routes(cfg: &mut web::ServiceConfig) {
    cfg.service(
        web::scope("/courses")
            .route("/", web::post().to(post_new_course))          // A POST request to /courses to create a new course
            .route("/{tutor_id}", web::get().to(get_courses_for_tutor))   // A GET request to /courses/{tutor_id} to retrieve all courses for a tutor
            .route("/{tutor_id}/{course_id}", web::get().to(
            get_course_details)),                                 // A GET request to /courses/{tutor_id}/{course_id} to retrieve the details for a particular course_id
    );
}
```

4.3.2 Setting up the application state and data model

Let's define the data model in src/iter2/models.rs under the project root. Here we'll define a data structure to represent a course. We'll also write a utility method that accepts the JSON data payload sent with the HTTP POST request and converts it into the Rust Course data structure.

Place the following code in the $PROJECT_ROOT/src/iter2/models.rs file.

Listing 4.2   Data model for the tutor web service

> The Course data structure contains the course ID, tutor ID, name of the course, and posted time as fields. Of these, the field posted_time is type Optional<T> because, for a new course posting, this field will be auto-populated by the tutor web service—the user does not need to provide this information.

> The From trait will extract the data payload sent with the POST HTTP request (for a new course) and convert it into the Rust Course data structure.

```rust
use actix_web::web;
use chrono::NaiveDateTime;
use serde::{Deserialize, Serialize};

#[derive(Deserialize, Serialize, Debug, Clone)]
pub struct Course {
    pub course_id: i32,
    pub tutor_id: i32,
    pub course_name: String,
    pub posted_time: Option<NaiveDateTime>,
}
impl From<web::Json<Course>> for Course {
    fn from(course: web::Json<Course>) -> Self {
        Course {
            course_id: course.course_id,
            tutor_id: course.tutor_id,
            course_name: course.course_name.clone(),
            posted_time: course.posted_time,
        }
    }
}
```

To connect to Postgres, we'll have to define a database connection pool and make it available across worker threads. We can achieve this by defining a connection pool as part of the application state. Add the following code to $PROJECT_ROOT/src/iter2/state.rs:

```rust
use sqlx::postgres::PgPool;
use std::sync::Mutex;
pub struct AppState {
    pub health_check_response: String,
    pub visit_count: Mutex<u32>,
    pub db: PgPool,
}
```

In the `AppState` struct, we have retained the two fields from the previous chapter that we need for the health-check response, and we have added an additional field, `db`, which represents the `sqlx` Postgres connection pool.

With the application state definition done, it's time to write the `main()` function for the web service.

4.3.3   *Setting up the connection pool using dependency injection*

In the `main()` function for the web service, we will perform the following:

- Retrieve the `DATABASE_URL` environment variable to get credentials to connect to the database.

- Create a `sqlx` connection pool.
- Create an application state, and add the connection pool to it.
- Create a new Actix web application, and configure it with routes. Inject the `AppState` struct as a dependency into the web application so it is made available to handler functions across threads.
- Initialize the Actix web server with the web application, and run the server.

The code for the `main()` function in $PROJECT_ROOT/src/bin/iter2.rs is shown in the following listing.

Listing 4.3 The tutor web service's `main()` function

```
use actix_web::{web, App, HttpServer};
use dotenv::dotenv;
use sqlx::postgres::PgPool;
use std::env;
use std::io;
use std::sync::Mutex;

#[path = "../iter2/handlers.rs"]
mod handlers;
#[path = "../iter2/models.rs"]
mod models;
#[path = "../iter2/routes.rs"]
mod routes;
#[path = "../iter2/state.rs"]
mod state;

use routes::*;
use state::AppState;

#[actix_rt::main]
async fn main() -> io::Result<()> {          Load environment
    dotenv().ok();                           variables.

    let database_url = env::var("DATABASE_URL").expect(                Create a new sqlx
        "DATABASE_URL is not set in .env file");                       connection pool.
    let db_pool = PgPool::connect(&database_url).await.unwrap();
    // Construct App State
    let shared_data = web::Data::new(AppState {
        health_check_response: "I'm good. You've already
        asked me ".to_string(),
        visit_count: Mutex::new(0),
        db: db_pool,
    });
    //Construct app and configure routes     Inject the connection pool into the
    let app = move || {                      Actix web application instance as a
        App::new()                           cross-application dependency. This will
            .app_data(shared_data.clone())   be made available to the handler
            .configure(general_routes)       functions by the Actix Web framework.
            .configure(course_routes)
    };
```

```
    //Start HTTP server

    HttpServer::new(app).bind("127.0.0.1:3000")?.run().await
}
```

The rest of the `main()` function is similar to what we wrote in the previous chapter. Let's also write the handler functions in $PROJECT_ROOT/src/iter2/handlers.rs.

Listing 4.4   Handler functions skeleton

```
use super::models::Course;
use super::state::AppState;
use actix_web::{web, HttpResponse};

pub async fn health_check_handler(app_state: web::Data<AppState>) ->
➥HttpResponse {
    let health_check_response = &app_state.health_check_response;
    let mut visit_count = app_state.visit_count.lock().unwrap();
    let response = format!("{} {} times", health_check_response,
    ➥visit_count);
    *visit_count += 1;
    HttpResponse::Ok().json(&response)
}

pub async fn get_courses_for_tutor(
    _app_state: web::Data<AppState>,
    _params: web::Path<(i32,)>,
) -> HttpResponse {
    HttpResponse::Ok().json("success")
}

pub async fn get_course_details(
    _app_state: web::Data<AppState>,
    _params: web::Path<(i32, i32)>,
) -> HttpResponse {
    HttpResponse::Ok().json("success")
}

pub async fn post_new_course(
    _new_course: web::Json<Course>,
    _app_state: web::Data<AppState>,
) -> HttpResponse {
    HttpResponse::Ok().json("success")
}
```

> The code for the health_check_handler function keeps track of how many times the handler is invoked and records that in the application state (as defined in $PROJECT_ROOT/src/iter2/state.rs). It returns the visit count as part of the HTTP response.

We've now written skeletal code for the three tutor handler functions. These don't do much yet except return a success response. Our goal is to verify that the code for the web service compiles without errors before we implement the database access logic in the next section.

Verify the code with the following command from the project root:

```
cargo check --bin iter2
```

The code should compile without errors, and the server should start up. You may see a few warnings related to unused variables, but we'll ignore those for now, as this is only an interim checkpoint. Next, we'll write the unit tests for the three handler functions.

4.3.4 Writing the unit tests

In the previous section, we wrote dummy handler functions that simply returned a success response. In this section, let's write the unit tests that invoke these handler functions. In the process, you'll learn how to simulate HTTP request parameters (which would otherwise come through external API calls), how to simulate application state being passed from the Actix framework to the handler function, and how to check for responses from the handler functions in test functions.

We'll write three unit test functions to test the three corresponding handler functions we wrote in the previous section: to get all courses for a tutor, to get course details for an individual course, and to post a new course.

Let's add the following unit test code to the $PROJECT_ROOT/src/iter2/handlers.rs file.

Listing 4.5 Unit tests for the handler functions

```
#[cfg(test)]
mod tests {
    use super::*;                  Module
    use actix_web::http::StatusCode;   imports
    use chrono::NaiveDate;
    use dotenv::dotenv;
    use sqlx::postgres::PgPool;
    use std::env;
    use std::sync::Mutex;

    #[actix_rt::test]
    async fn get_all_courses_success() {
        dotenv().ok();
        let database_url = env::var("DATABASE_URL").expect(
        ➥"DATABASE_URL is not set in .env file");
        let pool: PgPool = PgPool::connect(&database_url).await.unwrap();
        let app_state: web::Data<AppState> = web::Data::new(AppState {
            health_check_response: "".to_string(),
            visit_count: Mutex::new(0),
            db: pool,
        });
        let tutor_id: web::Path<(i32,)> = web::Path::from((1,));
        let resp = get_courses_for_tutor(app_state, tutor_id).await;
        assert_eq!(resp.status(), StatusCode::OK);
    }
}
```

Construct the application state that is to be passed as a parameter to the handler function. In an end-to-end test, the application state would be passed by the Actix Web framework to the handler function automatically. Here, in unit-test code, we have to do this step manually.

Read database access credentials from the .env file.

Create a new connection pool to talk to the Postgres database.

Construct the HTTP request parameter to pass to the handler function. In an end-to-end test, the Actix framework deserializes the incoming HTTP request parameters and passes them to the handler function. Here, in unit-test code, we have to do this step manually.

Verify that the returned HTTP response from the handler function shows the success status code.

Invoke the handler function with the application state and HTTP request parameter constructed in the previous steps.

```
#[actix_rt::test]
async fn get_course_detail_test() {
    dotenv().ok();
    let database_url = env::var("DATABASE_URL").expect(
    ➥"DATABASE_URL is not set in .env file");
    let pool: PgPool = PgPool::connect(&database_url).await.unwrap();
    let app_state: ...
    let params: web::Path<(i32, i32)> = web::Path::from((1, 2));
    let resp = get_course_details(app_state, params).await;
    assert_eq!(resp.status(), StatusCode::OK);
}
```

**An abridged section of
code—see the chapter's
source for the full code**

```
#[actix_rt::test]
async fn post_course_success() {
    dotenv().ok();
    let database_url = env::var("DATABASE_URL").expect(
    ➥"DATABASE_URL is not set in .env file");
    let pool: PgPool = PgPool::connect(&database_url).await.unwrap();
    let app_state: ...
    let new_course_msg = Course {
        course_id: 1,
        tutor_id: 1,
        course_name: "This is the next course".into(),
        posted_time: Some(NaiveDate::from_ymd(2020, 9, 17).and_hms(
        ➥14, 01, 11)),
    };
    let course_param = web::Json(new_course_msg);
    let resp = post_new_course(course_param, app_state).await;
    assert_eq!(resp.status(), StatusCode::OK);
}
}
```

The code in the preceding listing is annotated for the first of the test functions. The same concepts also apply to the other two test functions—you should be able to read and follow the test function code without much difficulty.

Let's run the unit tests with this command:

```
cargo test --bin iter2
```

You should see the three tests pass successfully with the following message:

```
running 3 tests
test handlers::tests::get_all_courses_success ... ok
test handlers::tests::post_course_success ... ok
test handlers::tests::get_course_detail_test ... ok

test result: ok. 3 passed; 0 failed; 0 ignored; 0 measured; 0 filtered out
```

The tests pass even though we haven't written any database access logic because we are returning unconditional success responses from the handlers. We'll fix that in the next section, but we have built the basic project structure with all the required pieces (routes, application state, a main() function, handlers, and unit tests), and you now know how to tie all of them together.

4.4 Creating and querying records from the database (iteration 3)

In this section, we'll write the database access code for the tutor APIs. Create a folder named iter3 under $PROJECT_ROOT/src. The code for this section will be organized as follows:

- *src/bin/iter3.rs*—Contains the `main()` function.
- *src/iter3/routes.rs*—Contains the routes.
- *src/iter3/handlers.rs*—Contains the handler functions.
- *src/iter3/models.rs*—Contains the data structure to represent a course and a few utility methods.
- *src/iter3/state.rs*—Application state containing the dependencies injected into each thread of application execution.
- *src/iter3/db_access.rs*—To adhere to the single responsibility principle, we don't want the database access logic to be part of the handler function, so we'll create a new $PROJECT_ROOT/src/iter3/db_access.rs file for the database access logic. Separating out database access will also be helpful if we want to switch databases (such as from Postgres to MySQL) in the future. We will be able to rewrite the database access functions with the new database, while retaining the same handler functions and database access function signatures.

Of the files listed for this iteration, we can reuse the code for routes.rs, state.rs, and models.rs from iteration 2. That leaves us to focus our efforts primarily on making the required adjustments to the `main()` function and handler code and on writing the core database access logic.

Let's look at the code for database access in three parts, each part corresponding to one of the APIs.

4.4.1 Writing database access functions

The steps for using `sqlx` to query records from Postgres tables are as follows:

1. Construct an SQL query using the SQL `query!` macro.
2. Execute the query using the `fetch_all()` method, passing the connection pool.
3. Extract the results, and convert them into a Rust struct that can be returned from the function.

The code in `$PROJECT_ROOT/src/iter3/db_access.rs` is shown in the following listing.

Listing 4.6 Database access code for retrieving all courses for a tutor

```
use super::models::Course;
use sqlx::postgres::PgPool;

pub async fn get_courses_for_tutor_db(pool: &PgPool, tutor_id: i32) ->
➥Vec<Course> {
```

```
// Prepare SQL statement
let course_rows = sqlx::query!(
    "SELECT tutor_id, course_id, course_name, posted_time FROM
    ➥ezy_course_c4 where tutor_id = $1",
    tutor_id
)
.fetch_all(pool)
.await
.unwrap();
// Extract result
course_rows
    .iter()
    .map(|course_row| Course {
        course_id: course_row.course_id,
        tutor_id: course_row.tutor_id,
        course_name: course_row.course_name.clone(),
        posted_time: Some(chrono::NaiveDateTime::from(
        ➥course_row.posted_time.unwrap())),
    })
    .collect()
}
```

Prepare the SQL statement for retrieving query results using the query! macro from the sqlx crate.

Execute the query.

Convert the query results into a Rust vector, which is returned from the function.

We're using the `fetch_all()` method to retrieve all records from the database that match the SQL query. The `fetch_all()` method accepts a Postgres connection pool as a parameter. The `await` keyword after `fetch_all()` denotes that we are making an asynchronous call to the Postgres database using the `sqlx` crate.

Note the use of the `iter()` method to convert the retrieved database records into a Rust iterator. The `map()` function then converts each database row (returned by the iterator) into a Rust data structure of type `Course`.

Finally, the results of applying the `map()` function on all the database records are accumulated into a Rust `Vec` data type by using the `collect()` method. The vector of `Course` struct instances is then returned from the function.

Note also the use of the `chrono` module to convert the `posted_time` value of a course retrieved from the database into a `NaiveDateTime` type from the `chrono` crate.

Overall, you'll notice that the code is quite concise due to the elegant functional programming constructs that Rust provides.

The code for retrieving the course details, given a `course-id` or `tutor-id`, is similar to the preceding implementation. The main difference is the use of the `fetch_one()` method instead of the `fetch_all()` that we used previously, as here we are retrieving the details for a single course. Place the following code in the same file ($PROJECT_ ROOT/src/iter3/db_access.rs).

Listing 4.7   Database access code for retrieving details for a single course

```
pub async fn get_course_details_db(pool: &PgPool, tutor_id: i32,
➥course_id: i32) -> Course {
    // Prepare SQL statement
    let course_row = sqlx::query!(
```

Prepare the query for execution.

```
      "SELECT tutor_id, course_id, course_name, posted_time FROM
   ➡ezy_course_c4 where tutor_id = $1 and course_id = $2",
      tutor_id, course_id
   )
   .fetch_one(pool)      ◁─┐   Execute the query. Note the use of the fetch_one
   .await                  │   method instead of fetch_all, which was used in listing
   .unwrap();              │   4.6, as here we only want details for one course.
   // Execute query
   Course {              ◁───────────────────────────┐   Return a Rust Course
      course_id: course_row.course_id,              │   data structure from
      tutor_id: course_row.tutor_id,                │   the function.
      course_name: course_row.course_name.clone(),
      posted_time: Some(chrono::NaiveDateTime::from(
   ➡course_row.posted_time.unwrap())),
   }
}
```

Lastly, we'll look at the database access code for posting a new course. The query is constructed and then executed. The inserted course is then retrieved, converted into a Rust struct, and returned from the function. Place the following code in $PROJECT_ROOT/src/iter3/db_access.rs.

Listing 4.8 Database access code for posting a new course

```
pub async fn post_new_course_db(pool: &PgPool, new_course: Course) ->
➡Course {

   let course_row = sqlx::query!("insert into ezy_course_c4 (
   ➡course_id,tutor_id, course_name) values ($1,$2,$3) returning
   ➡tutor_id, course_id,course_name, posted_time", new_course.course_id,
   ➡new_course.tutor_id, new_course.course_name)   ◁─┐   Prepare the query to
   .fetch_one(pool)    ◁─┐   After inserting, fetch     │   insert a new course into
   .await.unwrap();      │   the inserted course.       │   the database table.
   //Retrieve result
   Course {            ◁──────────────────┐   Return a Rust Course data
      course_id: course_row.course_id,   │   structure from the function.
      tutor_id: course_row.tutor_id,
      course_name: course_row.course_name.clone(),
      posted_time: Some(chrono::NaiveDateTime::from(
   ➡course_row.posted_time.unwrap())),
   }
}
```

Note that we're not passing the posted_time value to the insert query. This is because we have set the default value of this field to the system-generated current time. Refer to the $PROJECT_ROOT/src/database.sql file, where this default is defined as follows:

```
posted_time TIMESTAMP default now()
```

> ## Using MySQL instead of a Postgres database
>
> The `sql` crate supports both MySQL and SQLite, in addition to Postgres. If you prefer to follow along with this chapter using a MySQL database in place of Postgres, refer to the instructions for the `sqlx` crate repository at https://github.com/launchbadge/sqlx.
>
> One thing to note is that the SQL syntax supported by MySQL differs from that of Postgres, so the query statements listed in this chapter need some modifications for use with MySQL. For example, if you are using MySQL, the `$` sign used to denote parameters (e.g., $1) should be replaced with a question mark (?). Also, Postgres supports a `returning` clause in SQL statements that can be used to return values of columns modified by an insert, update, or delete operation, but MySQL does not support the `returning` clause directly.

This completes the code for database access. Next, let's look at the handler functions that invoke these database access functions.

4.4.2 Writing handler functions

We've looked at the code for database access. Now we need to invoke these database functions from the corresponding handler functions. Recall that the handler functions are invoked by the Actix framework based on the API routes (defined in routes.rs) on which the HTTP requests arrive (POST new course, GET courses for tutor, etc.).

The code for the handler functions, to be placed in $PROJECT_ROOT/src/iter3/handlers.rs, is shown in the following listing.

Listing 4.9   Handler function for retrieving query results

```
use super::db_access::*;
use super::models::Course;
use super::state::AppState;
use std::convert::TryFrom;

use actix_web::{web, HttpResponse};

pub async fn health_check_handler(app_state: web::Data<AppState>) ->
➥HttpResponse {
    let health_check_response = &app_state.health_check_response;
    let mut visit_count = app_state.visit_count.lock().unwrap();
    let response = format!("{} {} times", health_check_response, visit_count);
    *visit_count += 1;
    HttpResponse::Ok().json(&response)
}

pub async fn get_courses_for_tutor(
    app_state: web::Data<AppState>,
    params: web::Path<(i32,)>,
) -> HttpResponse {
    let tuple = params.0;
    let tutor_id: i32 = i32::try_from(tuple.0).unwrap();
```

web::Path is an extractor that allows you to extract typed information from the HTTP request's path.

The data type returned by the web::Path extractor for the get_courses_for_tutor() handler function is <(i32),>.

```
        let courses = get_courses_for_tutor_db(&app_state.db, tutor_id).await;
        HttpResponse::Ok().json(courses)
}

pub async fn get_course_details(
        app_state: web::Data<AppState>,
        params: web::Path<(i32, i32)>,
) -> HttpResponse {
        let tuple = params;
        let tutor_id: i32 = i32::try_from(tuple.0).unwrap();
        let course_id: i32 = i32::try_from(tuple.1).unwrap();
        let course = get_course_details_db(
        &app_state.db, tutor_id, course_id).await;
        HttpResponse::Ok().json(course)
}
pub async fn post_new_course(
        new_course: web::Json<Course>,
        app_state: web::Data<AppState>,
) -> HttpResponse {
        let course = post_new_course_db(&app_state.db, new_course.into()).await;

        HttpResponse::Ok().json(course)
}
```

> **Take the return value (the vector containing a list of courses) from the database function, convert it to JSON, and send an HTTP success response.**

> **Invoke the corresponding database access method to retrieve the list of courses for a tutor, passing in the application state and tutor-id.**

> **In the get_course_details() handler function, retrieve values for these two path parameters from the HTTP request: tutor-id and course-id.**

In listing 4.9, each of the handler functions is fairly straightforward and performs steps similar to those listed here:

1 Extract the connection pool from application state (appstate.db).

2 Extract the parameters sent as part of the HTTP request (the `params` argument).

3 Invoke the corresponding database access function (the function names suffixed with `db`)

4 Return the result from the database access function as an HTTP response.

Let's look at these steps using the example of the `get_course_details()` handler function, which is called whenever an HTTP request arrives on the route `/{tutor_id}/{course_id}`. An example would be the request http://localhost:3000/courses/1/2, where the HTTP client (the internet browser) is requesting to see the details of a course that has a `tutor-id` of 1 and a `course-id` of 2. Let's go through the code for this handler function in detail.

In order to extract the course details for a given `tutor-id` and `course-id`, we need to talk to the database. However, the handler function does not know (nor does it need to know, in keeping with the single responsibility principle of good software design) how to talk to the database. So it will have to rely on the `get_course_details_db()` database access function, which we wrote in the $PROJECT_ROOT/src/iter3/db_ access.rs source file.

This is the signature of the function:

```
pub async fn get_course_details_db(pool: &PgPool, tutor_id: i32,
course_id: i32) -> Course
```

In order to invoke the database access function, the handler function needs to pass three parameters: a database connection pool, the tutor-id, and the course-id.

The connection pool is available as part of the application state object. In the main() function of iteration 2, you saw how the application state is constructed with the connection pool and then injected into the Actix web application instance. Every Actix handler function will then automatically have access to the application state as a parameter (which is automatically populated by the Actix framework when the handler is invoked).

As a result, the first parameter in this handler, app_state, represents a value of type AppState, defined in $PROJECT_ROOT/src/iter3/state.rs and reproduced here:

```
pub struct AppState {
    pub health_check_response: String,
    pub visit_count: Mutex<u32>,
    pub db: PgPool,
}
```

Hence app_state.db refers to the db member of the AppState struct, and it represents the connection pool that can be passed to the database function get_course_details_db().

The next two parameters passed to the database access function are tutor-id and course-id. These are available as part of an incoming HTTP request of the form http(s)://{domain}:{port}/{tutor-id}/{course-id}. In order to extract the parameters from the request, the Actix Web framework provides utilities called *extractors*. An extractor can be accessed as an argument to the handler function (similar to application state). In our case, because we are expecting two numeric parameters from the HTTP request, the handler function signature has a parameter of type web::Path<(i32, i32)>, which basically yields a tuple containing two integers of type (i32, i32). To extract the value of the tutor-id and course-id from params, we will have to perform a two-step process.

The following line provides a tuple of form (i32, i32):

```
let tuple = params.0;
```

Then the next two lines are used to extract and convert the tutor-id and course-id from i32 to i32 type (which is the type expected by the database access function):

```
let tutor_id: i32 = i32::try_from(tuple.0).unwrap();
let course_id: i32 = i32::try_from(tuple.1).unwrap();
```

Now we can invoke the database access function with the application state, tutor-id, and course-id as shown here:

```
let course = get_course_details_db(&app_state.db, tutor_id,
    ➥course_id).await;
```

Finally, we take the return value of type Course from the database function, serialize it to Json type, and embed it into an HTTP response with a success status code, all in a succinct expression. (You can now see why Rust rocks!)

```
HttpResponse::Ok().json(course)
```

The other two handler functions are similar in structure to what you've just seen.

Recall that in the handlers.rs source file, we also had a handler function for health checks and the unit tests. These remain unchanged from the previous iteration. I've excluded error handling from this iteration so we could focus on database access.

4.4.3 *Writing the main() function for the database-backed web service*

We've written the database access and handler functions. Let's complete the final piece of code needed before we can test our web service. Add the following code to the `main()` function in $PROJECT_ROOT/src/bin/iter3.rs.

Listing 4.10   The `main()` function for iteration 3

```
use actix_web::{web, App, HttpServer};
use dotenv::dotenv;
use sqlx::postgres::PgPool;
use std::env;
use std::io;
use std::sync::Mutex;

#[path = "../iter3/db_access.rs"]
mod db_access;
#[path = "../iter3/handlers.rs"]
mod handlers;
#[path = "../iter3/models.rs"]
mod models;
#[path = "../iter3/routes.rs"]
mod routes;
#[path = "../iter3/state.rs"]
mod state;

use routes::*;
use state::AppState;

#[actix_rt::main]
async fn main() -> io::Result<()> {
    dotenv().ok();

    let database_url = env::var("DATABASE_URL").expect(
    "DATABASE_URL is not set in .env file");
    let db_pool = PgPool::connect(&database_url).await.unwrap();

    let shared_data = web::Data::new(AppState {
        health_check_response: "I'm good. You've already
        asked me ".to_string(),
        visit_count: Mutex::new(0),
        db: db_pool,
    });

    let app = move || {
        App::new()
            .app_data(shared_data.clone())
            .configure(general_routes)
            .configure(course_routes)
    };
```

Construct AppState.
Note that we are storing the connection pool as part of the application state in the db field.

Construct the app instance.

Inject the app state into the application instance.

Configure the routes.

```
//Start HTTP server

HttpServer::new(app).bind("127.0.0.1:3000")?.run().await
}
```

Start the Actix web server, load the constructed Actix web application instance, and bind the server running on localhost to port 3000. The await keyword indicates the asynchronous nature of the Actix web server.

We're now ready to test and run the web service. First, let's run the automated tests with this command:

```
cargo test --bin iter3
```

You should see the three test cases execute successfully as shown here:

```
running 3 tests
test handlers::tests::post_course_success ... ok
test handlers::tests::get_all_courses_success ... ok
test handlers::tests::get_course_detail_test ... ok
```

Note that if you run the `cargo test` command more than once, the program will exit with an error. This is because you are trying to insert a record with the same `course_id` twice. To get around this, log into the psql shell and run the following command:

```
delete from ezy_course_c4 where course_id=3;
```

You are inserting a record with a `course_id` value of 3 in the test function, so once you delete this database record, you can rerun the test.

To make this deletion step easier, the `delete` SQL statement can be placed within a script file. The file $PROJECT_ROOT/iter3-test-clean.sql contains this script, if you'd like to use it. Execute the script as follows:

```
psql -U $DATABASE_USER -d ezytutors --password <
➥ $PROJECT_ROOT/iter3-test-clean.sql
```

You can now rerun the test:

```
cargo test --bin iter3
```

Let's now run the server:

```
cargo run --bin iter3
```

From a browser, enter the following URL to retrieve query results for a `tutor` id of 1.

```
http://localhost:3000/courses/1
```

Or, if you are behind a firewall, you can use curl to run it:

```
curl localhost:3000/courses/1
```

You should see a response similar to what's shown here:

```
[{"course_id":1,"tutor_id":1,"course_name":"First course",
➥ "posted_time":"2020-12-17T05:40:00"},{"course_id":2,"tutor_id":1,
➥ "course_name":"Second course","posted_time":"2020-12-18T05:45:00"},
```

```
➡{"course_id":3,"tutor_id":1,"course_name":"Third course",
➡"posted_time":"2020-12-17T11:55:56.846276"}]
```

You will find three query results in your list. We added two courses as part of the database.sql script. We then added a new course using the unit tests.

Let's now test posting a new course using curl:

```
curl -X POST localhost:3000/courses/ \
-H "Content-Type: application/json" \
-d '{"tutor_id":1, "course_id":4, "course_name":"Fourth course"}'
```

You should see a response from the Actix web server similar to this:

```
{"course_id":4,"tutor_id":1,"course_name":"Fourth course",
➡"posted_time":"2021-01-12T12:58:19.668877"}
```

You can now try to retrieve the details for the newly posted course from a browser, as shown here:

```
http://localhost:3000/courses/1/4
```

> **NOTE** If you are behind a firewall, run this command with curl as previously suggested.

You'll see a result similar to this in the browser:

```
{"course_id":4,"tutor_id":1,"course_name":"Fourth course",
➡"posted_time":"2021-01-12T12:58:19.668877"}
```

This concludes iteration 3. We have now implemented three APIs for the tutor web service, backed by a database store. We have built the functionality to post a new course, persist it to the database, and then query the database for a list of courses and individual course details. Congratulations!

You now have two important tools at hand for implementing a wide spectrum of services: RESTful web services (from the previous chapter) and database persistence (from this chapter). Maybe you have already noticed that the vast majority of corporate applications are of the *CRUD* (create, read, update, delete) type. That is, they mainly offer users the possibility of creating, updating, and possibly deleting information. Armed with the knowledge you've acquired in the last two chapters, you can already go a long way.

You may also have noticed that this chapter covered only the *happy path* scenarios, and did not account for, or handle, any errors that might occur. This is unrealistic, as many things can go wrong in a distributed web application. We will also need to authenticate users making API calls. We'll discuss these topics in the next chapter.

Summary

- `sqlx` is a Rust crate that provides asynchronous database access to many databases including Postgres and MySQL. It has built-in connection pooling.

- Connecting to a database from Actix using `sqlx` involves the following three broad steps: in the `main()` function of the web service, create a `sqlx` connection pool and inject it into the application state; in the handler function, access the connection pool and pass it to the database access function; and in the database access function, construct the query and execute it on the connection pool.
- The web service with its three APIs was built in three iterations: In iteration 1, we configured the database, configured a `sqlx` connection to the database, and tested the connection through a vanilla Rust program (not with an Actix web server). In iteration 2, we set up the database model, routes, state, and the `main()` function for the web service. In iteration 3, we wrote the database access code for the three APIs along with the unit tests. The codebase for each of the iterations can be built and tested independently.

Handling errors

This chapter covers

- Setting up the project structure
- Handling errors in Rust and Actix Web
- Defining a custom error handler
- Error handling for the three APIs

In the previous chapter, we wrote the code to post and retrieve courses through APIs, but what we demonstrated and tested were the *happy path* scenarios. In the real world, however, many types of failures can occur. The database server may be unavailable, the tutor ID provided in the request may be invalid, there may be a web server error, and so on. It is important that our web service be able to detect errors, handle them gracefully, and send a meaningful error message back to the user or client sending the API request. This is done through *error handling*, which is the focus of this chapter. Error handling is important not just for the stability of our web service, but also to provide a good user experience.

Figure 5.1 summarizes the error-handling approach we will adopt in this chapter. We'll add custom error handling to our web service, unifying the different types of errors that can be encountered in the application. Whenever there is an invalid request or unexpected malfunction in the server code, the client will receive a meaningful and appropriate HTTP status code and error message. To achieve this, we will use a combination of the core Rust features for error handling and the features provided by Actix, while also customizing the error handling for our application.

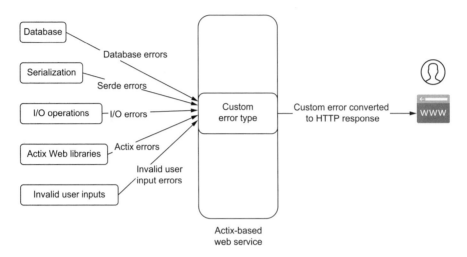

Figure 5.1   Unifying error handling in Rust

5.1   *Setting up the project structure*

We will use the code we built in the previous chapter as our starting point for adding error handling. If you've been following along, you can start with your own code from chapter 4. Alternatively, clone the repo from GitHub (https://github.com/peshwar9/rust-servers-services-apps), and use the code for iteration 3 from chapter 4 as your starting point.

We'll build the code in this chapter as *iteration 4*, so first go to the project root (ezytutors/tutor-db), and create a new folder called iter4 under src.

The code for this section will be organized as follows (see figure 5.2):

- *src/bin/iter4.rs*—The main() function
- *src/iter4/routes.rs*—Contains the routes
- *src/iter4/handlers.rs*—Handler functions
- *src/iter4/models.rs*—Data structure to represent a Course, and utility methods
- *src/iter4/state.rs*—Application state containing the dependencies that are injected into each thread of application execution
- *src/iter4/db_access.rs*—Database access code separated out from the handler function for modularity
- *src/iter4/errors.rs*—A custom error data structure and associated error-handling functions

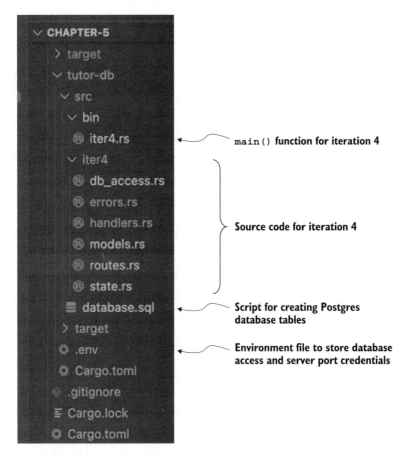

Figure 5.2   Project structure for chapter 5

We will not be changing the source code for routes.rs, models.rs, or state.rs, compared to chapter 4. For handlers.rs and db_access.rs, we will start with the code from chapter 4, but we will modify these files to incorporate custom error handling. Errors.rs is a new source file that we'll add.

Let's also create a new version of the database tables for this chapter by following these steps:

1   Amend the database.sql script from the previous chapter to look like this:

```
/* Drop table if it already exists*/
drop table if exists ezy_course_c5;
/* Create a table. */
/* Note: Don't put a comma after last field */
create table ezy_course_c5
(
    course_id serial primary key,
    tutor_id INT not null,
```

```
    course_name varchar(140) not null,
    posted_time TIMESTAMP default now()
);

/* Load seed data for testing */
insert into ezy_course_c5
    (course_id,tutor_id, course_name,posted_time)
values(1, 1, 'First course', '2021-03-17 05:40:00');
insert into ezy_course_c5
    (course_id, tutor_id, course_name,posted_time)
values(2, 1, 'Second course', '2021-03-18 05:45:00');
```

Note that the main change we are making in this script, compared to the last chapter, is to change the name of the table from ezy_course_c4 to ezy_course_c5.

2   Run the script from the command line as follows to create the table and load the sample data:

```
psql -U <user-name> -d ezytutors < database.sql
```

Ensure you provide the right path to the database.sql file, and enter the password if prompted.

3   Once the table is created, we need to give the database user permissions to this new table. Run the following commands from the terminal command line:

```
psql -U <user-name> -d ezytutors    // Login to psql shell
GRANT ALL PRIVILEGES ON TABLE __ezy_course_c5__ to <user-name>
\q                                  // Quit the psql shell
```

Replace the <user-name> with your own, and execute the commands.

4   Write the main() function: from the previous chapter, copy src/bin/iter3.rs into your project directory for this chapter under src/bin/iter4.rs, and replace the references to iter3 with iter4. The final code for iter4.rs should look like the following:

```
use actix_web::{web, App, HttpServer};
use dotenv::dotenv;
use sqlx::postgres::PgPool;
use std::env;
use std::io;
use std::sync::Mutex;

#[path = "../iter4/db_access.rs"]
mod db_access;
#[path = "../iter4/errors.rs"]
mod errors;
#[path = "../iter4/handlers.rs"]
mod handlers;
#[path = "../iter4/models.rs"]
mod models;
#[path = "../iter4/routes.rs"]
mod routes;
```

```
#[path = "../iter4/state.rs"]
mod state;

use routes::*;
use state::AppState;

#[actix_rt::main]
async fn main() -> io::Result<()> {
    dotenv().ok();

    let database_url = env::var("DATABASE_URL").expect(
    ➥"DATABASE_URL is not set in .env file");
    let db_pool = PgPool::connect(&database_url).await.unwrap();
    // Construct App State
    let shared_data = web::Data::new(AppState {
        health_check_response: "I'm good.
        ➥You've already asked me ".to_string(),
        visit_count: Mutex::new(0),
        db: db_pool,
    });
    //Construct app and configure routes
    let app = move || {
        App::new()
            .app_data(shared_data.clone())
            .configure(general_routes)
            .configure(course_routes)
    };

    //Start HTTP server
    let host_port = env::var("HOST_PORT").expect(
    ➥"HOST:PORT address is not set in .env file");
    HttpServer::new(app).bind(&host_port)?.run().await
}
```

Ensure that the modules being referred to in the code are under the src/iter4 folder. Also, make sure you add the environment variables for database access and server port numbers in the .env file.

Do a sanity check by running the server with this command:

```
cargo run --bin iter4
```

You now have recreated the end state of chapter 3 as the starting point for chapter 4.

Let's now take a quick tour of the basics of error handling in Rust, which we can then put to use to design the custom error handling for our web service.

5.2 *Basic error handling in Rust and Actix Web*

Broadly, programming languages use one of two approaches for error handling: *exception handling* or *return values*. Rust uses the latter approach. This is different from languages like Java, Python, and JavaScript, where exception handling is used. In Rust, error handling is seen as an enabler of the reliability guarantees provided by the language, so Rust wants the programmer to handle errors explicitly rather than to throw exceptions.

Toward this goal, Rust functions that might fail return a `Result` enum type whose definition is shown here:

```
enum Result<T, E> {
    Ok(T),
    Err(E),
}
```

A Rust function signature will contain a return value of type `Result<T,E>`, where `T` is the type of value that will be returned in the case of success, and `E` is the type of error value that will be returned in the case of a failure. A `Result` type is basically a way of saying that a computation or function can return one of two possible outcomes: a value in the case of a successful computation or an error in the case of failure.

Let's look at an example. The following simple function parses a string into an integer, squares it, and returns a value of type `i32`. If the parsing fails, it returns an error of type `ParseIntError`:

```
fn square(val: &str) -> Result<i32, ParseIntError> {
    match val.parse::<i32>() {
        Ok(num) => Ok(i32::pow(num, 2)),
        Err(e) => Err(e),
    }
}
```

The parse function in the Rust standard library returns a `Result` type, which we are unwrapping (i.e., extracting the value from) using a `match` statement. The return value from this function is of the pattern `Result<T,E>`, and in this case, `T` is `i32` and `E` is `ParseIntError`.

Let's write a `main()` function that calls the `square()` function:

```
use std::num::ParseIntError;

fn main() {
    println!("{:?}", square("2"));
    println!("{:?}", square("INVALID"));
}

fn square(val: &str) -> Result<i32, ParseIntError> {
    match val.parse::<i32>() {
        Ok(num) => Ok(i32::pow(num, 2)),
        Err(e) => Err(e),
    }
}
```

Run this code, and you will see the following output printed to the console:

```
Ok(4)
Err(ParseIntError { kind: InvalidDigit })
```

In the first case, the `square()` function is able to successfully parse the number 2 from the string, and it returns the squared value enclosed in the `Ok()` enum type. In the second case, an error of type `ParseIntError` is returned, as the `parse()` function is unable to extract a number from the string.

Let's now look at a special operator that Rust provides to make error handling less verbose: the ? operator. In the earlier code, we used the `match` clause to unwrap the `Result` type returned from the `parse()` method. We'll now see how the ? operator can be used to reduce boilerplate code:

```
use std::num::ParseIntError;

fn main() {
    println!("{:?}", square("2"));
    println!("{:?}", square("INVALID"));
}

fn square(val: &str) -> Result<i32, ParseIntError> {
    let num = val.parse::<i32>()?;
    Ok(i32::pow(num,2))
}
```

You'll notice that the `match` statement with the associated clauses has been replaced by the ? operator. This operator tries to unwrap the integer from the `Result` value and store it in the `num` variable. If unsuccessful, it receives the error from the `parse()` method, aborts the square function, and propagates the `ParseIntError` to the calling function (which in our case is the `main()` function).

We'll now take another step in exploring Rust's error handling by adding additional functionality to the `square()` function. The following code adds some lines of code to open a file and write the calculated square value to it:

```
use std::fs::File;
use std::io::Write;
use std::num::ParseIntError;

fn main() {
    println!("{:?}", square("2"));
    println!("{:?}", square("INVALID"));
}

fn square(val: &str) -> Result<i32, ParseIntError> {
    let num = val.parse::<i32>()?;
    let mut f = File::open("fictionalfile.txt")?;
    let string_to_write = format!("Square of {} is {}", num, i32::pow(num, 2));
    f.write_all(string_to_write.as_bytes())?;
    Ok(i32::pow(num, 2))
}
```

When you compile this code, you'll get an error message as follows:

```
the trait `std::convert::From<std::io::Error>` is not implemented
➥for `std::num::ParseIntError`
```

This error message may seem confusing, but it's trying to say that the `File::open` and `write_all` methods return a `Result` type containing an error of type `std::io::Error`, which should be propagated back to the `main()` function, as we have used the `?` operator. However, the function signature of `square()` specifically states that it returns an error of type `ParseIntError`. We seem to have a problem, as there are two possible error types that can be returned from the function—`std::num::ParseIntError` and `std::io::Error`, but our function signature can only specify one error type.

This is where custom error types come in. Let's define a custom error type that can be an abstraction over the `ParseIntError` and `io::Error` types. Modify the code as follows:

```rust
use std::fmt;
use std::fs::File;
use std::io::Write;

#[derive(Debug)]                         Define a custom error enum type
pub enum MyError {            ⭠⎯⎯⎯⎯  containing the set of error variants.
    ParseError,
    IOError,
}                                              By convention, error types in
                                               Rust implement the Error trait
impl std::error::Error for MyError {}   ⭠⎯⎯⎯  from the Rust standard library.

impl fmt::Display for MyError {                              ⭠⎯⎯⎯⎯⎯⎯┐  The Rust Error trait
    fn fmt(&self, f: &mut fmt::Formatter) -> fmt::Result {            requires the
        match self {                                                 implementation of the
            MyError::ParseError => write!(f, "Parse Error"),         Debug and Display
            MyError::IOError => write!(f, "IO Error"),               traits. The Debug trait
        }                                                            is auto-derived. The
    }                                                                Display trait is
}                                                                    implemented here.

fn main() {                              The square function is
    let result = square("INVALID");      called, and the result is
    match result {                       evaluated to print out
        Ok(res) => println!("Result is {:?}",res),   a suitable message.          The map_err method
        Err(e) => println!("Error in parsing: {:?}",e),                    transforms parsing, file
    };                                                                     open, and file write errors
}                                                                          into our MyError type,
                                                                           which is propagated back
                                                                           to the calling function
fn square(val: &str) -> Result<i32, MyError> {                             through the ? operator.
    let num = val.parse::<i32>().map_err(|_| MyError::ParseError)?;   ⭠⎯⎯⎯┐
    let mut f = File::open("fictionalfile.txt").map_err(
        |_| MyError::IOError)?;                                       ⭠⎯⎯⎯┤
    let string_to_write = format!("Square of {:?} is {:?}", num, i32::pow(
        num, 2));
    f.write_all(string_to_write.as_bytes())
        .map_err(|_| MyError::IOError)?;                              ⭠⎯⎯⎯┘
    Ok(i32::pow(num, 2))
}
```

We're making progress. We've so far seen how Rust uses the `Result` type to return errors, how we can use the `?` operator to reduce boilerplate code to propagate errors, and how we can define and implement custom error types to unify error handling at a function or application level.

> ### Rust's error handling makes code safe
>
> A Rust function can belong to the Rust standard library or to an external crate, or it can be a custom function written by the programmer. Whenever there is a possibility of error, Rust functions return a `Result` data type. The calling function must then handle the error in one of several ways:
>
> - *Propagating the error* further to its caller using the `?` operator
> - *Converting any errors* received into another type before bubbling them up
> - *Handling the* `Result::Ok` *and* `Result::Error` *variants* using the `match` block
> - *Simply panicking* on an error with `.unwrap()` or `.expect()`
>
> This makes programs safer because it is impossible to access invalid, null, or uninitialized data that's returned from a Rust function.

Let's now take a look at how Actix Web builds on top of the Rust error-handling philosophy to return errors for web services and applications.

Figure 5.3 shows the error-handling primitives in Actix. Actix Web has a general-purpose error struct, `actix_web::error::Error`, which, like any other Rust error type, implements the Rust standard library's `std::error::Error` error trait. Any error type that implements this Rust standard library `Error` trait can be converted into an Actix `Error` type with the `?` operator. The Actix `Error` type will then automatically be converted to an HTTP response message that goes back to the HTTP client.

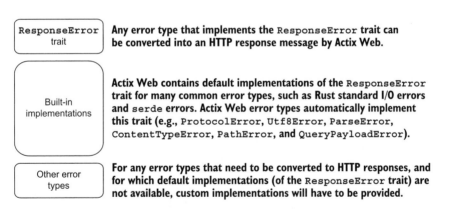

Figure 5.3   Converting errors to HTTP responses

Let's look at a basic Actix handler function that returns a `Result` type. Create a new Cargo project with `cargo new`, and add the following to the dependencies in Cargo.toml:

```
[dependencies]
actix-web = "3"
```

Add the following code to src/main.rs:

**The hello handler function can return one of two values:
HTTPResponse in the case of a successful computation,
or an Actix Error type in the case of failure.**

```
use actix_web::{error::Error, web, App, HttpResponse, HttpServer};

async fn hello() -> Result<HttpResponse, Error> {
    Ok(HttpResponse::Ok().body("Hello there!"))
}

#[actix_web::main]
async fn main() -> std::io::Result<()> {
    HttpServer::new(|| App::new().route("/hello", web::get().to(hello)))
        .bind("127.0.0.1:3000")?
        .run()
        .await
}
```

**The handler function returns
an HTTPResponse encapsulated
in the Ok() enum variant.**

Even though the handler function signature specifies that it can return an `Error` type, the handler function is so simple that there is little possibility of anything going wrong here.

Run the program with this command:

```
cargo run
```

From a browser, connect to the `hello` route:

```
http://localhost:3000/hello
```

You should see the following message displayed on your browser screen:

```
Hello there!
```

Now alter the handler function to include operations that can possibly fail:

```
use actix_web::{error::Error, web, App, HttpResponse, HttpServer};
use std::fs::File;
use std::io::Read;

async fn hello() -> Result<HttpResponse, Error> {
    let _ = File::open("fictionalfile.txt")?;
    Ok(HttpResponse::Ok().body("File read successfully"))
}

#[actix_web::main]
async fn main() -> std::io::Result<()> {
    HttpServer::new(|| App::new().route("/hello", web::get().to(hello)))
        .bind("127.0.0.1:3000")?
        .run()
        .await
}
```

**If the file open is successful, return an
HTTP response message with the success
status code and a text message.**

**Try to open a nonexistent file in the handler function. The
? operator propagates the error to the calling function
(which is the Actix web server itself, in this case).**

Run the program again, and connect to the `hello` route from the browser. You should see something like the following message:

```
No such file or directory (os error 2)
```

To a discerning reader, two immediate questions may come to mind:

1 The file operation returns an error of type `std::io::Error`, as seen in the earlier example. How is it possible to send an error of type `std::io::Error` from the handler function when the return type specified in the function signature is `actix_web::error::Error`?

2 How did the browser display a text error message when we returned an `Error` type from the handler function?

To answer the first question, anything that implements the `std::error::Error` trait (which the `std::io::Error` does), can be converted to the `actix_web::error::Error` type, as the Actix framework implements the `std::error::Error` trait for its own `actix_web::error::error` type. This allows a question mark (`?`) to be used on the `std::io::Error` type to convert it to the `actix_web::error::Error` type. See the Actix Web documentation of the `actix_web::error::Error` type for more details: http://mng.bz/lWXy.

To answer the second question, anything that implements the Actix Web `ResponseError` trait can be converted to an HTTP response. Interestingly, the Actix Web framework contains built-in implementations of this trait for many common error types, and `std::io::Error` is one of them. For more details about available default implementations, see the Actix Web documentation for the `actix_web::error::ResponseError` trait: http://mng.bz/D4zE. The combination of the Actix `Error` type and `ResponseError` trait provide the bulk of Actix's error-handling support for web services and applications.

In this section, we've seen that when an error of type `std::io::Error` is raised within the the `hello()` handler function, it gets converted into an HTTP response message. We will utilize these features of Actix Web to convert a custom error type into an HTTP response message in this chapter.

With this background, you are now ready to start implementing error handling in the tutor web service.

5.3 Defining a custom error handler

In this section, we'll define a custom error type for our web service. First, though, let's define our overall approach. We'll follow these steps:

1 Define a custom error `enum` type that encapsulates the various types of errors that we expect to encounter within the web service.

2 Implement the `From` trait (from the Rust standard library) to convert the other distinct error types into our custom error type.

3 Implement the Actix `ResponseError` trait for the custom error type. This enables Actix to convert the custom error into an HTTP response.

4 In the application code (the handler functions), return the custom error type instead of a standard Rust error type or Actix error type.

5 There is no step 5. Just sit back and watch Actix automatically convert any custom errors returned from the handler functions into valid HTTP responses that are sent back to the client.

Figure 5.4 illustrates these steps.

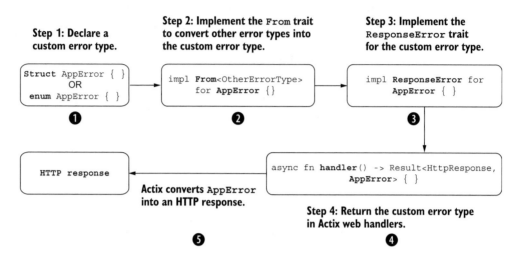

Figure 5.4   Steps in writing a custom error type

That's it. Let's start by creating a new file, src/iter4/errors.rs. We'll add the code for this file in three parts. Here is the code for part 1.

Listing 5.1   Error handling: part 1

```
use actix_web::{error, http::StatusCode, HttpResponse, Result};
use serde::Serialize;
use sqlx::error::Error as SQLxError;
use std::fmt;

#[derive(Debug, Serialize)]
pub enum EzyTutorError {        <──┐  Data structure to represent three types of errors that can
    DBError(String),                  occur in the web service: database-related errors, Actix
    ActixError(String),               server errors, and errors due to invalid client requests
    NotFound(String),
}
#[derive(Debug, Serialize)]
pub struct MyErrorResponse {    <──┐  Data structure to display a suitable
    error_message: String,            error message to the user or client
}                                     sending the API request.
```

We've defined two data structures for error handling: EzyTutorError, which is the primary error-handling mechanism within the web service, and MyErrorResponse, which is the user-facing message. To convert the former to the latter when an error occurs, let's write a method in the impl block of EzyTutorError. This code is shown in listing 5.2.

> ## `impl` **blocks**
>
> An `impl` block is Rust's way of allowing developers to specify functions associated with a data type. This is the only way in Rust to define a function that can be invoked on an instance of the type in a method-call syntax. For example, if `Foo` is a data type, `foo` is an instance of `Foo`, and `bar()` is the function defined within the `impl` block of `Foo`, then the function `bar()` can be invoked on instance `foo` as follows: `foo.bar()`.
>
> `impl` blocks also serve to group together functionality associated with a user-defined data type, which makes them easier to discover and maintain.
>
> Further, `impl` blocks allow the creation of *associated* functions, which are functions *associated with* the data type rather than an *instance* of the data type. For example, to create a new instance of `Foo`, an associated function, `new()`, can be defined such that `Foo:new()` creates a new instance of `Foo`.

Listing 5.2 Error handling: part 2

```
impl EzyTutorError {
    fn error_response(&self) -> String {
        match self {
            EzyTutorError::DBError(msg) => {
                println!("Database error occurred: {:?}", msg);
                "Database error".into()
            }
            EzyTutorError::ActixError(msg) => {
                println!("Server error occurred: {:?}", msg);
                "Internal server error".into()
            }
            EzyTutorError::NotFound(msg) => {
                println!("Not found error occurred: {:?}", msg);
                msg.into()
            }
        }
    }
}
```

We have now defined a method called `error_response()` on our custom `EzyTutorError` error struct. This method will be called when we want to send a user-friendly message to inform the user that an error has occurred. In this code, we are handling all three types of errors, with the goal of sending back a simpler, friendly error message to the user.

We have so far defined error data structures and have even written a method to convert a custom error struct to a user-friendly text message. The question that arises now is how we can propagate an error to an HTTP client from the web service. The only way an HTTP web service can communicate with a client is through an HTTP response message, right?

What's missing is a way to convert the custom error that is generated by the server into a corresponding HTTP response message. We saw in section 5.2 how to achieve this using the `actix_web::error::ResponseError` trait. If a handler returns an error that also implements the `ResponseError` trait, Actix Web will convert that error into an HTTP response, with the corresponding status code.

In our case, this boils down to implementing the `ResponseError` trait on the `EzyTutorError` struct. Implementing this trait means implementing two methods defined on the trait: `error_response()` and `status_code`. Let's look at the code.

Listing 5.3   Error handling: part 3

```
impl error::ResponseError for EzyTutorError {
    fn status_code(&self) -> StatusCode {         ◁─── Using this method, we can specify the
        match self {                                   HTTP status code that should be sent
          EzyTutorError::DBError(msg) | EzyTutorError::ActixError(msg) => {
              StatusCode::INTERNAL_SERVER_ERROR       as part of the HTTP response message.
          }
          EzyTutorError::NotFound(msg) => StatusCode::NOT_FOUND,
        }
    }
    fn error_response(&self) -> HttpResponse {                  ◁───
        HttpResponse::build(self.status_code()).json(MyErrorResponse {
          error_message: self.error_response(),
        })                                         This method will be used to
    }                                              determine the body of the HTML
}                                                  response in case of error scenarios.
```

NOTE The supported HTTP error codes are defined in the Actix Web documentation: http://mng.bz/V185.

Now that we've defined our custom error type, let's incorporate this into the handler and database access code for the web service's three APIs.

5.4   *Error handling for retrieving all courses*

In this section, we'll incorporate error handling for the API that retrieves the course list for a tutor. Let's focus on the db_access.rs file, which contains functions for database access.

Add the following import to db_access.rs:

```
use super::errors::EzyTutorError;
```

The `super` keyword refers to the parent scope (for the `db_access` module), which is where the `errors` module is located. Let's now look at a chunk of the existing code in the `get_courses_for_tutor_db` function:

```
let course_rows = sqlx::query!(
      "SELECT tutor_id, course_id, course_name,
      ⮩posted_time FROM ezy_course_c5 where tutor_id = $1",
      tutor_id
   )
```

```
    .fetch_all(pool)
    .await?
    .unwrap();
```

Note in particular the `unwrap()` method. This is a shortcut to handle errors in Rust. Whenever an error occurs in the database operation, the program thread will panic and exit. The `unwrap()` keyword in Rust means "If the operation is successful, return the result, which in this case is the list of courses. In case of error, just panic and abort the program."

This was fine in the previous chapter because you were just learning how to build the web service. But this is not the behavior expected from a production service. We cannot allow the program execution to panic and exit for every error in database access. What we want to do instead is handle the error in some way. If we know what to do with the error itself, we can do it there. Otherwise, we can propagate the error from the database access code to the calling handler function, which can then figure out what to do with the error.

To achieve this propagation, we can use the question mark operator (`?`) instead of the `unwrap()` keyword, as shown here:

```
let course_rows = sqlx::query!(
        "SELECT tutor_id, course_id, course_name,
        ➥posted_time FROM ezy_course_c5 where tutor_id = $1",
        tutor_id
    )
    .fetch_all(pool)
    .await?;
```

Note that the `.unwrap()` method, which operates on the result of the database fetch operation, has now been replaced with a question mark (`?`). While the earlier `unwrap()` operation told the Rust compiler to panic in the case of errors, the `?` tells the Rust compiler, "In case of errors, convert the `sqlx` database error into another error type and return from the function, propagating the error to the calling handler function." The question now is what type the question mark operator should convert the database error to. We'd have to specify that.

To propagate the error using `?`, we need to alter the database method signature to return a `Result` type. As you saw earlier, a `Result` type expresses the possibility of an error. It provides a way to represent one out of two possible outcomes in any computation or function call: `Ok(val)` in the case of success, where `val` is the result of the successful computation, or `Err(err)` in the case of errors, where `err` is the error returned from the computation.

In our database fetch function, let's define these two possible outcomes as follows:

- Return a vector of courses, `Vec<Course>`, if the database access is successful.
- Return an error of type `EzyTutorError` if the database fetch fails.

If we revisit the `await?` expression at the end of the database fetch operation, we can interpret it to mean that if the database access fails, we'll convert the `sqlx` database error into an error of type `EzyTutorError` and return from the function. In such a case of failure, the calling handler function would receive back an error of type `Ezy-TutorError` from the database access function.

Here is the modified code in db_access.rs. The changes are explained in the annotations.

Listing 5.4   Error handling in the method to retrieve courses for a tutor

```
pub async fn get_courses_for_tutor_db(
    pool: &PgPool,
    tutor_id: i32,
) -> Result<Vec<Course>, EzyTutorError> {
    // Prepare SQL statement
    let course_rows = sqlx::query!(
        "SELECT tutor_id, course_id, course_name,
        posted_time FROM ezy_course_c5 where tutor_id = $1",
        tutor_id
    )
    .fetch_all(pool)
    .await?;
    // Extract result

    let courses: Vec<Course> = course_rows
        .iter()
        .map(|course_row| Course {
            course_id: course_row.course_id,
            tutor_id: course_row.tutor_id,
            course_name: course_row.course_name.clone(),
            posted_time: Some(chrono::NaiveDateTime::from(
            course_row.posted_time.unwrap())),
        })
        .collect();
    match courses.len() {
        0 => Err(EzyTutorError::NotFound(
            "Courses not found for tutor".into(),
        )),
        _ => Ok(courses),
    }
}
```

The function returns a Result<T> type representing two possible outcomes: Vec<Course> in the case of success, or the EzyTutorError error type on failure.

Replace await.unwrap() with await?. This converts the sqlx error to an EzyTutorError and propagates it to the calling web handler function.

If there are no query results for the tutor_id, return an error of type EzyTutorError, which will generate a message for the user.

We could debate about whether finding no courses for a valid tutor ID is really an error. However, let's set this argument aside for now and use this as another opportunity to practice error handling in Rust.

Let's also alter the calling handler function (in iter4/handler.rs) to incorporate error handling. First, add the following import:

```
use super::errors::EzyTutorError;
```

Modify the get_courses_for_tutor() function to return a `Result` type:

```
pub async fn get_courses_for_tutor(
    app_state: web::Data<AppState>,
    path: web::Path<i32>,
```

```
) -> Result<HttpResponse, EzyTutorError> {
    let tutor_id = path.into_inner();
    get_courses_for_tutor_db(&app_state.db, tutor_id)
        .await
        .map(|courses| HttpResponse::Ok().json(courses))
}
```

Change the web handler method signature to return a Result type.

If the database call is successful, the map logic is processed and the list of query results is returned.

The call is made to the database access function. Any error returned is propagated by the handler function to the Actix Web framework, which converts it to an HTML response message.

It appears that we've completed the error-handling implementation for retrieving course lists. Compile and run the code with this command:

```
cargo run --bin iter4
```

You will notice there are compiler errors. This is because for the ? operator to work, each error raised in the program should be converted first to type EzyTutorError. For example, if there is an error in database access using sqlx, sqlx returns an error of type sqlx::error::DatabaseError, and Actix does not know how to deal with it. We must tell Actix how to convert the sqlx error to our custom EzyTutorError error type. Did you think Actix would do it for you? Sorry, you have to write the code.

The code in the following listing should be added to iter4/errors.rs.

Listing 5.5   Implementing From and Display traits for EzyTutorError

```
impl fmt::Display for EzyTutorError {
    fn fmt(&self, f: &mut fmt::Formatter) -> Result<(), fmt::Error> {
        write!(f, "{}", self)
    }
}
```

This enables us to print the EzyTutorError as a string that can be sent to the user.

```
impl From<actix_web::error::Error> for EzyTutorError {
    fn from(err: actix_web::error::Error) -> Self {
        EzyTutorError::ActixError(err.to_string())
    }
}
```

This enables Actix Web errors to be converted to EzyTutorError using the question mark (?) operator.

```
impl From<SQLxError> for EzyTutorError {
    fn from(err: SQLxError) -> Self {
        EzyTutorError::DBError(err.to_string())
    }
}
```

This enables database errors from sqlx to be converted to EzyTutorError using the question mark (?) operator.

We have now made the necessary changes to both the database access code and the handler code, incorporating error handling for retrieving course lists. Build and run the code:

```
cargo run --bin iter4
```

From a browser, access the following URL:

```
http://localhost:3000/courses/1
```

You should be able to see the list of courses. Let's test the error conditions now. Access the API with an invalid tutor ID as shown here:

```
http://localhost:3000/courses/10
```

You should see the following output displayed in the browser:

```
{"error_message":"Courses not found for tutor"}
```

This is as intended. Let's now try simulating another type of error—we will simulate an error in `sqlx` database access. In the .env file, change the database URL to an invalid user ID. An example is shown here:

```
DATABASE_URL=postgres://invaliduser:trupwd@127.0.0.1:5432/truwitter
```

Restart the web service:

```
cargo run --bin iter4
```

Access the valid URL as shown here:

```
http://localhost:3000/courses/1
```

You should see the following error message in the browser:

```
{"error_message":"Database error"}
```

Let's take a few minutes to understand what happened here. When we provided an invalid database URL, the web service database access function tried to create a connection from the connection pool and run the query. This operation failed, and an error of type `sqlx::error::DatabaseError` was raised by the `sqlx` client. This error was converted to our custom error type `EzyTutorError` due to the following `From` trait implementation in errors.rs:

```
impl From<SQLxError> for EzyTutorError {   }
```

The error of type `EzyTutorError` was then propagated from the database access function in db_access.rs to the handler function in handlers.rs. On receiving this error, the handler function propagated it further to the Actix Web framework, which then converted this error into an HTML response message with an appropriate error message.

Now, how do we check this error status code? This can be verified by accessing the URL using a command-line HTTP client. We'll use curl with the verbose option, as follows:

```
curl -v http://localhost:3000/courses/1
```

You should see a message in your terminal that's similar to the one shown here:

```
GET /courses/1 HTTP/1.1
> Host
```

```
: localhost:3000
> User-Agent: curl/7.64.1
> Accept: */*
>
< HTTP/1.1 500 Internal Server Error
```

Go back to the `status_code()` function in iter4/errors.rs. You'll notice that for database and Actix errors, we are returning a status code of `StatusCode::INTERNAL_SERVER_ERROR`, which translates to an HTML response status code of `500`. This matches the output generated by curl.

Before we move on, make sure you correct the database URL username to the right value in the .env file, or future tests will fail.

We have thus implemented custom error handling for the first API. Let's also ensure that the test scripts are not broken. Run the tests as follows:

```
cargo test --bin iter4
```

You will find that the compiler throws errors. This is because our test script must also be modified to receive an error response from the handler. Make changes to the test script in handlers.rs as shown in the following listing.

Listing 5.6 Test script for getting all courses for a tutor

```
#[actix_rt::test]
    async fn get_all_courses_success() {
        dotenv().ok();
        let database_url = env::var("DATABASE_URL").expect(
        ➥"DATABASE_URL is not set in .env file");
        let pool: PgPool = PgPool::connect(&database_url).await.unwrap();
        let app_state: web::Data<AppState> = web::Data::new(AppState {
            health_check_response: "".to_string(),
            visit_count: Mutex::new(0),
            db: pool,
        });
        let tutor_id: web::Path<i32> = web::Path::from(1);
        let resp = get_courses_for_tutor(
        ➥app_state, tutor_id).await.unwrap();      ◁─┐  Note the addition of .unwrap(). A
        assert_eq!(resp.status(), StatusCode::OK);     Result type is being returned from
    }                                                  the handler method, but we want
                                                       an HTTP Response, so we have
                                                       to "unwrap" the result.
```

NOTE Actix Web does not support propagating errors using the question mark (`?`) operator, so we have to use `unwrap()` or `expect()` to extract the HTTP response from the `Result` type.

Rerun the following command from the command line:

```
cargo test get_all_courses_success --bin iter4
```

You should now see the tests run successfully.

You'll notice that, in the previous command, we ran only the `get_all_courses_success` test case. If you run the entire test suite with `cargo test --bin iter4`, you may get an error similar to this:

```
DBError("duplicate key value violates unique constraint")
```

This is because every time the test suite is run, a new record with a `course_id` of 3 is inserted into the table. If the tests are run a second time, this record insertion will fail because `course_id` is the primary key in table, and there cannot be two records with the same `course_id`. In this case, simply log into the psql shell and delete the entry with a `course_id` of 3 from the `ezy_course_c5` table.

There is a simpler option, though. You can tell the Cargo test executor to ignore any specific test case in the test suite with the `#[ignore]` annotation. You can specify this annotation as follows:

```
#[ignore]
    #[actix_rt::test]
    async fn post_course_success() {
    }
```

Now you can run the entire test suite with `cargo test --bin iter4`, and you will see something similar to this printed on your console:

```
running 3 tests
test handlers::tests::post_course_success ... ignored
test handlers::tests::get_all_courses_success ... ok
test handlers::tests::get_course_detail_test ... ok

test result: ok. 2 passed; 0 failed; 1 ignored; 0 measured; 0 filtered out
```

You'll notice that the `post_course_success` test case has been ignored, and the other two tests have been run.

We now have to perform the same steps for the other two APIs, changing the database access functions, handler methods, and test scripts.

5.5 *Error handling for retrieving course details*

Let's look at the changes needed to incorporate error handling for the second API for getting course details. The following listing shows the updated database access code in db_access.rs.

Listing 5.7 Error handling in the function to get course details

```
pub async fn get_course_details_db(pool: &PgPool, tutor_id: i32,
➥course_id: i32) -> Result<Course, EzyTutorError> {      ◁─────────
    // Prepare SQL statement
    let course_row = sqlx::query!(
```

The function returns a Result type such that a course is returned from the function on success, and an error of type EzyTutorError is returned on failure.

```
        "SELECT tutor_id, course_id, course_name, posted_time
        ➥FROM ezy_course_c5 where tutor_id = $1 and course_id = $2",
        tutor_id, course_id
    )
    .fetch_one(pool)
    .await;
    if let Ok(course_row) = course_row {
    // Execute query
    Ok(Course {
        course_id: course_row.course_id,
        tutor_id: course_row.tutor_id,
        course_name: course_row.course_name.clone(),
        posted_time: Some(chrono::NaiveDateTime::from(
        ➥course_row.posted_time.unwrap())),
    })
} else {
    Err(EzyTutorError::NotFound("Course id not found".into()))
}
}
```

> If the specified course_id is not available in the database, it returns a custom error message.

Let's update the handler function:

```
pub async fn get_course_details(
    app_state: web::Data<AppState>,
    path:  web::Path<(i32, i32)>,
) -> Result<HttpResponse, EzyTutorError> {
    let (tutor_id, course_id) = path.into_inner();
    get_course_details_db(&app_state.db, tutor_id, course_id)
        .await
        .map(|course| HttpResponse::Ok().json(course))
}
```

> **Change the handler function signature to return a Result type.**

> **Invoke the database access function to retrieve the course details. If it's successful, return the course details in the body of the HTTP response.**

Restart the web service:

```
cargo run --bin iter4
```

Access the valid URL as follows:

```
http://localhost:3000/courses/1/2
```

You will see the course details displayed as before. Now try accessing the details for an invalid course ID:

```
http://localhost:3000/courses/1/10
```

You should see the following error message in the browser:

```
{"error_message":"Course id not found"}
```

Let's also alter the test script `async fn get_course_detail_test()` in handlers.rs to accommodate errors returned from the handler function:

```
let resp = get_course_details(app_state, parameters).await.unwrap();
```

> **Note the addition of .unwrap() in the call to the database access function to extract the HTTP Response from the Result type.**

Run the test with this command:

```
cargo test get_course_detail_test --bin iter4
```

The test should pass. Next, we'll incorporate error handling for posting a new course.

5.6   *Error handling for posting a new course*

We'll follow the same set of steps we used for the other two APIs: modify the database access function, the handler function, and the test script. Let's start with the database access function in db_access.rs.

Listing 5.8   Error handling in the database access function to post a new course

```
pub async fn post_new_course_db(
    pool: &PgPool,
    new_course: Course,
) -> Result<Course, EzyTutorError> {
    let course_row = sqlx::query!("insert into ezy_course_c5 (
    ➥course_id,tutor_id, course_name) values ($1,$2,$3)
    ➥returning tutor_id, course_id,course_name, posted_time",
    ➥new_course.course_id, new_course.tutor_id, new_course.course_name)
        .fetch_one(pool)
        .await?;
    //Retrieve result
    Ok(Course {
        course_id: course_row.course_id,
        tutor_id: course_row.tutor_id,
        course_name: course_row.course_name.clone(),
        posted_time: Some(chrono::NaiveDateTime::from(
        ➥course_row.posted_time.unwrap()))),
    })
}
```

> The function returns a Result type, wherein a successful insert into the database returns the new course details or an error is returned on failure.

> Note the use of ? to convert sqlx errors into EzyTutorError types and propagate them back to the calling handler function.

> Return a Result type with Ok(<Course>).

Next, update the handler function:

```
pub async fn post_new_course(
    new_course: web::Json<Course>,
    app_state: web::Data<AppState>,
) -> Result<HttpResponse, EzyTutorError> {
    post_new_course_db(&app_state.db, new_course.into())
        .await
        .map(|course| HttpResponse::Ok().json(course))
}
```

> Change the return value of the handler function into a Result type.

> If the call to the database access function is successful, return the new course details. On failure, propagate errors to the Actix Web framework.

Finally, update the test script `async fn post_course_success()` in handlers.rs to add unwrap() on the return value from the database access function:

```
#[actix_rt::test]
    async fn post_course_success() {
        /// all code not shown here
        let resp = post_new_course(course_param, app_state).await.unwrap();
```

```
        assert_eq!(resp.status(), StatusCode::OK);
}
```

**Add unwrap() on the result value returned by the handler
to extract the HTTP response from the Result type returned
by the post_new_course() database access function.**

Rebuild and restart the web service with the following command:

```
cargo run --bin iter4
```

Post a new course from the command line as follows:

```
curl -X POST localhost:3000/courses/ -H "Content-Type: application/json"
-d '{"course_id":4, "tutor_id": 1,
"course_name":"This is the fourth course!"}'
```

Verify that the new course has been added with the following URL on the browser:

```
http://localhost:3000/courses/1/4
```

Now run the tests:

```
cargo test --bin iter4
```

All three tests should successfully pass.

Let's do a quick recap. In this chapter, you have learned how to transform different types of errors encountered in the web service to a custom error type, and how to transform that to an HTTP response message, thus providing the client with a meaningful message in the case of server errors. Along the way, you have also picked up some of the finer concepts of error handling in Rust, which can be applied to any Rust application. More importantly, you now know how to handle failures gracefully, provide meaningful feedback to users, and build a solid and stable web service. You have also implemented error handling for the three APIs in the tutor web service. The web service can handle database and Actix errors, and it can also handle invalid input from users. Congratulations!

Our tutor web service is now functional with a full-fledged database to persist data, and it has a robust error-handling framework that can be customized further as the features evolve. In the next chapter, we will deal with another real-world situation: changes in product requirements from the management team, and additional feature requests from users. Will Rust stand up to the test of large-scale refactoring of code? You'll see in the next chapter.

Summary

- Rust provides a robust and ergonomic error-handling approach with features such as the `Result` type, combinator functions such as `map` and `map_err` that operate on the `Result` type, quick code prototyping options with `unwrap()` and `expect()`, the `?` operator to reduce boilerplate code, and the ability to convert errors from one error type to another using the `From` trait.

- Actix Web builds on top of Rust's error-handling features to include its own `Error` type and the `ResponseError` trait. These enable Rust programmers to define custom error types and have the Actix Web framework automatically convert them into meaningful HTTP response messages at runtime for sending back to the web client or user. Further, Actix Web provides built-in `From` implementations to convert Rust standard library error types to the Actix `Error` type, and it also provides default `ResponseError` trait implementations to convert Rust standard library error types into HTTP response messages.
- Implementing custom error handling in Actix involves the following steps:
  - Define a data structure to represent a custom error type.
  - Define possible values that the custom error type can take (for example, database errors, not-found errors, etc.).
  - Implement the `ResponseError` trait on the custom error type.
  - Implement `From` traits to convert various types of errors (such as `sqlx` errors or Actix Web errors) to the custom error type.
  - Change the return values of the database access and route handler functions to return the custom error type in the case of errors. The Actix Web framework will then convert the custom error type into an appropriate HTTP response and embed the error message within the body of the HTTP response.
- We incorporated custom error handling for each of the three APIs in the tutor web service.

Evolving the APIs and fearless refactoring

This chapter covers

- Revamping the project structure
- Enhancing the data model for course creation and management
- Enabling tutor registration and management

In the previous chapter, we covered the basics of error handling in Rust and how we can design custom error handling for our web service. After working through the last few chapters, you should now have a foundational understanding of how a web service is structured using the Actix Web framework, how you can talk to a relational database for CRUD activities, and how to handle any errors that occur while processing incoming data and requests. In this chapter, we will step up the pace and deal with something that we cannot avoid in the real world: *changes.*

Every actively used web service or application evolves significantly over its lifecycle, based on user feedback or business requirements. Many of these new requirements could mean breaking changes to the web service or application. In this chapter, you'll learn how Rust helps you cope with situations involving drastic design changes and the rewriting of significant parts of your existing code. You'll use the power of the Rust compiler and the features of the language to come out of this challenge with a smile on your face.

In this chapter, you will fearlessly make several changes to the web service. You'll redesign the data model for courses, add course routes, modify handler and database access functions, and update the test cases. You'll also design and build a new module in the application to manage tutor information and define the relationship between tutors and courses. You'll enhance the error-handling features of the web service to cover edge cases. And if that wasn't enough, you'll also fully revamp the project code and directory structure to neatly segregate the code across Rust modules.

There's no time to waste; let's get going.

6.1   *Revamping the project structure*

In the previous chapter, we focused on creating and maintaining basic course data. In this chapter, we'll enhance the course module and add functionality to create and maintain tutor information. As the size of the codebase will grow, this is a good time to rethink the project structure. So, we'll start by reorganizing the project into a structure that will aid in code development and maintenance as the application becomes larger and more complex.

Figure 6.1 shows two views. On the left is the project structure we'll start with (the structure from chapter 5). On the right is the structure that we'll end up with.

The main change you will notice is that in the proposed project structure, database access, handlers, and models are not single files but folders. The database access code for course and tutor will be organized under the dbaccess folder. Likewise for models and handlers. This approach will reduce the length of individual files while making it quicker to navigate to what we are looking for, though it adds some complexity to the project structure.

Before we begin, let's set up the PROJECT_ROOT environment variable to point to the full path of the project root (ezytutors/tutor_db):

```
export PROJECT_ROOT=<full-path-to ezytutors/tutor-db folder>
```

Verify that it is set correctly as follows:

```
echo $PROJECT_ROOT
```

Henceforth, the term *project root* will refer to the folder path stored in the $PROJECT_ ROOT environment variable. References to other files in this chapter will be made with respect to the project root.

Figure 6.1   Project structure for chapters 5 and 6

The code structure is described here:

- *$PROJECT_ROOT/src/bin/iter5.rs*—The `main()` function.
- *$PROJECT_ROOT/src/iter5/routes.rs*—Contains routes. This will continue to be a single file containing all the routes.
- *$PROJECT_ROOT/src/iter5/state.rs*—Application state containing the dependencies that are injected into each thread of application execution.
- *$PROJECT_ROOT/src/iter5/errors.rs*—A custom error data structure and associated error-handling functions.
- *$PROJECT_ROOT/.env*—Environment variables containing database access credentials. This file should not be checked into the code repository.

- *$PROJECT_ROOT/src/iter5/dbscripts*—Database table creation scripts for Postgres.
- *$PROJECT_ROOT/src/iter5/handlers*:
  - *$PROJECT_ROOT/src/iter5/handlers/course.rs*—Course-related handler functions.
  - *$PROJECT_ROOT/src/iter5/handlers/tutor.rs*—Tutor-related handler functions.
  - *$PROJECT_ROOT/src/iter5/handlers/general.rs*—Health-check handler function.
  - *$PROJECT_ROOT/src/iter5/handlers/mod.rs*—Converts the directory handlers into a Rust module so the Rust compiler knows how to find the dependent files.

- *$PROJECT_ROOT/src/iter5/models*:
  - *$PROJECT_ROOT/src/iter5/models/course.rs*—Course-related data structures and utility methods.
  - *$PROJECT_ROOT/src/iter5/models/tutor.rs*—Tutor-related data structures and utility methods.
  - *$PROJECT_ROOT/src/iter5/models/mod.rs*—Converts the directory models into a Rust module so the Rust compiler knows how to find the dependent files.

- *$PROJECT_ROOT/src/iter5/dbaccess*:
  - *$PROJECT_ROOT/src/iter5/dbaccess/course.rs*—Course-related database-access methods.
  - *$PROJECT_ROOT/src/iter5/dbaccess/tutor.rs*—Tutor-related database-access methods.
  - *$PROJECT_ROOT/src/iter5/dbaccess/mod.rs*—Converts the dbaccess directory into a Rust module so the Rust compiler knows how to find the dependent files.

Copy the code from chapter 5's iter4 folder as the starting point for this chapter. Then, without adding any new functionality, we'll reorganize the existing code of chapter 5 into this new project structure.

Follow these steps:

1 Rename $PROJECT_ROOT/src/bin/iter4.rs to $PROJECT_ROOT/src/bin/iter5.rs.
2 Rename the $PROJECT_ROOT/src/iter4 folder to $PROJECT_ROOT/src/iter5.
3 Under $PROJECT_ROOT/src/iter5, create three subfolders: dbaccess, models, and handlers.
4 Move and rename $PROJECT_ROOT/src/iter5/models.rs to $PROJECT_ROOT/src/iter5/models/course.rs.

5 Create two more files under the $PROJECT_ROOT/src/iter5/models folder: tutor.rs and mod.rs. Leave both files blank for now.

6 Move and rename $PROJECT_ROOT/src/iter5/dbaccess.rs to $PROJECT_ROOT/src/iter5/dbaccess/course.rs.

7 Create two more files under the $PROJECT_ROOT/src/iter5/dbaccess folder: tutor.rs and mod.rs. Leave both files blank for now.

8 Move and rename $PROJECT_ROOT/src/iter5/handlers.rs to $PROJECT_ROOT/src/iter5/handlers/course.rs.

9 Create three more files under the $PROJECT_ROOT/src/iter5/handlers folder: tutor.rs, general.rs, and mod.rs. Leave all three files blank for now.

10 Create a folder named $PROJECT_ROOT/src/iter5/dbscripts. Move and rename the existing database.sql file in the project folder to this directory, and rename it as course.sql. We'll modify this file later.

At this stage, ensure that your project structure looks similar to that shown in figure 6.1. Next, we'll modify the existing code to align to this new structure:

1 In the mod.rs files under the $PROJECT_ROOT/src/iter5/dbaccess and $PROJECT_ROOT/src/iter5/models folders, add the following code:

```
pub mod course;
pub mod tutor;
```

This tells the Rust compiler to consider the contents of the folders $PROJECT_ROOT/src/iter5/models and $PROJECT_ROOT/src/iter5/dbaccess to be Rust modules. This allows us to, for example, refer and use the `Course` data structure in another source file like this:

```
use crate::models::course::Course;
```

Note the similarity between the folder structure and module organization.

2 Similarly, in the mod.rs file under $PROJECT_ROOT/src/iter5/handlers, add the following code:

```
pub mod course;
pub mod tutor;
pub mod general;
```

3 Add the following imports to $PROJECT_ROOT/src/iter5/handlers/general.rs:

```
use super::errors::EzyTutorError;
use super::state::AppState;
use actix_web::{web, HttpResponse};
```

Further, move the function `pub async fn health_check_handler() {..}` from $PROJECT_ROOT/src/iter5/handlers/course.rs to $PROJECT_ROOT/src/iter5/handlers/general.rs.

4   Let's now move to the `main()` function. In $PROJECT_ROOT/src/bin/iter5, adjust the module declaration paths to look like this:

```
#[path = "../iter5/dbaccess/mod.rs"]
mod dbaccess;
#[path = "../iter5/errors.rs"]
mod errors;
#[path = "../iter5/handlers/mod.rs"]
mod handlers;
#[path = "../iter5/models/mod.rs"]
mod models;
#[path = "../iter5/routes.rs"]
mod routes;
#[path = "../iter5/state.rs"]
mod state;
```

5   Adjust the module import paths in $PROJECT_ROOT/src/iter5/dbaccess/course.rs as follows:

```
use crate::errors::EzyTutorError;
use crate::models::course::Course;
```

6   Adjust the module import paths in $PROJECT_ROOT/src/iter5/handlers/course.rs as follows:

```
use crate::dbaccess::course::*;
use crate::errors::EzyTutorError;
use crate::models::course::Course;
```

7   Lastly, adjust the module paths in $PROJECT_ROOT/src/iter5/routes.rs as shown here:

```
use crate::handlers::{course::*, general::*};
```

In this code refactoring exercise, ensure you do not delete any of the other existing import statements, such as those related to Actix Web. I didn't mention these because there is no change to their module paths.

Now, from the project root, check for compilation errors with the following command:

```
cargo check
```

You can also run the test script, which should execute successfully:

```
cargo test
```

If there are any errors, revisit the steps.

Congratulations, you've successfully completed the refactoring of the project code into the new structure.

By way of a recap, we have split the code into multiple smaller files, each performing a specific function (in line with the single responsibility principle in software engineering). Also, we have grouped related files under common folders. For example, the database access code for tutors and courses is now in separate source files, while both the source files are placed together under a dbaccess folder. We have clearly separated the namespaces (through the use of Rust modules) for handler functions, database access, the data model, routes, errors, database scripts, application state, and error handling. This kind of intuitive project structure and file naming enables collaboration among the multiple developers who may be involved in reviewing and modifying a code repository, it improves ramp-up time for new team members, and it reduces the time to release for defect fixes and code enhancements.

Note that this type of structure could be overkill for small projects. Your decisions on refactoring your code should be based on how the code and functional complexity evolve over time.

We can now focus on the functionality enhancements, starting in the next section.

6.2 Enhancing the data model for course creation and management

In this section, we'll enhance the course-related APIs. This will involve changes to the Rust data model, database table structure, routes, handlers, and database access functions.

Figure 6.2 shows the final code structure for the course-related APIs. In the figure, the course-related API routes are listed, along with the names of the respective handler and database access functions.

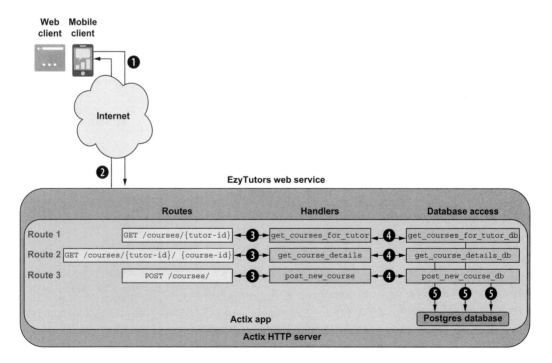

Figure 6.2 Code structure for the course-related APIs

Note the general naming convention for the database access functions: they are named by using the corresponding handler function name and suffixing it with db.

Let's start by looking at the current Course data model in $PROJECT_ROOT/src/iter5/models/course.rs:

```
pub struct Course {
    pub course_id: i32,
    pub tutor_id: i32,
    pub course_name: String,
    pub posted_time: Option<NaiveDateTime>,
}
```

This data structure has served its purpose, but it is elementary. It's time to add more real-world attributes to describe the courses. Let's enhance the Course struct to add the following details:

- *Description*—Textual information describing the course so prospective students can decide if the course is for them.
- *Format*—The course can be delivered in multiple formats, such as a self-paced video course, an e-book format, or instructor-led in-person training.
- *Structure of course*—For now, we'll allow the tutor to upload a document that describes the course (such as a brochure in PDF format).
- *Duration of course*—The length of the course. This is typically described in terms of the duration of video recordings for video-based courses, the duration of in-person training hours, or the recommended study hours in the case of e-books.
- *Price*—We'll specify the course price in US dollars.
- *Language*—Since we expect to have an international audience for the web app, let's allow courses in multiple languages.
- *Level*—This denotes the level of the student the course is targeted at. Possible values include Beginner, Intermediate, and Expert.

In the next subsection, we'll make the changes to the Rust data model.

6.2.1 *Making changes to the data model*

Let's begin to make the changes, starting with file imports. Here is the original set of imports:

```
use actix_web::web;
use chrono::NaiveDateTime;
use serde::{Deserialize, Serialize};
```

Let's alter the Course data structure to incorporate the additional data elements that we wish to capture. Here is the updated Course data structure in $PROJECT_ROOT/src/iter5/models/course.rs:

```
#[derive(Serialize, Debug, Clone, sqlx::FromRow)]
pub struct Course {
    pub course_id: i32,
```

```
    pub tutor_id: i32,
    pub course_name: String,
    pub course_description: Option<String>,
    pub course_format: Option<String>,
    pub course_structure: Option<String>,
    pub course_duration: Option<String>,
    pub course_price: Option<i32>,
    pub course_language: Option<String>,
    pub course_level: Option<String>,
    pub posted_time: Option<NaiveDateTime>,
}
```

Note that we've declared a struct that has three mandatory fields: `course_id`, `tutor_id`, and `course_name`. The rest of the fields are optional (denoted by the `Option<T>` type). This reflects the possibility that a course record in the database may not have values for these optional fields.

We've also auto-derived a few traits. `Serialize` enables us to send the fields of the `Course` struct back to the API client. `Debug` enables the printing of struct values during the development cycle. `Clone` will help us duplicate string values while complying with the Rust ownership model. `sqlx::FromRow` enables the automatic conversion of a database record into the `Course` struct while reading values from the database. We'll look at how we can implement this feature when we write the database access functions.

If we look at the `Course` data structure, there are a couple of fields, `posted_time` and `course_id`, which we plan to auto-generate at the database level. While we need these fields to fully represent a `Course` record, we don't need these values to be sent by the API client. So how can we handle these different representations of a `Course`?.

Let's create a separate data structure that will only contain the fields relevant to the frontend for the creation of a new course. Here is the new `CreateCourse` struct:

```
#[derive(Deserialize, Debug, Clone)]
pub struct CreateCourse {
    pub tutor_id: i32,
    pub course_name: String,
    pub course_description: Option<String>,
    pub course_format: Option<String>,
    pub course_structure: Option<String>,
    pub course_duration: Option<String>,
    pub course_price: Option<i32>,
    pub course_language: Option<String>,
    pub course_level: Option<String>,
}
```

In this struct, we are specifying that for creating a new course, `tutor_id` and `course_id` are mandatory fields; the rest are optional, as far as the API client is concerned. However, for the tutor web service, both `course_id` and `posted_time` are also mandatory fields for creating a new course—these will be auto-generated internally.

You'll also notice that we've auto-derived the `Deserialize` trait for `CreateCourse`, whereas we auto-derived the `Serialize` trait for the `Course` struct. Why do you think we've done this?

This is because the `CreateCourse` struct will be used as the data structure to carry inputs from the user to the web service as part of an HTTP request body. Hence, the Actix Web framework needs a way to deserialize the data coming in over the wire into the `CreateCourse` Rust struct.

Note that for HTTP requests, the API client *serializes* the data payload for transmission, while the Actix framework at the receiving end will *deserialize* the data back into a suitable form for processing by the application. To be more precise, the Actix Web framework serializes the incoming data payload into an Actix `web::Json<Create-Course>` data type, but our application does not understand this type. We'll have to convert this Actix type into a regular Rust struct.

We'll implement the Rust `From` trait to write the conversion function, which we can then invoke at runtime, whenever an HTTP request is received to create a new course:

```
impl From<web::Json<CreateCourse>> for CreateCourse {

    fn from(new_course: web::Json<CreateCourse>) -> Self {
        CreateCourse {
            tutor_id: new_course.tutor_id,
            course_name: new_course.course_name.clone(),
            course_description: new_course.course_description.clone(),
            course_format: new_course.course_format.clone(),
            course_structure: new_course.course_structure.clone(),
            course_level: new_course.course_level.clone(),
            course_duration: new_course.course_duration.clone(),
            course_language: new_course.course_language.clone(),
            course_price: new_course.course_price,
        }
    }
}
```

This conversion is relatively straightforward, but if there is any possibility of errors during the conversion, we would use the `TryFrom` trait instead of the `From` trait. Errors can occur, for example, if we call a Rust standard lib function that returns a `Result` type, such as for converting a string value to an integer.

You can import the `TryFrom` trait from the Rust standard library:

```
use std::convert::TryFrom;
```

Then you'll need to implement the `try_from` function and declare the type for `Error` that will be returned if there are problems in processing:

```
impl TryFrom<web::Json<CreateCourse>> for CreateCourse {
    type Error = EzyTutorError;

    fn try_from(new_course: web::Json<CreateCourse>) ->
    Result<Self, Self::Error> {
        Ok(CreateCourse {
            tutor_id: new_course.tutor_id,
            course_name: new_course.course_name.clone(),
            course_description: new_course.course_description.clone(),
            course_format: new_course.course_format.clone(),
```

```
            course_structure: new_course.course_structure.clone(),
            course_level: new_course.course_level.clone(),
            course_duration: new_course.course_duration.clone(),
            course_language: new_course.course_language.clone(),
            course_price: new_course.course_price,
        })
    }
}
```

Note that `Error` is a type placeholder associated with the `TryFrom` trait. We are declaring it to be of type `EzyTutorError` since we would like to unify all the error handling with the `EzyTutorError` type. Within the function, we can then raise errors of type `EzyTutorError` in the case of faults.

However, for our purposes here, it would suffice to use the `From` trait, as we do not anticipate any failure conditions during this conversion. The use of the `TryFrom` trait is only shown here to demonstrate how you can use it if the need arises.

We now have a way to receive data from an API client for creating a new course. What about course updates? Can we use the same `CreateCourse` struct? We cannot. While updating a course, we don't want to allow the `tutor_id` to be modified, as we don't want the course created by one tutor to be switched to another tutor. Also, the `course_name` field in the `CreateCourse` struct is mandatory. When we are updating a course, we don't want to force the user to update the name every time.

Let's create another struct that's more suitable for updating course details:

```
#[derive(Deserialize, Debug, Clone)]
pub struct UpdateCourse {
    pub course_name: Option<String>,
    pub course_description: Option<String>,
    pub course_format: Option<String>,
    pub course_structure: Option<String>,
    pub course_duration: Option<String>,
    pub course_price: Option<i32>,
    pub course_language: Option<String>,
    pub course_level: Option<String>,
}
```

Note that all the fields here are optional, which is the way it should be for a good user experience.

We'll also have to write a `From` trait implementation for `UpdateCourse`, similar to the one for `CreateCourse`. Here is the code:

```
impl From<web::Json<UpdateCourse>> for UpdateCourse {
    fn from(update_course: web::Json<UpdateCourse>) -> Self {
        UpdateCourse {
            course_name: update_course.course_name.clone(),
            course_description: update_course.course_description.clone(),
            course_format: update_course.course_format.clone(),
            course_structure: update_course.course_structure.clone(),
            course_level: update_course.course_level.clone(),
            course_duration: update_course.course_duration.clone(),
```

```
            course_language: update_course.course_language.clone(),
            course_price: update_course.course_price,
        }
    }
}
```

Before we forget, in the $PROJECT_ROOT/src/iter5/models/course.rs file, delete the From trait implementation that converts from web::Json<Course> to the Course struct, which we wrote in the previous chapter. We now have separate structs for receiving data from users (CreateCourse and UpdateCourse) and for sending data back (Course).

This concludes the data model changes for the Course data struct, but we're not done yet. We have to change the model of the physical database tables to add the new fields.

In the course.sql file, under $PROJECT_ROOT/src/iter5/dbscripts, add the following database scripts:

```
/* Drop tables if they already exist*/

drop table if exists ezy_course_c6;

/* Create tables. */
/* Note: Don't put a comma after last field */

create table ezy_course_c6
(
    course_id serial primary key,
    tutor_id INT not null,
    course_name varchar(140) not null,
    course_description varchar(2000),
    course_format varchar(30),
    course_structure varchar(200),
    course_duration varchar(30),
    course_price INT,
    course_language varchar(30),
    course_level varchar(30),
    posted_time TIMESTAMP default now()

);
```

Note the main changes compared to the script we wrote in the previous chapter:

- The database table name now has the c6 suffix. This allows us to test the code for each chapter independently.
- The additional data elements we designed in the Course data structure are reflected in the table-creation script.
- The NOT NULL constraint is specified for tutor_id and course_name. This will be enforced by the database, and we won't be able to add a record without these columns. In addition, course_id, which is marked as the primary key, and posted_time, which is automatically set to current time by default, are also enforced at the database level. The fields that do not have a NOT NULL constraint

are optional columns. If you refer back to the Course struct, you'll notice that these columns are also the ones marked as the Option<T> type in the Course struct definition. In this way, we have aligned the database column constraints with the Rust struct.

To test the database script, run the following command from the command line. Make sure the right path to the script file is specified:

```
psql -U <user-name> -d ezytutors < <path.to.file>/course.sql
```

Replace <user-name> and <path.to-file> with the appropriate values, and enter the password if prompted. You should see the scripts execute successfully.

To verify that the tables have indeed been created according to the script specification, log in to the psql shell with the following command:

```
psql -U <user-name> -d ezytutors          Display the list of
\d                                         relations (tables).
\d+ ezy_course_c6            Display column
\q              Quit the     names in the table.
                psql shell.
```

After creating the new table, we need to give permissions to the database user. Run the following commands from the terminal command line:

```
psql -U <user-name> -d ezytutors     // Login to psql shell
GRANT ALL PRIVILEGES ON TABLE __ezy_course_c6__ to <user-name>
\q                                   // Quit the psql shell
```

Replace <user-name> with your username, which should be the same one you configured in the .env file. Note that you can also choose to execute this step directly as part of the database scripts after creating the table.

With this, we conclude the data model changes. In the next subsection, we'll make the changes to the API processing logic to accommodate the data model changes.

6.2.2 Making changes to the course APIs

In the previous section, we enhanced the data model for Course and created new database scripts to create the new structure for the Course we designed.

We'll now have to modify the application logic to incorporate the data model changes. To verify this, just run the following command from the project root:

```
cargo check
```

You'll see that there are errors in the database access and handler functions that need to be fixed. Let's do that now.

We'll start with the routes in $PROJECT_ROOT/src/iter5/routes.rs. Modify the code to look like this:

```
use crate::handlers::{course::*, general::*};
use actix_web::web;
```

```
pub fn general_routes(cfg: &mut web::ServiceConfig) {
    cfg.route("/health", web::get().to(health_check_handler));
}

pub fn course_routes(cfg: &mut web::ServiceConfig) {
    cfg.service(
        web::scope("/courses")
        .route("", web::post().to(post_new_course))
        .route("/{tutor_id}", web::get().to(get_courses_for_tutor))
        .route("/{tutor_id}/{course_id}", web::get().to(get_course_details))
        .route(
            "/{tutor_id}/{course_id}",
            web::put().to(update_course_details),
        )
        .route("/{tutor_id}/{course_id}", web::delete().to(delete_course)),
    );
}
```

Display the list of relations (tables).

HTTP GET request to retrieve all courses for a given tutor

HTTP PUT request to update course details

HTTP GET request to get details for a given course

HTTP DELETE request to delete a course entry

There are a few things you should notice in this code:

- We are importing the handler functions from two modules—`crate::handlers::course` and `crate::handlers::general`.
- We are using the appropriate HTTP methods for the various routes—the `post()` method to create a new course, the `get()` method to retrieve a single course or a list of courses, the `put()` method to update a course, and the `delete()` method to delete a course.
- We are using URL path parameters, `{tutor_id}` and `{course_id}`, to identify specific resources on which to operate.

You may be wondering about the `CreateCourse` and `UpdateCourse` structs that we designed as part of the data model to enable the creation and updating of course records. Why are they not visible in the route definitions? That's because these structs are sent as part of the HTTP request payload, which is automatically extracted by Actix and made available to the respective handler functions. Only the URL path parameters, HTTP methods, and names of handler functions for a route are specified as part of the routes declaration in Actix Web.

Let's next focus on the handler functions in $PROJECT_ROOT/src/iter5/handlers/course.rs. Here are the module imports:

```
use crate::dbaccess::course::*;
use crate::errors::EzyTutorError;
use crate::models::course::{CreateCourse, UpdateCourse};
use crate::state::AppState;
use actix_web::{web, HttpResponse};
```

First, recall that the handler functions are called whenever an HTTP request arrives at one of the routes defined in routes.rs. In the case of `courses`, for example, it can be a GET request to retrieve a list of courses for a tutor or a POST request to create a new course. The handler functions corresponding to each of the valid course routes will be stored in this file. The handler functions, in turn, make use of the `Course` data models and database access functions, and these are reflected in the module imports.

Here we're importing the database access functions (as the handlers will invoke them), a custom error type, data structures from the `Course` model, `AppState` (for the database connection pool), and the Actix utilities needed for HTTP communications with the client frontend.

Let's write the various handler functions corresponding to the routes, one by one. Here is the handler method to retrieve all courses for a tutor:

```
pub async fn get_courses_for_tutor(
    app_state: web::Data<AppState>,
    path: web::Path<i32>,
) -> Result<HttpResponse, EzyTutorError> {
    let tutor_id = path.into_inner();
    get_courses_for_tutor_db(&app_state.db, tutor_id)
        .await
        .map(|courses| HttpResponse::Ok().json(courses))
}
```

This function accepts a URL path parameter that refers to the `tutor_id`, which is encapsulated in the Actix data structure `web::Path<i32>`. The function returns an HTTP response containing either the data requested or an error message.

The handler function, in turn, invokes the `get_courses_for_tutor_db` database access function to access the database and retrieve the course list. The return value from the database access function is handled through the `map` construct in Rust, which constructs a valid HTTP response message with the success code and sends the list of courses back as part of the HTTP response body.

If there are errors while accessing the database, the database access functions raise an error of type `EzyTutorError`, which is then propagated back to the handler functions, where this error is transformed into an Actix error type and sent back to the client through a valid HTTP response message. This error translation is handled by the Actix framework, provided the application implements the Actix `ResponseError` trait on the `EzyTutorError` type, which we did in the previous chapter.

Let's next look at the code for retrieving an individual course record:

```
pub async fn get_course_details(
    app_state: web::Data<AppState>,
    path: web::Path<(i32, i32)>,
) -> Result<HttpResponse, EzyTutorError> {
    let (tutor_id, course_id) = path.into_inner();
    get_course_details_db(&app_state.db, tutor_id, course_id)
        .await
        .map(|course| HttpResponse::Ok().json(course))
}
```

Similar to the previous function, this function is invoked in response to an `HTTP::GET` request. The difference is that here we will receive the `tutor_id` and `course_id` as part of the URL path parameters, which will help us uniquely identify a single course record in the database.

Note the use of the `.await` keyword in these handler functions when invoking the corresponding database access functions. Since the database access library we use, `sqlx`, uses an asynchronous connection to the database, we use the `.await` keyword to denote an asynchronous call to communicate with the database.

Moving on, here is the code for the handler function that posts a new course:

```
pub async fn post_new_course(
    new_course: web::Json<CreateCourse>,
    app_state: web::Data<AppState>,
) -> Result<HttpResponse, EzyTutorError> {
    post_new_course_db(&app_state.db, new_course.into()?)
        .await
        .map(|course| HttpResponse::Ok().json(course))
}
```

This handler function is invoked for an `HTTP::POST` request received on the route specified in the routes.rs file. The Actix framework deserializes the HTTP request body of this POST request and makes the data available to the `post_new_course()` handler function within the `web::Json<CreateCourse>` data structure.

Recall that we wrote a method to convert from `web::Json<CreateCourse>` to the `CreateCourse` struct as part of the `From` trait implementation in the models/course.rs file, which we are invoking within the handler function using the expression `new_course.into()?`. If we had implemented the conversion function using the `TryFrom` trait instead of the `From` trait, we would invoke the conversion using `new_course.try_into()?`, with the `?` denoting the possibility of an error being returned from the conversion function.

In this handler function, after a new course is created, the database access function returns the newly created course record, which is then sent back from the web service within the body of an HTTP response message.

Next, let's look at the handler function to delete a course:

```
pub async fn delete_course(
    app_state: web::Data<AppState>,
    path: web::Path<(i32, i32)>,
) -> Result<HttpResponse, EzyTutorError> {
    let (tutor_id, course_id) = path.into_inner();
    delete_course_db(&app_state.db, tutor_id, course_id)
        .await
        .map(|resp| HttpResponse::Ok().json(resp))
}
```

This handler function is invoked in response to an `HTTP::DELETE` request. The handler function invokes the `delete_course_db` database access function to perform the actual deletion of the course record in the database. On receiving a message confirming successful deletion, the handler function sends it back as part of the HTTP response.

Here is the handler function to update the details for a course:

```
pub async fn update_course_details(
    app_state: web::Data<AppState>,
    update_course: web::Json<UpdateCourse>,
    path: web::Path<(i32, i32)>,
) -> Result<HttpResponse, EzyTutorError> {
    let (tutor_id, course_id) = path.into_inner();
    update_course_details_db(&app_state.db, tutor_id,
    ➥course_id, update_course.into())
        .await
        .map(|course| HttpResponse::Ok().json(course))
}
```

This handler function is invoked in response to an `HTTP::PUT` request on the specified route in the routes.rs file. It receives two URL path parameters, `tutor_id` and `course_id`, which are used to uniquely identify a course in the database. The input parameters for the course to be modified are sent from the web frontend to the Actix web server route as part of the HTTP request body, and this is made available by Actix to the handler function as `web::Json::UpdateCourse`.

Note the use of the `update_course.into()` expression. This is used to convert `web::json::UpdateCourse` to `UpdateCourse struct`. To achieve this, we previously implemented the `From` trait in the models/course.rs file.

The updated course details are then sent back as part of the HTTP response message.

Let's also write unit test cases for the handler functions. In the handlers/course.rs file, we'll add the test cases and module imports (after the code for handler functions) within the `test` module as shown here:

```
#[cfg(test)]
mod tests {
    //write test cases here
}
```

Let's add the module imports first:

```
use super::*;
use actix_web::http::StatusCode;
use actix_web::ResponseError;
use dotenv::dotenv;
use sqlx::postgres::PgPool;
use std::env;
use std::sync::Mutex;
```

Now let's start with the test case for getting all courses for a tutor:

```
#[actix_rt::test]
async fn get_all_courses_success() {
    dotenv().ok();
    let database_url = env::var("DATABASE_URL").expect(
    ➥"DATABASE_URL is not set in .env file");
```

Load the environment variables from the .env file. ←┘

Retrieve the DATABASE_URL from the environment variable. If the variable is not set, the code will panic with an error message. ←┘

Construct a Postgres
database connection pool.

Construct the application state, which is injected as a
dependency by Actix Web into each of the handler functions.
The database connection pool is part of the application
state, and this is needed by the database access functions.

```
let pool: PgPool = PgPool::connect(&database_url).await.unwrap();
let app_state: web::Data<AppState> = web::Data::new(AppState {
    health_check_response: "".to_string(),
    visit_count: Mutex::new(0),
    db: pool,
});
let tutor_id: web::Path<i32> = web::Path::from(1);
let resp = get_courses_for_tutor(
    app_state, tutor_id).await.unwrap();
assert_eq!(resp.status(), StatusCode::OK);
}
```

Simulate the URL Path parameter
tutor_id by constructing a
web::Path extractor with a value
of 1, using the from() method.

Invoke the
handler
function.

Check the return value of the
handler function call with
the expected status code.

Here is the test case to retrieve an individual course:

```
#[actix_rt::test]
async fn get_course_detail_success_test() {
    dotenv().ok();
    let database_url = env::var("DATABASE_URL").expect(
        "DATABASE_URL is not set in .env file");
    let pool: PgPool = PgPool::connect(&database_url).await.unwrap();
    let app_state: web::Data<AppState> = web::Data::new(AppState {
        health_check_response: "".to_string(),
        visit_count: Mutex::new(0),
        db: pool,
    });
    let parameters: web::Path<(i32, i32)> = web::Path::from((1, 2));
    let resp = get_course_details(app_state, parameters).await.unwrap();
    assert_eq!(resp.status(), StatusCode::OK);
}
```

Construct path parameters
representing tutor_id and course_id.

The preceding test function is mostly similar to the previous one, except that here we
are retrieving a single course from the database.

What happens if we provide an invalid `course id` or `tutor id`? In the handler and
database access functions, we handle such a case by returning an error. Let's see if we
can verify this scenario:

```
#[actix_rt::test]
async fn get_course_detail_failure_test() {
    dotenv().ok();
    let database_url = env::var("DATABASE_URL").expect(
        "DATABASE_URL is not set in .env file");
    let pool: PgPool = PgPool::connect(&database_url).await.unwrap();
    let app_state: web::Data<AppState> = web::Data::new(AppState {
        health_check_response: "".to_string(),
        visit_count: Mutex::new(0),
        db: pool,
    });
    let parameters: web::Path<(i32, i32)> = web::Path::from((1, 21));
    let resp = get_course_details(app_state, parameters).await;
```

Note the call to the handler function,
which returns a Result<T,E> type.

```
        match resp {
            Ok(_) => println!("Something wrong"),
            Err(err) => assert_eq!(err.status_code(),
            ➥StatusCode::NOT_FOUND),
        }
}
```

We use the match clause to check if the handler function returns successfully or returns an Error. In this case, we are trying to retrieve details for a non-existent course-id, so we're expecting an error to be returned.

We are asserting that the error status code returned from the handler function is of type StatusCode::NOT_FOUND.

Next, we'll write the test case to post a new course:

```
#[ignore]
#[actix_rt::test]
async fn post_course_success() {
    dotenv().ok();
    let database_url = env::var("DATABASE_URL").expect(
    ➥"DATABASE_URL is not set in .env file");
    let pool: PgPool = PgPool::new(&database_url).await.unwrap();
    let app_state: web::Data<AppState> = web::Data::new(AppState {
        health_check_response: "".to_string(),
        visit_count: Mutex::new(0),
        db: pool,
    });
    let new_course_msg = CreateCourse {
        tutor_id: 1,
        course_name: "Third course".into(),
        course_description: Some("This is a test course".into()),
        course_format: None,
        course_level: Some("Beginner".into()),
        course_price: None,
        course_duration: None,
        course_language: Some("English".into()),
        course_structure: None,
    };
    let course_param = web::Json(new_course_msg);
    let resp = post_new_course(course_param, app_state).await.unwrap();
    assert_eq!(resp.status(), StatusCode::OK);
}
```

Construct a data structure representing the attributes of the course to be created.

Encapsulate the constructed CreateCourse struct in a web::Json object to simulate what happens in a client API call.

The rest of the code is similar to the previous test cases. Note the use of [ignore] at the top of the preceding test case. This ensures that the `cargo test` command will ignore this test case whenever it is invoked. This is because we may not want to create a new test case every time we run test cases for sanity checks. In such a case, we can use the [ignore] annotation.

Shown next is the test case to update a course:

```
#[actix_rt::test]
async fn update_course_success() {
    dotenv().ok();
    let database_url = env::var("DATABASE_URL").expect(
    ➥"DATABASE_URL is not set in .env file");
    let pool: PgPool = PgPool::connect(&database_url).await.unwrap();
    let app_state: web::Data<AppState> = web::Data::new(AppState {
        health_check_response: "".to_string(),
        visit_count: Mutex::new(0),
```

```
        db: pool,
    });
    let update_course_msg = UpdateCourse {
        course_name: Some("Course name changed".into()),
        course_description: Some(
        ➡"This is yet another test course".into()),
        course_format: None,
        course_level: Some("Intermediate".into()),
        course_price: None,
        course_duration: None,
        course_language: Some("German".into()),
        course_structure: None,
    };
    let parameters: web::Path<(i32, i32)> = web::Path::from((1, 2));
    let update_param = web::Json(update_course_msg);
    let resp = update_course_details(app_state,
    ➡update_param, parameters)
        .await
        .unwrap();
    assert_eq!(resp.status(), StatusCode::OK);
}
```

> Similar to the **CreateCourse** struct in the previous test case, we are using the **UpdateCourse** struct to provide the data elements to modify the Course record in the database.

> Simulate the URL path parameters to uniquely identify a course record in the database using tutor_id and course_id.

Here is the test case to delete a course:

```
#[ignore]
#[actix_rt::test]
async fn delete_test_success() {
    dotenv().ok();
    let database_url = env::var("DATABASE_URL").expect(
    ➡"DATABASE_URL is not set in .env file");
    let pool: PgPool = PgPool::connect(&database_url).await.unwrap();
    let app_state: web::Data<AppState> = web::Data::new(AppState {
        health_check_response: "".to_string(),
        visit_count: Mutex::new(0),
        db: pool,
    });
    let parameters: web::Path<(i32, i32)> = web::Path::from((1, 5));
    let resp = delete_course(app_state, parameters).await.unwrap();
    assert_eq!(resp.status(), StatusCode::OK);
}
```

> Ensure that a valid tutor-id and course-id are provided in the URL path parameters before invoking this test case.

What if we were to provide an invalid `tutor-id` or `course-id`? Let's write a test case for that:

```
#[actix_rt::test]
async fn delete_test_failure() {
    dotenv().ok();
    let database_url = env::var("DATABASE_URL").expect(
    ➡"DATABASE_URL is not set in .env file");
    let pool: PgPool = PgPool::connect(&database_url).await.unwrap();
    let app_state: web::Data<AppState> = web::Data::new(AppState {
        health_check_response: "".to_string(),
        visit_count: Mutex::new(0),
        db: pool,
    });
```

```
let parameters: web::Path<(i32, i32)> = web::Path::from((1, 21));
let resp = delete_course(app_state, parameters).await;
match resp {
    Ok(_) => println!("Something wrong"),
    Err(err) => assert_eq!(err.status_code(),
    StatusCode::NOT_FOUND),
}
}
```

Provide an invalid course-id or tutor-id in the path parameters.

Expect an error to be returned from the handler function, and compare the error status code returned by the handler with the expected value.

This concludes our unit test cases for the various handler functions. However, we're not yet ready to run the tests, as we have not implemented the database access functions. Let's look at them now in $PROJECT_ROOT/src/iter5/dbaccess/course.rs.

Let's begin with the database access function to retrieve all courses for a tutor, along with all the module imports for the file:

```
use crate::errors::EzyTutorError;
use crate::models::course::*;
use sqlx::postgres::PgPool;


pub async fn get_courses_for_tutor_db(
    pool: &PgPool,
    tutor_id: i32,
) -> Result<Vec<Course>, EzyTutorError> {
    // Prepare SQL statement

    let course_rows: Vec<Course> = sqlx::query_as!(
        Course,
        "SELECT * FROM ezy_course_c6 where tutor_id = $1",
        tutor_id
    )
    .fetch_all(pool)
    .await?;

    Ok(course_rows)
}
```

Construct a query using the sqlx query_as!

Execute the SELECT query statement to retrieve all rows that match the selection clause in SQL.

Indicates an async function that internally uses Rust futures. In Rust, futures are lazily evaluated, which means that until the .await keyword is called, the query is not executed.

The sqlx library automatically converts the database row into a Rust Course data struct, and a vector of these courses is returned from this function.

The query_as! macro comes in handy to map the columns in the database record to the Course data struct. This mapping is done automatically by sqlx if the sqlx::FromRow trait is implemented for the Course struct. We did this in the models module by auto-deriving this trait as outlined here:

```
#[derive(Deserialize, Serialize, Debug, Clone, sqlx::FromRow)]
pub struct Course {
// fields
}
```

Without the query_as! macro, we would have to manually perform the mapping of each database column to the corresponding Course struct field.

Here is the next function to retrieve a single course from the database:

```
pub async fn get_course_details_db(
    pool: &PgPool,
    tutor_id: i32,
    course_id: i32,
) -> Result<Course, EzyTutorError> {
    // Prepare SQL statement
    let course_row = sqlx::query_as!(
      Course,
      "SELECT * FROM ezy_course_c6 where tutor_id = $1 and course_id = $2",
      tutor_id,
      course_id
    )
    .fetch_optional(pool)
    .await?;

    if let Some(course) = course_row {
      Ok(course)
    } else {
      Err(EzyTutorError::NotFound("Course id not found".into()))
    }
}
```

The query_as! macro is used to map the returned database record into a Course struct.

fetch_optional returns an Option type, indicating that there may not be a record in the database for the specified SELECT clause.

If a record is found in the database, return the course details encapsulated in the OK(T) variant of the Result type.

If no record is found for the criteria specified, return an Err type with a suitable error message. This error is then propagated back to the calling handler function and sent to the API client as part of an HTTP response message.

The code for adding a new course to the database is shown next:

```
pub async fn post_new_course_db(
    pool: &PgPool,
    new_course: CreateCourse,
) -> Result<Course, EzyTutorError> {
    let course_row= sqlx::query_as!(Course,"insert into ezy_course_c6 (
    tutor_id, course_name, course_description,course_duration,
    course_level, course_format, course_language, course_structure,
    course_price) values ($1,$2,$3,$4,$5,$6,$7,$8,$9) returning
    tutor_id, course_id,course_name, course_description,
    course_duration, course_level, course_format, course_language,
    course_structure, course_price, posted_time",
    new_course.tutor_id, new_course.course_name,
    new_course.course_description,
    new_course.course_duration, new_course.course_level,
    new_course.course_format, new_course.course_language,
    new_course.course_structure, new_course.course_price)
    .fetch_one(pool)
    .await?;

    Ok(course_row)
}
```

First, a standard insert SQL statement is constructed using the parameters passed from the handler function.

After inserting a record, the fetch_one() method is called to return the inserted record. The retrieved database row is automatically converted into the Course data type due to the use of the query_as! macro. The newly created course is returned to the handler function in the form of the Course struct.

Note the use of the `returning` keyword in the SQL insert statement. This is a feature supported by the Postgres database that enables us to retrieve the newly inserted course details as part of the same insert query (instead of having to write a separate SQL query).

Let's look at the function to delete a course from the database:

```
pub async fn delete_course_db(
    pool: &PgPool,
    tutor_id: i32,
    course_id: i32,
) -> Result<String, EzyTutorError> {
    // Prepare SQL statement
    let course_row = sqlx::query!(
        "DELETE FROM ezy_course_c6 where tutor_id = $1 and course_id = $2",
        tutor_id,
        course_id,
    )
    .execute(pool)
    .await?;
    Ok(format!("Deleted {:#?} record", course_row))
}
```

Construct a SQL query to delete the specified course from the database.

Execute the query statement. Note that because this is an async function, the query is actually executed only when .await() is invoked.

Return a message confirming deletion.

Lastly, let's look at the code to update the details of a course:

```
pub async fn update_course_details_db(
    pool: &PgPool,
    tutor_id: i32,
    course_id: i32,
    update_course: UpdateCourse,
) -> Result<Course, EzyTutorError> {
    // Retrieve current record

    let current_course_row = sqlx::query_as!(
        Course,
        "SELECT * FROM ezy_course_c6 where tutor_id = $1 and course_id = $2",
        tutor_id,
        course_id
    )
    .fetch_one(pool)
    .await
    .map_err(|_err| EzyTutorError::NotFound(
        "Course id not found".into()))?;

    // Construct the parameters for update:

    let name: String = if let Some(name) = update_course.course_name {
        name
    } else {
        current_course_row.course_name
    };
    let description: String = if let Some(desc) = ...
    let format: String = if let Some(format) = ...
    let structure: String = if let Some(structure) = ...
    let duration: String = if let Some(duration) = ...
    let level: String = if let Some(level) = ...
    let language: String = if let Some(language) = ...
    let price = if let Some(price) = ...
```

Construct a SQL query to verify if a record exists in the database for the criteria specified.

Fetch a single record.

If no record is found for the specified tutor_id and course_id, return an error message.

Construct the values to update the database.

Abridged source code—for the full code, see the GitHub source.

```
        // Prepare SQL statement
        let course_row =
            sqlx::query_as!(                ◄──────────────────────   Construct the query statement
            Course,                                                    to update the database.
            "UPDATE ezy_course_c6 set course_name = $1,
            ➡course_description = $2, course_format = $3,
            course_structure = $4, course_duration = $5, course_price = $6,
            ➡course_language = $7,
            course_level = $8 where tutor_id = $9 and course_id = $10
            ➡returning tutor_id, course_id,
            course_name, course_description, course_duration, course_level,
            ➡course_format,
            course_language, course_structure, course_price, posted_time ",
            ➡name, description, format,
            structure, duration, price, language,level, tutor_id, course_id
        )
            .fetch_one(pool)    ◄──┤  Retrieve the updated record.
            .await;
        if let Ok(course) = course_row {      ◄──┐  Verify whether the update is successful.
            Ok(course)                             │  If it is, return the updated course
        } else {                                   │  record to the calling handler function.
            Err(EzyTutorError::NotFound
            ➡("Course id not found".into()))   ◄──┐  If the update operation fails,
        }                                           │  return an error message.
}
```

The UpdateCourse struct contains a set of optional fields, so we first need to verify which fields have been sent by the API client. If a new value has been sent for a field, we need to update it. Otherwise, we need to retain the value in the database. To achieve this, we first extract the current course record, containing all the fields. Then, if the value of a particular field is sent by the API client, we use it to update the database. Otherwise, we use the existing value to update it.

We've now completed the code changes to the data model, routes, handlers, test cases, and database access functions for courses. You can now check for any compilation errors by running this command from the project root:

```
cargo check
```

If it compiles successfully, you can build and run the server with this command:

```
cargo run
```

You can test the HTTP::GET related APIs from the browser:

```
http://localhost:3000/courses/1        ◄──────────────────────   Retrieve all courses
http://localhost:3000/courses/1/2   ◄──┐                          for tutor-id=1.
                                        │  Retrieve course details for
                                        │  tutor-id=1, course-id=2.
```

The POST, PUT, and DELETE APIs can be tested with curl or from a GUI tool such as Postman. The curl commands shown here can be executed on the command line from the project root:

```
curl -X POST localhost:3000/courses -H "Content-Type: application/json" \
 -d '{"tutor_id":1, "course_name":"This is a culinary course",
 "course_level":"Beginner"}'

curl -X PUT localhost:3000/courses/1/5 -H "Content-Type: application/json"
 -d '{"course_name":"This is a master culinary course",
 "course_duration":"8 hours of training", course_format:"online"}'

curl -X DELETE http://localhost:3000/courses/1/6
```

Post a new course for tutor-id = 1. Note that the JSON field names must correspond to the CreateCourse struct, where tutor_id and course_name are mandatory, and the rest are optional fields.

Delete the course record identified by tutor-id = 1 and course-id = 6.

Update the course corresponding to tutor -id = 1 and course-id = 5. The JSON field names should correspond to the UpdateCourse struct.

Ensure you change the `course_id` and `tutor_id` values based on your database data setup.

Further, you can run the test cases with this command:

```
cargo test
```

You can selectively disable the tests to be ignored with the `#[ignore]` annotation at the beginning of a test case function declaration.

With this, we have come to the end of the changes for the course-related functionality. We've covered a lot of ground:

- We made changes to the `Course` data model to add additional fields, some of which are optional values requiring the use of the `Option<>` type in the struct member declaration.
- We added data structures for creating and updating a course.
- We implemented conversion methods from Actix JSON data structs to the `CreateCourse` and `UpdateCourse` structs. We saw how to use both the `TryFrom` and `From` traits.
- We modified the routes to cover create, retrieve, update, and delete functions for course data.
- We wrote the handler functions for each of these routes.
- We wrote the unit test cases for the handler functions. We wrote a couple of test cases where errors are returned from the handler functions, instead of a success response.
- We wrote database access functions corresponding to each handler method. We used the `query_as!` macro to significantly reduce the boilerplate code for mapping columns from a database record into Rust struct fields.

Are you exhausted already? Writing real-world web services and applications involves considerable work, for sure. In the next section, we'll add functionality for maintaining tutor data.

6.3 Enabling tutor registration and management

In this section, we'll design and write the code for the tutor-related APIs, which will include the Rust data models for tutors, the database table structure, routes, handlers, and database access functions for managing the tutor data.

Figure 6.3 shows the overall code structure for tutor-related APIs. You'll notice that we have five routes. There is also a handler function and a database access function corresponding to each route.

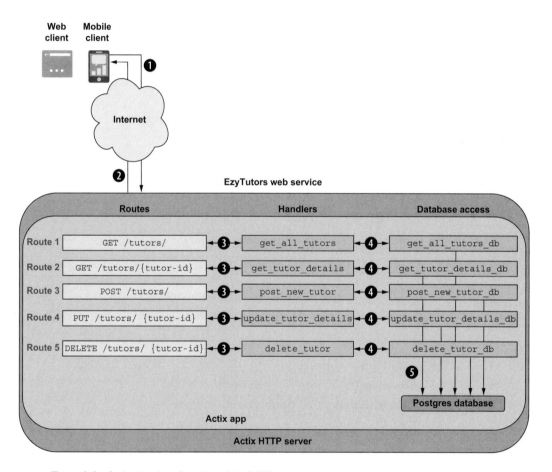

Figure 6.3 Code structure for tutor-related APIs

Let's first look at the data model and routes.

6.3.1 Data model and routes for tutors

Let's first add a new Tutor struct to the data model in the $PROJECT_ROOT/src/ iter5/models/tutor.rs file.

We'll start with the module imports:

```
use actix_web::web;
use serde::{Deserialize, Serialize};
```

Define the struct as shown next:

```
#[derive(Deserialize, Serialize, Debug, Clone)]
pub struct Tutor {
    tutor_id: i32,
    tutor_name: String,
    tutor_pic_url: String,
    tutor_profile: String
}
```

We've defined a `Tutor` struct that contains the following information:

- *Tutor ID*—This will be a unique ID to represent a tutor, and it will be autogenerated by the database.
- *Tutor name*—The full name of the tutor.
- *Tutor picture URL*—The URL of the tutor image.
- *Tutor profile*—A brief profile of the tutor.

Let's create two more structs—one to define the fields needed to create a new course, and another for updating it:

```
#[derive(Deserialize, Debug, Clone)]
pub struct NewTutor {
    pub tutor_name: String,
    pub tutor_pic_url: String,
    pub tutor_profile: String,
}
#[derive(Deserialize, Debug, Clone)]
pub struct UpdateTutor {
    pub tutor_name: Option<String>,
    pub tutor_pic_url: Option<String>,
    pub tutor_profile: Option<String>,
}
```

We need two separate structs because when we are creating a tutor, we will require all the fields, but for updating, all fields are optional.

And much like for the `Course` data struct, here are the functions to convert from `web::Json<NewTutor>` to `NewTutor` and from `web::Json<UpdateTutor>` to `Update-Tutor`:

```
impl From<web::Json<NewTutor>> for NewTutor {
    fn from(new_tutor: web::Json<NewTutor>) -> Self {
        NewTutor {
            tutor_name: new_tutor.tutor_name.clone(),
            tutor_pic_url: new_tutor.tutor_pic_url.clone(),
            tutor_profile: new_tutor.tutor_profile.clone(),
        }
    }
}
```

```
impl From<web::Json<UpdateTutor>> for UpdateTutor {
    fn from(new_tutor: web::Json<UpdateTutor>) -> Self {
        UpdateTutor {
            tutor_name: new_tutor.tutor_name.clone(),
            tutor_pic_url: new_tutor.tutor_pic_url.clone(),
            tutor_profile: new_tutor.tutor_profile.clone(),
        }
    }
}
```

This completes the data model changes for Tutor. Next, let's add the tutor-related routes in $PROJECT_ROOT/src/iter5/routes.rs:

```
pub fn tutor_routes(cfg: &mut web::ServiceConfig) {
    cfg.service(
        web::scope("/tutors")
            .route("/", web::post().to(post_new_tutor))
            .route("/", web::get().to(get_all_tutors))
            .route("/{tutor_id}", web::get().to(get_tutor_details))
            .route("/{tutor_id}", web::put().to(update_tutor_details))
            .route("/{tutor_id}", web::delete().to(delete_tutor)),
    );
}
```

Route to create a new tutor with an HTTP::POST request

Route to retrieve a list of all tutors using HTTP::GET

Route to update tutor details using HTTP::PUT

Route to delete a tutor entry using HTTP::DELETE

Route to get details for an individual tutor using HTTP::GET

Don't forget to update the module imports to import the handler functions for tutors, which we will shortly write, in the $PROJECT_ROOT/src/iter5/routes.rs file:

```
use crate::handlers::{course::*, general::*, tutor::*};
```

We'll have to register the new tutor routes in the main() function. Otherwise, the Actix framework will not recognize requests coming in on the tutor routes and will not know how to route them to their handlers.

In $PROJECT_ROOT/src/bin/iter5.rs, add the tutor routes after the course routes while constructing the Actix app, as shown here:

```
.configure(course_routes)
.configure(tutor_routes)
```

We can now move on to the handler functions.

6.3.2   *Handler functions for tutor routes*

You've already seen how to write the handler functions for Course. Let's move quickly through the tutor routes, only slowing down to look at any differences.

Here is the first handler method to retrieve all tutors, along with the module imports. Add this code to the $PROJECT_ROOT/src/iter5/handlers/tutor.rs file:

```
use crate::dbaccess::tutor::*;
use crate::errors::EzyTutorError;
use crate::models::tutor::{NewTutor, UpdateTutor};
use crate::state::AppState;
```

```
use actix_web::{web, HttpResponse};

pub async fn get_all_tutors(app_state: web::Data<AppState>) ->
➥Result<HttpResponse, EzyTutorError> {
    get_all_tutors_db(&app_state.db)
        .await
        .map(|tutors| HttpResponse::Ok().json(tutors))
}

pub async fn get_tutor_details(
    app_state: web::Data<AppState>,
    web::Path(tutor_id): web::Path<i32>,
) -> Result<HttpResponse, EzyTutorError> {
    get_tutor_details_db(&app_state.db, tutor_id)
        .await
        .map(|tutor| HttpResponse::Ok().json(tutor))
}
```

The two functions linked to the `HTTP::GET` request are shown here: `get_all_tutors()` takes no parameters, while `get_tutor_details()` takes a `tutor_id` as a path parameter. Both invoke database access functions with the same names as the handler functions, but with a `db` suffix. The return value from the database access function is returned to the web client in the body of an `HttpResponse` message.

Here are the handler functions for posting a new tutor entry, updating tutor details, and deleting a tutor from the database:

```
pub async fn post_new_tutor(
    new_tutor: web::Json<NewTutor>,
    app_state: web::Data<AppState>,
) -> Result<HttpResponse, EzyTutorError> {
    post_new_tutor_db(&app_state.db, NewTutor::from(new_tutor))
        .await
        .map(|tutor| HttpResponse::Ok().json(tutor))
}

pub async fn update_tutor_details(
    app_state: web::Data<AppState>,
    web::Path(tutor_id): web::Path<i32>,
    update_tutor: web::Json<UpdateTutor>,
) -> Result<HttpResponse, EzyTutorError> {
    update_tutor_details_db(&app_state.db, tutor_id,
    ➥UpdateTutor::from(update_tutor))
        .await
        .map(|tutor| HttpResponse::Ok().json(tutor))
}

pub async fn delete_tutor(
    app_state: web::Data<AppState>,
    web::Path(tutor_id): web::Path<i32>,
) -> Result<HttpResponse, EzyTutorError> {
    delete_tutor_db(&app_state.db, tutor_id)
        .await
        .map(|tutor| HttpResponse::Ok().json(tutor))
}
```

These three functions are similar to the ones for courses. The functional syntax of Rust makes the code crisp and pleasant to read.

As an exercise, you can write the test cases for these handler methods. Refer back to the test cases for courses if you have any doubts. Also, the test cases are available as part of the Git repo for the chapter.

Next, we'll address the database access layer.

6.3.3   *Database access functions for tutor routes*

We'll now look at the database access functions for tutors. These should be placed in the \$PROJECT_ROOT/src/iter5/dbaccess/tutor.rs file.

Here is the database access function to get the list of tutors, along with the module imports:

```
use crate::errors::EzyTutorError;
use crate::models::tutor::{NewTutor, Tutor, UpdateTutor};
use sqlx::postgres::PgPool;

pub async fn get_all_tutors_db(pool: &PgPool) ->
➥Result<Vec<Tutor>, EzyTutorError> {
    // Prepare SQL statement
    let tutor_rows =
        sqlx::query!("SELECT tutor_id, tutor_name, tutor_pic_url,
        ➥tutor_profile FROM ezy_tutor_c6")
            .fetch_all(pool)
            .await?;
    // Extract result

    let tutors: Vec<Tutor> = tutor_rows
        .iter()
        .map(|tutor_row| Tutor {
            tutor_id: tutor_row.tutor_id,
            tutor_name: tutor_row.tutor_name.clone(),
            tutor_pic_url: tutor_row.tutor_pic_url.clone(),
            tutor_profile: tutor_row.tutor_profile.clone(),
        })
        .collect();
    match tutors.len() {
        0 => Err(EzyTutorError::NotFound("No tutors found".into())),
        _ => Ok(tutors),
    }
}
```

Note that we're not using the `query_as!` macro to map the retrieved database records into the `Tutor` struct. Instead, we are manually performing this mapping within the `map` method. You may wonder why we are taking this more tedious approach, compared to having the mapping automatically done by `sqlx` using the `query_as!` macro. There are two main reasons for this:

- The `query_as!` macro works as long as the field names in the struct match the database column names. However, there may be situations where this may not be feasible.

- You may have additional fields in the struct compared to the database columns. For example, you may want to have a derived or computed field, or you may want a Rust struct to represent a tutor along with the list of their courses. In such cases, you'll need to know how to perform this database-to-struct mapping manually. We are taking this approach as a learning exercise, as it is always useful to have a wider repertoire of tools.

Here is the database function to retrieve details for an individual tutor:

```
pub async fn get_tutor_details_db(pool: &PgPool, tutor_id: i32) ->
➥Result<Tutor, EzyTutorError> {
    // Prepare SQL statement
    let tutor_row = sqlx::query!(
        "SELECT tutor_id, tutor_name, tutor_pic_url,
        ➥tutor_profile FROM ezy_tutor_c6 where tutor_id = $1",
        tutor_id
    )
    .fetch_one(pool)
    .await
    .map(|tutor_row|
        Tutor {
            tutor_id: tutor_row.tutor_id,
            tutor_name: tutor_row.tutor_name,
            tutor_pic_url: tutor_row.tutor_pic_url,
            tutor_profile: tutor_row.tutor_profile,
        }
    )
    .map_err(|_err| EzyTutorError::NotFound("Tutor id not found".into()))?;

Ok(tutor_row)

}
```

Note the use of `map_err` here. If no record is found in the database, a `sqlx` error is returned, which we are converting to an `EzyTutorError` type using `map_err` before propagating the error back to the calling handler function using the `?` operator.

Here is the function to post a new tutor:

```
pub async fn post_new_tutor_db(pool: &PgPool, new_tutor: NewTutor) ->
➥Result<Tutor, EzyTutorError> {
    let tutor_row = sqlx::query!("insert into ezy_tutor_c6 (
    ➥tutor_name, tutor_pic_url, tutor_profile) values ($1,$2,$3)
    ➥returning tutor_id, tutor_name, tutor_pic_url, tutor_profile",
    ➥new_tutor.tutor_name, new_tutor.tutor_pic_url,
    ➥new_tutor.tutor_profile)
    .fetch_one(pool)
    .await?;
    //Retrieve result
    Ok(Tutor {
        tutor_id: tutor_row.tutor_id,
        tutor_name: tutor_row.tutor_name,
        tutor_pic_url: tutor_row.tutor_pic_url,
```

```
            tutor_profile: tutor_row.tutor_profile,
    })
}
```

Here we're constructing a query to insert a new tutor record in the `ezy_tutor_c6` table. Then we're fetching the inserted row and mapping it to the Rust tutor struct, which is returned to the handler function.

The code for updating and deleting a tutor is not shown here. I suggest you write it as an exercise. The complete code is available in the code repo for this chapter, which you can refer to if necessary.

6.3.4 *Database scripts for tutors*

We're done with the application logic for the APIs. We now have to create a new table in the database for tutors before we can compile this code. `sqlx` performs compile-time checking of database table names and columns, so the compilation will fail if any of these don't exist or if the table description does not match the SQL statements.

Place the following database script under $PROJECT_ROOT/src/iter5/dbscripts/tutor-course.sql:

```
/* Drop tables if they already exist*/

drop table if exists ezy_course_c6 cascade;      ⟵┐  Delete old versions of the tables.
drop table if exists ezy_tutor_c6;                   This is convenient in the
                                                     development cycle, but if the
/* Create tables. */                                 database is in production, the tables
                                         ┌─ Create the   will have to be migrated to a new
create table ezy_tutor_c6 (      ⟵──┘   tutor table.  schema to protect any existing data.
    tutor_id serial primary key,
    tutor_name varchar(200) not null,
    tutor_pic_url varchar(200) not null,
    tutor_profile varchar(2000) not null
);
                                         ┌─ Create the
create table ezy_course_c6       ⟵──┘   course table.
(
    course_id serial primary key,
    tutor_id INT not null,
    course_name varchar(140) not null,
    course_description varchar(2000),
    course_format varchar(30),
    course_structure varchar(200),
    course_duration varchar(30),
    course_price INT,
    course_language varchar(30),
    course_level varchar(30),
    posted_time TIMESTAMP default now(),
    CONSTRAINT fk_tutor                   Mark the tutor_id column of
    FOREIGN KEY(tutor_id)                 ezy_course_c6 as a foreign key of the
        REFERENCES ezy_tutor_c6(tutor_id) tutor_id column in the ezy_tutor_c6 table.
    ON DELETE cascade
);
```

Grant privileges to the database user for the newly
created tables. Replace <user-name> with your own.

```
grant all privileges on table ezy_tutor_c6 to <username>;
grant all privileges on table ezy_course_c6 to <username>;
grant all privileges on all sequences in schema public to <username>;;

/* Load seed data for testing */
insert into ezy_tutor_c6(tutor_id, tutor_name, tutor_pic_url,tutor_profile)
values(1,'Merlene','http://s3.amazon.aws.com/pic1',
'Merlene is an experienced finance professional');

insert into ezy_tutor_c6(tutor_id, tutor_name, tutor_pic_url,tutor_profile)
values(2,'Frank','http://s3.amazon.aws.com/pic2',
'Frank is an expert nuclear engineer');

insert into ezy_course_c6
    (course_id,tutor_id, course_name,course_level, posted_time)
values(1, 1, 'First course', 'Beginner' , '2021-04-12 05:40:00');
insert into ezy_course_c6
    (course_id, tutor_id, course_name, course_format, posted_time)
values(2, 1, 'Second course', 'ebook', '2021-04-12 05:45:00');
```

Load seed data for testing
the HTTP::GET based APIs.

6.3.5   *Run and test the tutor APIs*

Run the following command from the command line to execute the database script:

```
psql -U <user-name> -d ezytutors < <path.to.file>/tutor-course.sql
```

Replace <user-name> and <path.to-file> with your own values, and enter the password when prompted. You should see the scripts execute successfully. To verify that the tables have indeed been created according to the script specification, log in to the psql shell:

```
psql -U <user-name> -d ezytutors
\d
\d+ ezy_tutor_c6
\d+ ezy_course_c6
\q
```

Display the list of
relations (tables).

Display column names in the table.

Quit the
psql shell.

Compile the program to check for errors. After resolving any errors, build and run the web server with these commands:

```
cargo check
cargo run --bin iter5
```

You can then run the automated tests:

```
cargo test
```

Before running the test scripts, ensure the data being queried for in the test cases is present in the database, or prepare the data appropriately.

You can also manually execute the tutor-related CRUD APIs from curl as follows:

```
curl -X POST localhost:3000/tutors/ -H "Content-Type: application/json"
➥-d '{ "tutor_name":"Jessica", "tutor_pic_url":
➥"http://tutor1.com/tutor1.pic", "tutor_profile":        Create a new
➥"Experienced professional"}'                        ◄── tutor record.
```

```
curl -X PUT localhost:3000/tutors/8 -H "Content-Type: application/json"
➥-d '{"tutor_name":"James", "tutor_pic_url":"http://james.com/pic",
➥"tutor_profile":"Expert in thermodynamics"}'    ◄──┐ Update a tutor record for
                                                     │ tutor-id=8 (assuming this
curl -X DELETE http://localhost0/tutors/8   ◄──────┐ │ exists in the database).
                                                   │ │
              Delete the tutor with tutor-id=8 ────┘
              (assuming this exists in the database).
```

From a browser, you can execute the HTTP::GET APIs as follows:

```
http://localhost:3000/tutors/      ◄─────────┐  Retrieve the list of all
http://localhost:3000/tutors/2  ◄──┐         │  tutors in the database.
                                   │ Retrieve the details
                                   │ for tutor-id 2.
```

As an exercise, you can also try deleting a tutor for which course records exist. You should receive an error message. This is because courses and tutors are linked by a foreign-key constraint in the database. Once you delete all courses for a `tutor-id`, that tutor can be deleted from the database.

Another exercise you can try is to provide invalid JSON as part of creating or updating a tutor or course (for example, remove a double quote or a curly brace from the JSON data for creating or updating a tutor). You'll find that neither does the command get executed on the server nor do you get any error message stating that the JSON is invalid. This is not user-friendly. To fix this, let's make a few changes.

In the ezytutors/tutor-db/src/iter5/errors.rs file, add a new `Invalid-Input(String)` entry in the `EzyTutorError` enum, which will then look like this:

```
#[derive(Debug, Serialize)]
pub enum EzyTutorError {
    DBError(String),
    ActixError(String),
    NotFound(String),
    InvalidInput(String),
}
```

`InvalidInput(String)` denotes that the `EzytutorError` enum can take a new invariant, `InvalidInput`, that in turn can accept a `string` value as a parameter. For all errors arising from invalid parameters sent by the API client, we'll use this new variant.

Also, in the same errors.rs file, make the following additional changes, required by the addition of the new enum variant. First, in the `error_response()` function, add code to deal with the `EzyTutorError::InvalidInput` type:

```
fn error_response(&self) -> String {
    match self {
        EzyTutorError::DBError(msg) => {
            println!("Database error occurred: {:?}", msg);
            "Database error".into()
```

```
        }
        EzyTutorError::ActixError(msg) => {
            println!("Server error occurred: {:?}", msg);
            "Internal server error".into()
        }
        EzyTutorError::NotFound(msg) => {
            println!("Not found error occurred: {:?}", msg);
            msg.into()
        }
        EzyTutorError::InvalidInput(msg) => {
            println!("Invalid parameters received: {:?}", msg);
            msg.into()
        }
    }
}
```

In the `ResponseError` trait implementation, add code to deal with the new enum variant:

```
fn status_code(&self) -> StatusCode {
    match self {
        EzyTutorError::DBError(_msg) | EzyTutorError::ActixError(_msg) => {
            StatusCode::INTERNAL_SERVER_ERROR
        }
        EzyTutorError::InvalidInput(_msg) => StatusCode::BAD_REQUEST,
        EzyTutorError::NotFound(_msg) => StatusCode::NOT_FOUND,
    }
}
```

We're now ready to make use of this new error variant in our code. Add the following code in $PROJECT_ROOT/src/bin/iter5.rs, while creating an Actix app instance, to raise an error if the JSON data received at the server is invalid:

```
let app = move || {
  App::new()
    .app_data(shared_data.clone())
    .app_data(web::JsonConfig::default().error_handler(|_err, _req| {
      EzyTutorError::InvalidInput(
      ➥"Please provide valid Json input".to_string()).into()
  }))
    .configure(general_routes)
    .configure(course_routes)
    .configure(tutor_routes)
};
```

Now, whenever you provide invalid JSON data, you'll receive the specified error message.

With that, we'll conclude this chapter on refactoring code in Rust and Actix Web and adding functionality while you, as the developer, retain complete control over the entire process. For refactoring, there isn't a specific sequence of steps that can be prescribed, but it generally helps to start from the outside (the user interface), and work your way through the various layers of the application. For example, if some new information is requested from the web service, start by defining the new route, define the handler function, and then define the data model and database access function. If this necessitates changes to the database schema, modify the database creation and update scripts along with any associated migration scripts. The database access functions provide a layer of abstraction if you need to switch to a different database as part of your refactoring.

Our tutor web service is now more complex and aligned to the real world, rather than being just an academic example. It has two types of entities (tutors and courses) that have a defined relationship between them at the database level, and eleven API endpoints. It can handle five broad classes of errors: database-related errors, Actix-related errors, bad user-input parameters, requests on resources that do not exist (not found errors), and badly formatted JSON in input requests. It can seamlessly process concurrent requests, as it uses async calls both in the Actix layer and database access layer without any bottlenecks. The project code is well organized, which will enable further evolution of the web service over time, and more importantly, it will be easily understandable as newer developers take charge of the existing codebase. The project code and configuration are separated by using the .env file, which contains database access credentials and other such config information. Dependency injection is built into the project through application state (in the state.rs file), which serves as a placeholder in which we can add any dependencies that need to be propagated to the various handler functions. The project itself does not use too many external crates and eschews shortcuts and magical crates (such as crates that automate code generation for error handling or database functions). However, you are encouraged to experiment with other third-party crates now that you have the foundational knowledge of doing things the hard way.

You'll observe that, throughout this process, the Rust compiler has been a great friend and guide to help you achieve your goals. Your next best friend will be the automated test scripts, which will help to ensure there is no regression of functionality.

If you have been able to follow this chapter successfully, I applaud your perseverance. I hope this chapter has given you the confidence to fearlessly enhance any Rust web codebase, even if you were not the original author of the code.

With this, we also conclude the first part of the book, which focused on developing a web service using Rust. We will revisit a few related topics in the last part of the book when we discuss how to prepare web services and applications for production deployment.

In the next part of the book, we'll move on to the client side, where we'll discuss how to develop server-rendered web frontends using Rust and Actix Web.

Summary

- In this chapter, we enhanced the data model for courses, added more course API routes, and evolved the code for handlers and database access along with the test cases.
- We also added functionality to allow for the creation, updating, deletion, and querying of tutor records. We created a database model and scripts to store

tutor data, and we defined the relationship between tutors and courses with foreign-key constraints. We created new routes for tutor-related CRUD APIs and wrote the handler functions, database access code, and test cases.

- In the handler code, you saw how to create separate data structures for the creation and updating of tutor and course data, as well as how to use the `From` and `TryFrom` traits to write functions for converting between data types. You also saw how to mark fields in data structures as optional using the `Option<T>` type and how to map this to the corresponding column definitions in the database.

- In the database code, we used the `query_as!` macro to simplify and reduce boilerplate code by auto-deriving `sqlx::FromRow` for the `Course` struct, where the mapping between database columns and the fields of the `Course` struct is defined. We also performed this mapping from database records to Rust structs manually, which is useful when using the `query_as!` macro is not possible or desirable.

- We wrote code in the handler and database access layers in a concise but highly readable manner using Rust's functional constructs.

- We explored error-handling concepts, revisiting the entire error-management workflow and fine-tuning the error handling to make the user experience more interactive and meaningful.

- We restructured the project code's organization to better support projects as they get larger and more complex, with separate and clearly marked areas for code for handlers, database access functions, data models, and database scripts. We also separated the source files that contain tutor- and course-related functionality by organizing them into Rust modules.

- We looked at testing code using automated test scripts that can automatically handle both success and error conditions. We also tested the API scenarios using both curl commands and commands from the browser.

Part 2

Server-side web applications

Part 1 focused on the business logic of our web application. It set the foundations on which a user-friendly user interface (UI) can be built. In line with best practices, the various concerns were separated: HTTP processing, route definitions, application logic, and database logic.

In this part, we will tackle the interaction with users. In a web application, this interaction takes place in the user's browser, using the combined power of HTML, CSS, and JavaScript (or TypeScript). There are currently several ways to implement a web user interface.

At one end of the spectrum are the popular single-page application (SPA) frameworks, like React, Angular, and Vue. Such frameworks provide for a very rich user experience (UX)—in many cases as rich as the ones provided by desktop applications. At the other end of the spectrum, there is server-side rendering. In a typical SPA, the UI is built dynamically in the browser as the user starts to interact with the application. With server-side rendering, the UI's HTML pages are delivered "fully baked" by the server. This does not mean that these pages cannot exhibit some dynamic behavior (such as showing or hiding sections), but each page's structure is defined on the server and does not change in the browser. Both SPAs and server-side rendering have their pros and cons. In this book, we'll use server-side rendering based on templates because that is the most straightforward path for a Rust-exclusive approach.

Once you have completed part 2, you will have gained a solid foundation for developing web application UIs using server-side rendering. You will also have gained more insight into the merits of server-side rendering as an approach to web application development.

7
Introducing server-side web apps in Rust

This chapter covers

- Serving a static web page with Actix
- Rendering a dynamic web page with Actix and Tera
- Adding user input with forms
- Displaying a list with templates
- Writing and running client-side tests
- Connecting to the backend web service

In chapters 3 to 6 of the book, we built the tutor web service from scratch using Rust and the Actix Web framework. In this section, we'll focus on learning the basics of building a web application in Rust. It may sound strange to use a system programming language to create a web application, but that's the power of Rust. It can straddle the worlds of system and application programming with ease.

In this chapter, you will be introduced to concepts and tools you can use with Rust to build web applications. At this point, it is important to recall that there are two broad techniques for building web applications—*server-side rendering* (SSR) and *single-page application* (SPA)—each possibly taking the form of a *progressive web*

169

application (PWA). In this section, we'll focus on the former technique, and in later chapters, we'll cover the latter. We will not cover PWAs in this book.

More specifically, our focus for chapters 7 to 9 is to learn how develop a simple web application that can be used to register and log in to a web application, view lists and detail views, and perform standard CRUD (create, read, update, and delete) operations on data using web-based forms. Along the way, you will learn how to render dynamic web pages using the Actix Web framework along with a template engine. While we can use any Rust web framework to achieve the same goal (Actix Web, Rocket, or Warp, to name a few), staying with Actix Web will help us use what you've learned in previous chapters.

7.1   *Introducing server-side rendering*

SSR is a web development technique where web pages are rendered on the server and then sent to the client (such as a web browser). In this approach, a web application running on the server combines static HTML pages (such as those from a web designer) with data (fetched from a database or from other web services) and sends a fully rendered web page to the user's browser for display. Web applications that use such a technique are called *server-rendered* or *server-side* web apps. With this approach, websites load faster, and the web page content reflects the latest data, as every request typically involves fetching the latest copy of the user data (an exception is when caching techniques are adopted on the server). To keep such data specific to the user, websites either require users to log in to identify themselves, or they use cookies to personalize the content for a user.

Web pages can either be *static* or *dynamic*:

- An example of a *static* web page is the home page of your bank's website, which typically serves as a marketing tool for the bank and also provides useful links to the bank's services. This page is the same for whoever accesses the bank's home page. In this sense, it is a static web page.
- A *dynamic* web page is what you see when you log in to your bank with your authorized credentials (such as a username and password) and view your account balances and statements. This page is dynamic in the sense that each customer views their own balance, but the page may also contain static components, such as the bank's logo and other common styling (such as colors, fonts, layout, etc.), which are shown to all customers viewing account balances.

We know how to create a static web page. A web designer can do this either by writing the HTML and CSS scripts by hand or by using one of the many available tools for this purpose. But how does one convert a *static* web page to a *dynamic* web page? This is where a *template engine* comes in. (Figure 7.1 shows the various components that go into rendering a dynamic web page.)

A *template engine* is one of the primary tools for converting a static web page into a dynamic web page. It expects a *template* file as input and generates an HTML file as output. In the process, it embeds data (passed to it by the web application) into the

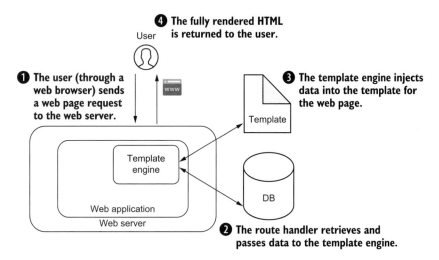

Figure 7.1 Server-side rendering of web pages

template file to generate an HTML file. This process is dynamic in two ways: the data is loaded on demand, and the data is tailored to the individual user requesting the data.

In this chapter, we'll explore SSR with Rust by writing some example code. If a picture is worth a thousand words, a few lines of code are worth several times that. We will look at small snippets of code and see how the various pieces fit together to construct a web application. In the next chapter, we will actually design and build the *tutor web application*.

Here is a outline of the examples we will be building in this chapter. These examples represent the most common tasks in any web application where users can view and maintain data from a browser-based user interface:

- Section 7.2 will show you how to serve static web pages with Actix Web.
- Section 7.3 will cover the generation of dynamic web pages using Tera, a popular template engine in the web development world.
- In section 7.4, you'll learn to capture user input with an HTML form.
- Section 7.5 will display lists of information using Tera HTML templates.
- You learned earlier how to write automated tests for the server-side web service, and in section 7.6, you'll learn to write client-side tests.
- Section 7.7 will connect the frontend web application with the backend web service using an HTTP client.

To develop server-side web apps in Rust, we will use the following tools and components:

- *Actix web server*—This will host a web application running at a specific port on the server, and it will route requests to the handler functions provided by the web application.

- *A web application*—This will serve content in response to requests from a browser. It will be written in Rust and deployed on the Actix web server. It will contain the core handler logic that knows how to respond to various types of HTTP requests.
- *Tera*—This is a template engine that's popular in the Python world, and it has been ported to Rust.
- *Our backend tutor web service*—This is the tutor web service we developed in the previous chapters. It will fetch data from the database and manage database interactions. The web application will talk to the tutor web service to retrieve data and perform transactions, rather than deal with the database itself.
- *A built-in HTTP client from the Actix Web framework*—This will talk to the tutor web service.

With this background, let's get to our first example.

7.2   *Serving a static web page with Actix*

In the previous chapters, we used the Actix web server to host our tutor web service. In this section, we'll use Actix to serve a static web page. Consider this the "Hello World" program for web application development.

Let's first set up the project structure:

1 Make a copy of the `ezytutors` workspace repo from chapter 6 to work with in this chapter.
2 Create a new Rust cargo project with `cargo new tutor-web-app-ssr`
3 Rename the tutor-db folder under the `ezytutors` workspace to tutor-web-service. This way, the two repos under the workspace can be referred to unambiguously as "web service" and "web app".
4 In the Cargo.toml file of the workspace folder, edit the workspace section to look like this:

```
[workspace]
members = ["tutor-web-service","tutor-web-app-ssr"]
```

We now have two projects in the workspace: one for the tutor web service (which we developed earlier) and another for the tutor web app, which is rendered on the server side (and which we have yet to develop).

5 Switch to the tutor-web-app-ssr folder: `cd tutor-web-app-ssr`. That's where we'll write the code for this section. Henceforth, let's refer to this folder as the project root folder. To avoid confusion, set this as an environment variable in each of the terminal sessions you will be working with for this project, as shown here:

```
export $PROJECT_ROOT=.
```

6 Update Cargo.toml to add the following dependencies:

```
[dependencies]
actix-web = "4.2.1"
actix-files="0.6.2"
```

actix-web is the core Actix Web framework, and actix-files helps in serving static files from the web server.

7 Create a folder named static under $PROJECT_ROOT. Create a static-web-page.html file under $PROJECT_ROOT/static with the following HTML code:

```
<!DOCTYPE html>
<html>
<head>
  <title>XYZ Bank Website</title>
</head>
<body>
  <h1>Welcome to XYZ bank home page!</h1>
  <p>This is an example of a static web page served from Actix
  ➥Web server.</p>
</body>
</html>
```

This is a simple static web page. You'll see how to serve this page with the Actix server.

8 Create a bin folder under $PROJECT_ROOT/src. Create a new source file, static.rs, under $PROJECT_ROOT/src/bin, and add the following code:

```
                                    Import actix_files, which provides a
                                    service to serve static files from a disk.
use actix_files as fs;      ◁──┘
use actix_web::{error, web, App, Error, HttpResponse, HttpServer, Result};

#[actix_web::main]                              The main function
async fn main() -> std::io::Result<()> {  ◁──── returns a Result type.
    let addr = env::var("SERVER_ADDR").unwrap_or_else(|_|
    ➥"127.0.0.1:8080".to_string());
    println!("Listening on: {}, open browser and visit have a try!",addr);
    HttpServer::new(|| {
        App::new().service(fs::Files::new(
        ➥"/static", "./static").show_files_listing())      ◁──────┐
    })
    .bind(addr)?    │ Run the
    .run()   ◁──────┘ web server.
    .await   ◁─────┐
}               The await keyword triggers an async
                operation and keeps polling until a
                future is successfully completed.
```

The web server binds to a port. [pointing to .bind(addr)?]

Register the actix_files service with the web application. show_files_listing() allows subdirectory listings to be shown to users.

The Result type is needed as a return value of the main() function because any function that uses a ? operator within its code to propagate errors must return a Result type. The return value of Result<()> indicates that successful execution returns a unit type, (); in the case of errors, an Error type is returned.

Also note in the preceding code that the route /static indicates that resource requests starting with the /static route have to be served from the ./static subfolder in the project root folder.

In summary, the preceding program creates a new web application and registers a service with the application. The service serves files from the filesystem (on disk) when a GET request on a route starting with /static is made to the web server. The web application is then deployed on the web server, and the web server is started:

1   Run the web server with cargo run --bin static.
2   From a browser, visit the following URL:

    http://localhost:8080/static/static-web-page.html

You should see the web page appear in your browser.

Let's try to understand what we just did. We wrote a program to serve a static web page from an Actix web server. When we requested a particular static file, the actix_files service looked for it within the /static folder and returned it to the browser, and it was then displayed to the user.

This is an example of a static page because the content of this page does not change depending on which user requests this page. In the next section, we'll look at how to build dynamic web pages with Actix.

7.3   Rendering a dynamic web page with Actix and Tera

What if we want to show custom content for each user? How would you write an HTML page that presents content dynamically? Displaying a dynamic web page does not mean *everything* in the page changes for every user, but that the web page has both static and dynamic parts to it.

Figure 7.1 showed a generic view of SSR, but figure 7.2 shows how dynamic web pages can be implemented using Actix Web and the Tera template engine. The figure shows a local database as the source of data for the dynamic web page, but it is also possible to retrieve data from an external web service. In fact, that is the design approach that we will use in this book.

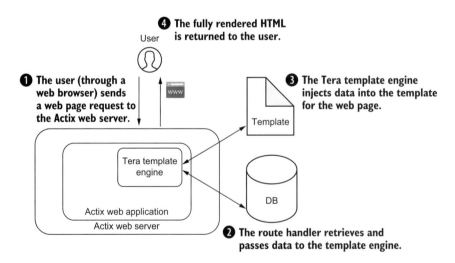

Figure 7.2   Dynamic web pages with Actix and Tera

We will define the HTML file in a specific Tera template format—a simple example is shown here. Add this to $PROJECT_ROOT/static/iter1/index.html:

```
<!DOCTYPE html>
<html>

<head>
    <title>XYZ Bank Website</title>
</head>

<body>
  <h1>Welcome {{ name }}, to XYZ bank home page!</h1>
  <p>This is an example of a dynamic web page served with Actix and
  Tera templates.</p>
</body>
</html>
```

Note the use of the {{name}} tag. At runtime, when the web page is requested by the browser, Tera replaces this tag with the actual name of the user. Tera can retrieve this value from wherever you want it to—from a file, a database, or hardcoded values.

> **NOTE** For more details on the Tera template format, see the Tera documentation: https://tera.netlify.app/docs/.

Let's modify the program we wrote earlier to cater to dynamic web page requests using Tera. In $PROJECT_ROOT/Cargo.toml, add the following dependencies:

```
tera = "1.17.0"
serde = { version = "1.0.144", features = ["derive"] }
```

We're adding the tera crate for templating support and the serde crate to enable custom data structures to be serialized and deserialized between the web browser and web server.

In $PROJECT_ROOT/src/bin, copy the contents of the static.rs file we wrote earlier into a new file called iter1.rs, and modify the code to look like this:

```
use tera::Tera;

#[actix_web::main]
async fn main() -> std::io::Result<()> {

    println!("Listening on: 127.0.0.1:8080, open browser and visit
    have a try!");
    HttpServer::new(|| {
        let tera = Tera::new(concat!(        ⟵┐  Create a new Tera instance. The Tera
            env!("CARGO_MANIFEST_DIR"),          templates are under the /static/iter1/ folder
            "/static/iter1/**/*"                 where we earlier placed the index.html file
        ))                                       containing the Tera {{name}} tag.
        .unwrap();
                                    ┌─ Inject the Tera instance as a dependency
        App::new()                  │  into the application. This will allow Tera to
            .data(tera)    ⟵────────┘  be accessed within all route handlers.       ┌─ Serve static
            .service(fs::Files::new(                                                │  files from the
            "/static", "./static").show_files_listing())   ⟵─────────────────────────┘  /static route.
```

```
        .service(web::resource("/").route(web::get().to(index)))    ◄────┐
    })                                                                     │
    .bind("127.0.0.1:8080")?                                              │
    .run()                                                                 │
    .await                                                                 │
}
```

> **Serve a dynamic web page from the / route, which invokes the index handler.**

Let's now write the `index` handler:

> **Access the Tera instance as part of the arguments passed to the index handler. Create a new Tera Context object, which will be used to inject data into the web page.**

> **In the index handler, assign a value to the name variable.**

```
async fn index(tmpl: web::Data<tera::Tera>) -> Result<HttpResponse, Error> {
    let mut ctx = tera::Context::new();                              ◄────┐
    ctx.insert("name", "Bob");                                            │
    let s = tmpl
        .render("index.html", &ctx)    ◄──┐ Invoke Tera's web page rendering
        .map_err(|_| error::ErrorInternalServerError("Template error"))?;

    Ok(HttpResponse::Ok().content_type("text/html").body(s))    ◄──────┐
}
```

> **Invoke Tera's web page rendering function, passing the context object.**

> **Return an HTTP response from the index handler function, passing the constructed dynamic web page as part of the HTTP response body.**

Run the server with `cargo run --bin iter1`. Then, from a web browser, access the following URL:

```
http://localhost:8080/
```

You should see the following message displayed on the web page:

```
Welcome Bob, to XYZ bank home page!
```

This is a trivial example, but it serves to illustrate how dynamic web pages can be constructed using Actix. Tera has a lot of features that can be used in templates, including control statements, such as `if` and `for` loops, which you can explore at leisure.

So far, we've seen how to render both static and dynamic HTML pages, but the examples have dealt with displaying information to a user. Does Actix also support writing HTML pages that accept user input? You'll find out in the next section.

7.4   Adding user input with forms

In this section, we'll create a web page that accepts user input through a form. This form is as simple as it can get.

Create a $PROJECT_ROOT/static/iter2 folder, and place the following HTML in a new form.html file in this folder. This HTML code contains a form that accepts a tutor name, and then it submits a POST request, containing the tutor name, to the Actix web server:

```
<!doctype html>
<html>

<head>
    <meta charset=utf-8>
```

```
    <title>Forms with Actix & Rust</title>
</head>

<body>
    <h3>Enter name of tutor</h3>
    <form action=/tutors method=POST>
        <label>
            Tutor name:
            <input name="name">
        </label>
        <button type=submit>Submit form</button>
    </form>

    <hr>
</html>
```

Note the `<input>` HTML element that is used to accept user input for a tutor name. The `<button>` tag is used to submit the form to the web server. This form is encapsulated in an HTTP POST request sent to the web server on the route `/tutors`, which is specified in the `<form action="">` attribute.

Let's create a second HTML file under the $PROJECT_ROOT/static/iter2 folder called user.html. This will display the name submitted by the user in the previous form:

```
<!DOCTYPE html>
<html>

<head>
    <meta charset="utf-8" />
    <title>Actix web</title>
</head>

<body>
    <h1>Hi, {{ name }}!</h1>
    <p>
        {{ text }}
    </p>
</body>

</html>
```

This HTML file has a template variable, `{{name}}`. When this page is shown to the user, the value of the `{{name}}` template variable is replaced with the actual tutor name that was entered by the user in the previous form.

Let's now add the route and a handler to deal with this POST request. In $PROJECT_ROOT/src/bin, create a new iter2.rs file, and add the following code to it:

```
... // imports removed for concision; see full source code from GitHub

// store tera template in application state
async fn index(                          ◁————————
    tmpl: web::Data<tera::Tera>
) -> Result<HttpResponse, Error> {
```

> The Index handler function is invoked for HTTP requests coming on route /. This shows the form where the user can enter a tutor name.

Render the form.html file with a new Tera Context object.
We are not inserting any data into the context because the
form.html file does not have any template variables.

```
    let s = tmpl
        .render("form.html", &tera::Context::new())
        .map_err(|_| error::ErrorInternalServerError("Template error"))?;

    Ok(HttpResponse::Ok().content_type("text/html").body(s))
}

#[derive(Serialize, Deserialize)]
pub struct Tutor {
    name: String,
}
```

The Tutor serializable struct represents the data
to be captured in the form. This is a custom data
structure, and you can define it any way you
want. We just define a tutor name in the struct.

```
async fn handle_post_tutor(
    tmpl: web::Data<tera::Tera>,
    params: web::Form<Tutor>,
) -> Result<HttpResponse, Error> {
    let mut ctx = tera::Context::new();
    ctx.insert("name", &params.name);
    ctx.insert("text", "Welcome!");
    let s = tmpl
        .render("user.html", &ctx)
        .map_err(|_| error::ErrorInternalServerError("Template error"))?;

    Ok(HttpResponse::Ok().content_type("text/html").body(s))
}
```

This second handler function is invoked
when the user enters the tutor name
and presses the Submit Form button.

The form data (tutor name) submitted by
the user is made available to this handler
function by Actix in the web::Form<T>
extractor; T is the Tutor struct in this case.

```
#[actix_web::main]
async fn main() -> std::io::Result<()> {

    println!("Listening on: 127.0.0.1:8080");
    HttpServer::new(|| {
        let tera = Tera::new(concat!(
            env!("CARGO_MANIFEST_DIR"),
            "/static/iter2/**/*"
        ))
        .unwrap();

        App::new()
            .data(tera)
            .configure(app_config)
    })
    .bind("127.0.0.1:8080")?
    .run()
    .await
}

fn app_config(config: &mut web::ServiceConfig) {
    config.service(
        web::scope("")
            .service(web::resource("/").route(web::get().to(index)))
            .service(web::resource("/tutors").route(web::post().to(
            ➡handle_post_tutor)))
    );
}
```

The main function to
set up and run an
Actix web server

The Tera template is injected into the
web application and made available as a
parameter to the web handler functions.

Web application routes
aggregated into an app_config
object. This is another way of
organizing routes.

We used an Actix extractor in the preceding code. Extractors are utility functions that let handler functions extract the parameters sent with the HTTP request. Recall that earlier we defined an input field called `name` in the form.html template. When the user fills out the form and presses the Submit Form button, an HTTP POST request that contains the value entered by the user is generated by the browser. The value for this `name` parameter is accessible to the handler function using the Actix extractor `web::Form<T>`.

To recap, in the preceding code, when a user visits the / route, form.html is displayed, which contains a form. When the user enters a name in the form and presses the Submit Form button, a POST request is generated on the route /tutors, which invokes a `handle_post_tutor` handler function. In this handler, the name entered by the user is accessible through the `web::Form` extractor. The handler injects this name into a new Tera `Context` object. The Tera `render` function is then invoked with the context object to show the user.html page to the user.

Run the web server with this command:

```
cargo run --bin iter2
```

Access this URL from a browser:

```
http://localhost:8080/
```

You should first see the form displayed. Enter a name, and click the Submit Form button. You should see the second HTML page displayed, containing the name you entered.

That concludes this section on accepting user input and processing it. In the next section, we'll cover another common feature of the template engine—the ability to display lists.

7.5   *Displaying a list with templates*

In this section, we'll display a list of data elements dynamically on a web page. In the tutor web app, one of the things a user will want to see is a list of tutors or courses. This list is dynamic because the user may want to see a list of all tutors in the system or a subset of tutors based on some criteria. Likewise, the user may want to see a listing of all courses available on the site or the courses for a particular tutor. How can we use Actix and Tera to show such information? Let's find out.

Create an iter3 folder under $PROJECT_ROOT/static. Create a new list.html file here, and add the following HTML:

```
<!DOCTYPE html>
<html>

<head>
    <meta charset="utf-8" />
    <title>Actix web</title>
</head>
```

```
<body>
    <h1>Tutors list</h1>
    <ol>
        {% for tutor in tutors %}
        <li>
                <h5>{{tutor.name}}</h5>
        </li>
        {% endfor %}
    </ol>
</body>

</html>
```

Display an ordered list.

Display the name of the tutor.

Display each tutor as an HTML list item.

End of for loop block

A Tera template control statement using a for loop to go through each item in the list of tutors. The tutors object containing a list of tutors will be passed into the template by the handler function.

The preceding code includes an example of a Tera template control statement using a for loop. The tutors object containing a list of tutors will be passed into the template by the handler function. This template control statement loops through each item in the list of tutors and performs some actions. See the Tera documentation for a list of other template control statements: https://tera.netlify.app/docs/#control-structures.

We have now written an HTML file that contains a template control statement (using a for loop) that loops through each tutor in a list and displays the tutor name on the web page. Next, let's write the handler function to implement this logic, as well as the main function for the web server.

Create a new iter3.rs file under $PROJECT_ROOT/src/bin, and add the following code:

```
use actix_files as fs;
use actix_web::{error, web, App, Error, HttpResponse, HttpServer, Result};
use serde::{Deserialize, Serialize};
use tera::Tera;

#[derive(Serialize, Deserialize)]
pub struct Tutor {
    name: String,
}

async fn handle_get_tutors(tmpl: web::Data<tera::Tera>) ->
    Result<HttpResponse, Error> {
    let tutors: Vec<Tutor> = vec![
        Tutor {
            name: String::from("Tutor 1"),
        },
        ...
    ];
    let mut ctx = tera::Context::new();
    ctx.insert("tutors", &tutors);
    let rendered_html = tmpl
        .render("list.html", &ctx)
        .map_err(|_| error::ErrorInternalServerError("Template error"))?;

    Ok(HttpResponse::Ok().content_type("text/html").body(rendered_html))
}

#[actix_web::main]
async fn main() -> std::io::Result<()> {
```

Create a serializable custom data struct to define the structure of the tutor data. The tutor struct will contain only the tutor name for simplicity.

The handle_get_tutors handler function will be called when an HTTP GET request is made on the route /tutors.

Load a list of tutors as mock data (hardcoded for convenience).

Create a new Tera Context object.

Abridged source code for concision—see the GitHub source for the unabridged version.

Inject the tutors list into the Tera Context

Render list.html along with the Context object containing the mock tutor data.

```
        println!("Listening on: 127.0.0.1:8080");
        HttpServer::new(|| {
            let tera = Tera::new(concat!(
                env!("CARGO_MANIFEST_DIR"),
                "/static/iter3/**/*"
            ))
            .unwrap();

            App::new()
                .data(tera)
                .service(fs::Files::new(
                ➥"/static", "./static").show_files_listing())
                .service(web::resource("/tutors").route(web::get().to(
                ➥handle_get_tutors)))              ◁──┐ The route to invoke the
        })                                             │ handle_get_tutors handler
        .bind("127.0.0.1:8080")?
        .run()
        .await
}
```

In the preceding code, we used hardcoded tutor data. In a future section of this chapter, we'll replace this mock data with actual data retrieved from the web service.

Run the web server with this command:

```
cargo run --bin iter3
```

From a web browser, access the following URL:

```
http://localhost:8080/tutors
```

You should see the list of tutors displayed. After the initial euphoria of seeing the tutor list displayed has waned, you will start to notice that the web page isn't particularly impressive or aesthetic. You will most certainly want to add some CSS to the web page. Here is some example CSS for illustration purposes. Place this code in styles.css under the /static folder, which we already declared in the main function to be the source of static assets:

```
/* css */
ul {
    list-style: none;
    padding: 0;
  }
  li {
    padding: 5px 7px;
    background-color: #FFEBCD;
    border: 2px solid #DEB887;
  }
```

In list.html under $PROJECT_ROOT/iter3, add the CSS file to the head block of HTML as follows:

```
<head>
    <meta charset="utf-8" />
```

```
    <link rel="stylesheet" type="text/css" href="/static/styles.css" />
    <title>Actix web</title>
</head>
```

Run the web server again, and visit the /tutors route from a web browser. You should now see the CSS styles reflected on the web page. This still may not be the prettiest of pages, but you now understand how you can add your own styling to the web page.

But if you're like me, and you don't want to write your own custom CSS, you can import one of your preferred CSS frameworks. Change the head section of the list.html file to import tailwind.css, a popular modern CSSS library. You can alternatively import Bootstrap, Foundation, Bulma, or any other CSS framework of your choice:

```
<!DOCTYPE html>
<html>

<head>
    <meta charset="utf-8" />
    <title>Actix web</title>
    <link href="https://unpkg.com/tailwindcss@^1.0/dist/tailwind.min.css"
    ➥rel="stylesheet">
</head>

<body>
    <h1 class="text-2xl font-bold mt-8 mb-5">Tutors list</h1>
    <ul class="list-disc list-inside my-5 pl-2">
        {% for tutor in tutors %}
        <ol class="list-decimal list-inside my-5 pl-2">
            <h5 class="text-1xl font-bold mb-4 mt-0">{{tutor.name}}</h5>
        </ol>
        {% endfor %}
    </ul>
</body>

</html>
```

Compile and run the server again, and this time you should see something a little more appealing to your eye.

We will not spend much time on CSS styles in this book, but CSS is an integral part of web pages, so it is important for you to know how to use it with Actix and templates.

We've seen different ways to show dynamic content in web pages using Actix and Tera. Let's now shift gears and focus on one more important aspect of developing frontend web apps: automated unit and integration tests. We were able to write test cases for the backend tutor web service, but is it also possible to write test cases for the frontend web app in Rust with Actix and Tera? Let's find out.

7.6   *Writing and running client-side tests*

In this section, we won't be writing any new application code. Instead, we'll reuse one of the handler functions we've previously written and write unit test cases for the handler.

Let's use the code we wrote in iter2.rs. This is the handler function we'll focus on:

```
async fn handle_post_tutor(
    tmpl: web::Data<tera::Tera>,
    params: web::Form<Tutor>,
) -> Result<HttpResponse, Error> {
    let mut ctx = tera::Context::new();
    ctx.insert("name", &params.name);
    ctx.insert("text", "Welcome!");
    let s = tmpl
        .render("user.html", &ctx)
        .map_err(|_| error::ErrorInternalServerError("Template error"))?;

    Ok(HttpResponse::Ok().content_type("text/html").body(s))
}
```

This handler can be invoked from the command line using a curl POST request as follows:

```
curl -X POST localhost:8080/tutors -d "name=Terry"
```

Let's write a unit test case for this handler function. In $PROJECT_ROOT/Cargo.toml, add the following section:

```
[dev-dependencies]
actix-rt = "2.2.0"
```

actix-rt is the Actix async runtime, which is needed to execute the asynchronous test functions.

In $PROJECT_ROOT/src/bin/iter2.rs, add the following test code toward the end of the file (as a convention, Rust unit test cases are located toward the end of the source file).

```
#[cfg(test)]          ⟵── Standard Rust annotation for test cases
mod tests {           ⟵──────────────── Start of the standard Rust tests module
    use super::*;
    use actix_web::http::{header::CONTENT_TYPE, HeaderValue, StatusCode};
    use actix_web::web::Form;
                              This annotation indicates to the Actix runtime
                              that the function following it is a test function
    #[actix_rt::test]   ⟵──  that must be executed by the Actix runtime.
    async fn handle_post_1_unit_test() {
        let params = Form(Tutor {            ⟵┐  Simulate user entry by creating a
            name: "Terry".to_string(),           Tutor object and embedding it in
        });                                       the Actix web::Form extractor.
        let tera = Tera::new(concat!(
            env!("CARGO_MANIFEST_DIR"),
            "/static/iter2/**/*"
        ))
        .unwrap();
        let webdata_tera = web::Data::new(tera);   ⟵┐  Inject the Tera instance
        let resp = handle_post_tutor(                   as a dependency in the
        ⟶webdata_tera, params).await.unwrap();          web application.
    }
```

Create a new Tera instance.

Invoke the handler function with the Tera instance and form parameters. This simulates what happens when a user submits a form.

Check
the return
status code.
```
assert_eq!(resp.status(), StatusCode::OK);
assert_eq!(
    resp.headers().get(CONTENT_TYPE).unwrap(),
    HeaderValue::from_static("text/html")
);
    }
}
```
Check the return
content type.

Run the tests from $PROJECT_ROOT with this command:

```
cargo test --bin iter2
```

You should see that the test passes.

We've just written a unit test by invoking the handler function directly. We were able to do this because we knew the handler function signature. This is OK for a unit test case, but how would we simulate a web client posting an HTTP request with the form data?

That's the domain of integration testing. Let's write an integration test to simulate a user's form submission. Add the following to the tests module in $PROJECT_ROOT/src/bin/iter2.rs:

```
use actix_web::dev::{HttpResponseBuilder, Service, ServiceResponse};
use actix_web::test::{self, TestRequest};

// Integration test case
#[actix_rt::test]
async fn handle_post_1_integration_test() {
    let tera = Tera::new(concat!(
        env!("CARGO_MANIFEST_DIR"),
        "/static/iter2/**/*"
    ))
    .unwrap();
    let mut app = test::init_service(App::new().data(tera).configure(
    ➥app_config)).await;

    let req = test::TestRequest::post()
        .uri("/tutors")
        .set_form(&Tutor {
            name: "Terry".to_string(),
        })
        .to_request();
    let resp: ServiceResponse = app.call(req).await.unwrap();
    assert_eq!(resp.status(), StatusCode::OK);
    assert_eq!(
        resp.headers().get(CONTENT_TYPE).unwrap(),
        HeaderValue::from_static("text/html")
    );
}
```

init_service() creates an Actix Service for testing. We can post HTTP messages to this service to simulate a web client sending a request to the web server. It takes a regular app builder as a parameter, so we can pass the Tera instance and application routes to it, like we do for a regular Actix web application.

to_request() converts the parameters passed to the TestRequest::post() builder to a regular formatted HTTP request message.

The HTTP request message is constructed using TestRequest::post(), which can be used to send regular POST requests to the test server.

Check for the expected status code.

The test server is called with the HTTP request message.

Check for the expected content type.

You'll notice that Actix provides rich support for testing in the form of built-in services, modules, and functions, which we can use to write unit or integration tests.

Run the tests from $PROJECT_ROOT:

```
cargo test --bin iter2
```

You should see both unit and integration tests pass.

That concludes this section on writing unit and integration test cases for frontend web apps built with Actix and Tera. We'll use what you have learned here to write the actual test cases for the tutor web application.

7.7 *Connecting to the backend web service*

In section 7.5, we displayed a list of tutors on a web page using mock data. In this section, we'll fetch data from the backend tutor web service to display on the web page, instead of using mock data. Technically, we can directly talk to a database from the Actix web application, but that's not what we want to do, mainly because we do not want to duplicate database access logic that is already present in the web service. Another reason is that we do not want to expose the database access credentials in both the web service and web application, which could increase the surface area of any security or hacking attacks.

We know that the backend tutor web service exposes various REST APIs. To talk to the web service from the web application, we need an HTTP client that can be embedded within the web application. While there are external crates available for this, let's use the built-in HTTP client in the Actix Web framework. We also need a way to parse and interpret the JSON data that is returned from the web service. For this, we'll use the `serde_json` crate.

Add the following to $PROJECT_ROOT/Cargo.toml:

```
serde_json = "1.0.64"
```

Let's now write the code to connect, make a GET request to the tutor web service, and retrieve the list of tutors. Create a new file called iter4.rs under $PROJECT_ROOT/src/bin, and copy the contents of iter3.rs to it to get a head start.

Using the `serde_json` crate, we can deserialize the incoming JSON payload in the HTTP response into a strongly typed data structure. In our case, we want to convert the JSON sent by the tutor web service into a `Vec<Tutor>` type. We also want to define the structure of the `Tutor` struct to match the incoming JSON data. Remove the old definition of the `Tutor` struct in the $PROJECT_ROOT/src/bin/iter4.rs file, and replace it with the following:

```
#[derive(Serialize, Deserialize, Debug)]
pub struct Tutor {
    pub tutor_id: i32,
    pub tutor_name: String,
    pub tutor_pic_url: String,
    pub tutor_profile: String,
}
```

Within the same source file, in the `handle_get_tutors` handler function, we'll connect to the tutor web service to retrieve the tutor list. That means we can remove the hardcoded values. Import the `actix_web` client module, and modify the code for the `handle_get_tutors` handler function as follows:

```
use actix_web::client::Client;

async fn handle_get_tutors(tmpl: web::Data<tera::Tera>) ->
Result<HttpResponse, Error> {
    let client = Client::default();
```

Construct an instance of the Actix Web HTTP client to talk to the web service.

```
    // Create request builder and send request
```

Construct a GET request with the URL endpoint. Adjust your URL endpoint as appropriate.

Send the HTTP request to the server.

```
    let response = client
        .get("http://localhost:3000/tutors/")
        .send()
        .await
        .unwrap()
        .body()
        .await
        .unwrap();
```

Asynchronous network requests require the await keyword.

We're unwrapping the result of the network response using the unwrap() keyword as a shortcut. When we write the tutor web application, we'll deal with errors in a production-compliant manner. Unwrap terminates the current process and is not suitable for production use, but it simplifies the earlier stages of software development.

From the HTTP response, extract the body() of the response. This contains the tutor list.

```
    let str_list = std::str::from_utf8(&response.as_ref()).unwrap();
    let tutor_list: Vec<Tutor> = serde_json::from_str(str_list).unwrap();
    let mut ctx = tera::Context::new();
```

Deserialize the str slice into a vector of Tutor objects using the serde_json crate.

```
    ctx.insert("tutors", &tutor_list);
    let rendered_html = tmpl
        .render("list.html", &ctx)
        .map_err(|_| error::ErrorInternalServerError("Template error"))?;

    Ok(HttpResponse::Ok().content_type("text/html").body(rendered_html))
}
```

Pass the deserialized tutor list into the Tera Context object.

The body() of the response is received as bytes. Convert it to a str slice.

The rest of the code related to rendering Tera templates is similar to what you've seen before.

Next, create a new $PROJECT_ROOT/static/iter4 folder. Under this folder, place a copy of the list.html file from $PROJECT_ROOT/static/iter3. Alter the list.html file to change the template variable {{tutor.name}} to {{tutor.tutor_name}} because that's the structure of the data sent back from the tutor web service.

Here is the updated list.html listing from the iter4 folder:

```
<!DOCTYPE html>
<html>

<head>
    <meta charset="utf-8" />
    <title>Actix web</title>
    <link href="https://unpkg.com/tailwindcss@^1.0/dist/tailwind.min.css"
    rel="stylesheet">
</head>

<body>
    <h1 class="text-2xl font-bold mt-8 mb-5">Tutors list</h1>
    <ul class="list-disc list-inside my-5 pl-2">
        {% for tutor in tutors %}
        <ol class="list-decimal list-inside my-5 pl-2">
```

```
            <h5 class="text-1xl font-bold mb-4 mt-0">{{tutor.tutor_name}}</h5>
          </ol>
          {% endfor %}
      </ul>
  </body>

</html>
```

We also need to alter the `main()` function in iter4.rs to look for Tera templates in the $PROJCT_ROOT/static/iter4 folder. Here is the updated `main()` function:

```
#[actix_web::main]
async fn main() -> std::io::Result<()> {
  println!("Listening on: 127.0.0.1:8080!");
  HttpServer::new(|| {
    let tera = Tera::new(concat!(env!("CARGO_MANIFEST_DIR"),
    ➥"/static/iter4/**/*")).unwrap();

    App::new()
      .data(tera)
      .service(fs::Files::new("/static", "./static").show_files_listing())
      .service(web::resource("/tutors").route(web::get().to(
      ➥handle_get_tutors)))
  })
    .bind("127.0.0.1:8080")?
    .run()
    .await
}
```

What we have done so far is fetch the tutor list from the tutor web service instead of using the hardcoded values as in iteration 3. We use it to display the tutor list in the list.html file, which is rendered when an HTTP request arrives from a client at route `/tutors`.

To test this, go to the tutor_web_service folder under the `ezytutors` workspace, and run the server in a separate terminal. This server should now be listening on `localhost:3000`. Test the server with the following command:

```
cargo run --bin iter6
```

iter6 was the last iteration we built for the tutor web service.

Then, from another terminal, run the `tutor_ssr_app` web server from $PROJECT_ROOT with the following command:

```
cargo run --bin iter4
```

We now have the tutor web service running on port 3000, and the tutor web app running on port 8080, both on localhost. Here's what should happen: When the user visits the `/tutors` route on port 8080, the request will go to the web handler of the web app, which will then call out to the tutor web service to retrieve the tutor list. The tutor web app handler will then inject this data into the Tera template and display the web page to the user.

To test this from a browser, visit this URL:

```
localhost:8080/tutors
```

You should see the list of tutor names, retrieved from our tutor web service, populated in the web page. If you have reached this point, congratulations! If you encounter any errors, just retrace the code back to the last point when you had it working, and reapply the changes in again.

You have now learned the critical aspects of developing a client-side application with Actix. In the next chapter, we will use the knowledge and skills gained in this chapter to write the code for the frontend tutor web application.

Summary

- Rust can be used to not just build backend *web services*, but also frontend *web applications*.
- Server-side rendering (SSR) is a web architectural pattern that involves creating a fully rendered web page on the server and sending it to the browser for display. SSR typically involves serving a mix of static and dynamic content on a web page.
- Actix Web and the Tera template engine are powerful tools for implementing SSR in Rust-based web applications.
- The Tera template engine is instantiated and injected into the web application in the `main()` function. The Tera instance is made available to all the handler functions by the Actix Web framework. The route handler functions, in turn, can use Tera templates to construct dynamic web pages that are sent back to the browser client as part of the HTTP response body.
- HTML forms are used to capture user input and post that input to a route on the Actix web application. The corresponding route handler then processes the HTTP request and sends back an HTTP response containing the dynamic web page.
- The control flow features of Tera templates can be used to display lists of information on a web page. The contents of the list can be retrieved either from a local database or an external web service and then be injected into the web page template.
- An Actix Web client can be used as an HTTP client to communicate between the Actix web application frontend and Actix web service backend.

Working with templates for tutor registration

This chapter covers

- Designing a tutor registration feature
- Setting up the project structure
- Displaying the registration form
- Handling registration submission

In the previous chapter, we covered the basics of working with Actix to develop a server-side web application. In this chapter, you'll more about how to work with templates as we create a tutor registration form using Actix and Tera.

Templates and forms are an important feature of web applications. They are commonly used for registration, signing in, capturing user profiles, providing payment information or know-your-customer details for regulatory purposes, and performing CRUD (create, read. update, and delete) operations on data. While capturing user input, it is also necessary to validate that data and provide feedback to the user in the case of errors. If the forms involve data updates, existing information has to be presented to the user allowing the user to change it. Elements of styling must also be added for aesthetic appeal. When forms are submitted, the form data needs to be serialized into an HTTP request, which should then invoke the

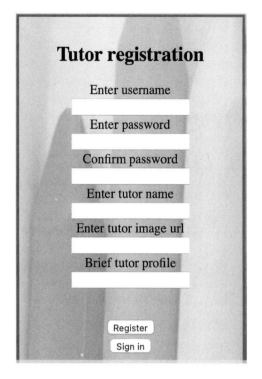

Figure 8.1   Tutor registration form

right handler functions for processing and storing the form data. Finally, the user needs to be given feedback on the success of the form submission and then optionally be taken to the next screen. You'll learn how to do all that in this chapter using Actix Web, the Tera template engine, and a few other components.

In this chapter, we'll write an HTML template and associated code to allow tutors to register. Figure 8.1 shows the tutor registration form.

For registration, we'll accept six fields: username, password, password confirmation, tutor name, tutor image URL, and a brief tutor profile. The first three are needed for user management functions, and the others will be used to send a request to the tutor web service and create a new tutor in the database. We'll first set up the project code structure and basic scaffolding.

8.1   *Writing the initial web application*

First, copy the code from chapter 7. We'll build on this code structure.

The tutor-web-app-ssr folder represents the project root, so we can set the PROJECT_ROOT environment variable to /path-to-folder/ezytutors/tutor-web-app-ssr. Henceforth, we'll refer to this folder as $PROJECT_ROOT.

Let's organize the code under the project root as follows:

1   Create an iter5 folder under $PROJECT_ROOT/src. This will contain the data model, routes, handler functions, definitions for custom error types and application state, and database SQL scripts.

2   Create an iter5 folder under $PROJECT_ROOT/static. This folder will contain the HTML and Tera templates.

3   Create an iter5-ssr.rs file under $PROJECT_ROOT/bin. This is the main function that will configure and start up the Actix web server (to serve the web application we are building).

4   Under $PROJECT_ROOT/src/iter5, create the following files:

   – *routes.rs*—Stores the routes for the web application on which HTTP requests can be received.

   – *model.rs*—Contains the data model definitions.

– *handler.rs*—Contains the handler functions associated with the various routes to process the incoming HTTP requests.

– *state.rs*—Stores the data structure representing the application state, which will be injected into the handlers (a process known as dependency injection).

– *errors.rs*—Contains the custom error type and associated functions to construct suitable error messages for users.

– *dbaccess.rs*—Contains the functions that access the database for reading and writing tutor data.

– *dbscripts/user.sql*—Create a dbscripts folder under $PROJECT_ROOT/src/iter5, and create a user.sql file under it. This will contain the SQL scripts to create a database table.

– *mod.rs*—Configures the $PROJECT_ROOT/src/iter5 directory as a Rust module that can be imported into other files.

We're now ready to start coding. Let's begin with the routes definition in $PROJECT_ROOT/src/iter5/routes.rs:

> **Import the handler functions that display the registration form and handle form submission. We'll write the code for these functions shortly.**

```
use crate::handler::{handle_register, show_register_form};
use actix_files as fs;              ◄──┐  actix-files is used to
use actix_web::web;                     │  serve static files.

pub fn app_config(config: &mut web::ServiceConfig) {
  config.service(
    web::scope("")
      .service(fs::Files::new(
      ➥"/static", "./static").show_files_listing())
      .service(web::resource("/").route(web::get().to(
      ➥show_register_form)))
      .service(web::resource("/register").route(web::post().to(
      ➥handle_register)))),
  );
}
```

> **Create a service configuration to specify routes and associated handlers.**

> **HTTP requests for static resources on routes with the /static prefix will be served from the /static folder under $PROJECT_ROOT.**

> **This route handles a POST request for a registration form submission.**

> **The index route displays the registration form in response to a GET request.**

We can now move on to the model definition in $PROJECT_ROOT/src/iter5/model.rs. Add the following data structures to model.rs.

Listing 8.1 Data model

```
use serde::{Deserialize, Serialize};

#[derive(Serialize, Deserialize, Debug)]
pub struct TutorRegisterForm {          ◄──┐  Struct to hold the details
    pub username: String,                   │  that will be captured in the
    pub password: String,                   │  tutor registration form
    pub confirmation: String,
    pub name: String,
```

```
        pub imageurl: String,
        pub profile: String,
}

#[derive(Serialize, Deserialize, Debug)]
pub struct TutorResponse {
        pub tutor_id: i32,
        pub tutor_name: String,
        pub tutor_pic_url: String,
        pub tutor_profile: String,
}

#[derive(Serialize, Deserialize, Debug, sqlx::FromRow)]
pub struct User {
        pub username: String,
        pub tutor_id: Option<i32>,
        pub user_password: String,
}
```

> **Struct to store the response from the tutor web service, received in response to creating a new tutor**

> **Struct to store user credentials for authentication purposes**

Let's next define the application state in $PROJECT_ROOT/src/iter5/state.rs:

```
use sqlx::postgres::PgPool;

pub struct AppState {
        pub db: PgPool,
}
```

AppState will hold the Postgres connection pool object, which will be used by the database access functions. AppState will be injected into each handler function by Actix Web, and you'll see later how to configure this while creating the Actix application instance.

Let's also create an error.rs file under $PROJECT_ROOT/src/iter5 to define a custom error type. This is similar to the error definition we earlier created for the tutor web service, but with some minor changes.

Listing 8.2   Custom error type

```
use ...

#[derive(Debug, Serialize)]
pub enum EzyTutorError {
        DBError(String),
        ActixError(String),
        NotFound(String),
        TeraError(String),
}
#[derive(Debug, Serialize)]
pub struct MyErrorResponse {
        error_message: String,
}
impl std::error::Error for EzyTutorError {}
```

> **Code elided for concision; see the GitHub source files for the complete code.**

> **Define a custom error type, EzyTutorError.**

> **Define a MyErrorResponse error type to send the response back to the user.**

> **Implement Rust's standard error trait for our custom error type. This allows for the custom error type to be converted to an HTTP response by Actix.**

```
impl EzyTutorError {
    fn error_response(&self) -> String {
        match self {
            EzyTutorError::DBError(msg) => {
                println!("Database error occurred: {:?}", msg);
                "Database error".into()
            }
            EzyTutorError::ActixError(msg) => { ... }
            EzyTutorError::TeraError(msg) => { ... }
            EzyTutorError::NotFound(msg) => { ... }
        }
    }
}
```

> **Construct the error response message (to the user) for various types of errors that can occur in the tutor web application.**

> **Code elided for concision; see the GitHub source files for the complete code.**

```
impl error::ResponseError for EzyTutorError {
    fn status_code(&self) -> StatusCode {
        match self {
            EzyTutorError::DBError(_msg)
            | EzyTutorError::ActixError(_msg)
            | EzyTutorError::TeraError(_msg) =>
              StatusCode::INTERNAL_SERVER_ERROR,
            EzyTutorError::NotFound(_msg) => StatusCode::NOT_FOUND,
        }
    }
    fn error_response(&self) -> HttpResponse {
        HttpResponse::build(self.status_code()).json(MyErrorResponse {
            error_message: self.error_response(),
        })
    }
}
```

> **Implement Actix's ResponseError trait, which specifies how to convert EzyTutorError to an HTTP response.**

> **Implement the Display trait from the Rust standard library for EzyTutorError. This allows for the printing of errors.**

```
impl fmt::Display for EzyTutorError {
    fn fmt(&self, f: &mut fmt::Formatter) -> Result<(), fmt::Error> {
        write!(f, "{}", self)
    }
}
```

> **Implementing the Actix Web Error trait for EzyTutorError allows for the conversion of the former to the latter using the question mark (?) operator.**

```
impl From<actix_web::error::Error> for EzyTutorError {
    fn from(err: actix_web::error::Error) -> Self {
        EzyTutorError::ActixError(err.to_string())
    }
}
```

> **Code elided for concision; see the GitHub source files for the complete code. Implementing the sqlx error trait for EzyTutorError allows for the conversion of the former to the latter using the question mark (?) operator.**

```
impl From<SQLxError> for EzyTutorError { ... }
```

We've so far defined the routes, data model, application state, and error type. Let's next write the scaffolding for the various handler functions. These won't do much, but they will establish the code structure, which we can build on in future sections.

In $PROJECT_ROOT/src/iter5/handler.rs, add the following:

```
use actix_web::{Error, HttpResponse, Result};

pub async fn show_register_form() -> Result<HttpResponse, Error> {
    let msg = "Hello, you are in the registration page";
```

> **Handler function to show the registration form to the user**

```
        Ok(HttpResponse::Ok().content_type("text/html").body(msg))
}

pub async fn handle_register() -> Result<HttpResponse, Error> {          ◁─────┐
        Ok(HttpResponse::Ok().body(""))
}
```

> **Handler function to handle registration requests**

As you can see, the handler functions don't really do much, but this is sufficient for us to establish an initial code structure that we can build on.

Lastly, let's write the `main()` function that will configure the web application with the associated routes and launch the web server. Add the following code to $PROJECT_ROOT/bin/iter5-ssr.rs.

Listing 8.3   The `main()` function

> **Module definition to import application-specific code**

```
#[path = "../iter5/mod.rs"]
mod iter5;
use iter5::{dbaccess, errors, handler, model, routes, state::AppState};
use routes::app_config;
use actix_web::{web, App, HttpServer};          ◁──────┐
use dotenv::dotenv;      ┌──────────────────────────────────┐
use std::env;            │ Packages to work with environment variables │
use sqlx::postgres::PgPool;          ◁───┐

use tera::Tera;

#[actix_web::main]
async fn main() -> std::io::Result<()> {
        dotenv().ok();          ◁──
        //Start HTTP server
        let host_port = env::var("HOST_PORT").expect(
        ➥"HOST:PORT address is not set in .env file");          ◁──
        println!("Listening on: {}", &host_port);
        let database_url = env::var("DATABASE_URL").expect(
        ➥"DATABASE_URL is not set in .env file");          ◁──
        let db_pool = PgPool::connect(&database_url).await.unwrap();          ◁───┐
        // Construct App State
        let shared_data = web::Data::new(AppState { db: db_pool });          ◁────┐

        HttpServer::new(move || {          ◁───┐
        let tera = Tera::new(concat!(env!("CARGO_MANIFEST_DIR"),
        ➥"/static/iter5/**/*")).unwrap();
                App::new()
                        .data(tera)
                        .app_data(shared_data.clone())
                        .configure(app_config)
        })
        .bind(&host_port)?
        .run()
        .await
}
```

> **Core Actix modules to set up a web application and web server**

> **Import the sqlx Postgres connection pool.**

> **Import the env module from the Rust standard library to read the environment variables.**

> **Import host, port, and database access credentials from the .env file.**

> **Create a new Postgres connection pool and embed it in the application state.**

> **Configure the Actix web application with the routes, application state, and Tera.**

> **Bind the web server to the host and port configuration, and run it.**

We still have to do a couple more things. First, add the `dotenv` package to the Cargo.toml file in $PROJECT_ROOT. Make sure the Cargo.toml file looks similar to this:

```
[dependencies]
actix-web = "4.2.1"
actix-files="0.6.2"
tera = "1.17.0"
serde = { version = "1.0.144", features = ["derive"] }
serde_json = "1.0.85"
awc = "3.0.1"
sqlx = {version = "0.6.2", default_features = false, features =
➡ ["postgres","runtime-tokio-native-tls", "macros", "chrono"]}
rust-argon2 = "1.0.0"
dotenv = "0.15.0"

[dev-dependencies]
actix-rt = "2.7.0"
```

Configure the host, port, and database details in the .env file in $PROJECT_ROOT as shown:

```
HOST_PORT=127.0.0.1:8080
DATABASE_URL=postgres://ssruser:mypassword@127.0.0.1:5432/ezytutor_web_ssr
```

The `DATABASE_URL` specifies the username (`ssruser`) and password (`mypassword`) for database access. It also specifies the port number at which the Postgres database processes are running and the name of the database (`ezytutor_web_ssr`) to connect to.

Lastly, add the following entries to mod.rs under $PROJECT_ROOT/src/iter5. This will export the functions and data structures we have defined and allow them to be imported and used elsewhere in the application:

```
pub mod dbaccess;
pub mod errors;
pub mod handler;
pub mod model;
pub mod routes;
pub mod state;
```

We're now ready to test. Run the following from $PROJECT_ROOT:

```
cargo run --bin  iter5-ssr
```

You should see the Actix web server start up and listen on the host:port combination specified in the .env file.

From a browser, try the following URL route (adjust the port number to the one in your own .env file):

```
localhost:8080/
```

You should see the following message displayed on your browser screen:

```
Hello, you are in the registration page
```

We have now established the basic project structure and are ready to implement the logic to display the registration form to the user.

8.2   *Displaying the registration form*

In earlier chapters, we built APIs on the tutor web service for adding, updating, and deleting tutor information. We tested these APIs using command-line tools. In this chapter, we're going to add the following two features:

- Provide a web user interface where tutors can register.
- Store user credentials in a local database (for user management).

Note that the user management in the second point can be done in different ways. It can be built directly into the backend web service, or it can be handled in the frontend web application.

In this chapter, we'll adopt the latter approach, mainly to demonstrate how you can implement a separation of responsibilities between the backend web service and frontend web application as a design choice. In this model, the backend web service will take care of the core business and data access logic to store and apply rules on tutor and course data, while the frontend web application will handle the user authentication and session management functions. In such a design, we will have the tutor web service running in a trusted zone behind the firewall, receiving HTTP requests only from the trusted frontend web application.

Figure 8.2 shows the tutor registration workflow, which involves several steps:

1   The user visits the landing page URL. The web browser will make a GET request on the index route, /, which is routed by the Actix web server to the `show_register_form()` handler function. This function will send the registration form back to the web browser as an HTTP response. The tutor registration form is now displayed to the user.

2   The user fills out the registration form. There may be invalid inputs from users that need to be corrected (e.g., the password may not meet minimum length criteria).

3   The HTML specifications allow us a few types of basic validation checks to be made within the browser, rather than making a round trip to the server every time. We'll make use of this to enforce mandatory fields and field lengths, so that for these errors, feedback can be provided to the user within the browser.

4   The user submits the registration form, and a POST request is sent to the Actix web server on the /register route. The Actix Web framework routes the request to the `handle_register()` web handler.

5   The `handle_register()` function checks to see if the password and password confirmation fields match. If they don't, the registration form is displayed back to the user with an appropriate error message. This is a case of validating user input on the server rather than within the browser. (Note that it would be possible to perform this validation using custom jQuery or JavaScript in the browser,

but we're avoiding that approach in this book, if only to demonstrate that it is possible to write complete web applications in Rust without JavaScript. You can use JavaScript if you prefer.)

6 If the passwords match, the `handle_register()` function makes a POST request on the backend tutor web service to create a new tutor entry in the database.

7 The username and password provided by the user in the registration form are stored in a local database on the tutor web application (not in the tutor web service), for the purpose of authenticating the user in the future.

8 A confirmation page is returned to the web browser by the `handle_register()` function as an HTTP response.

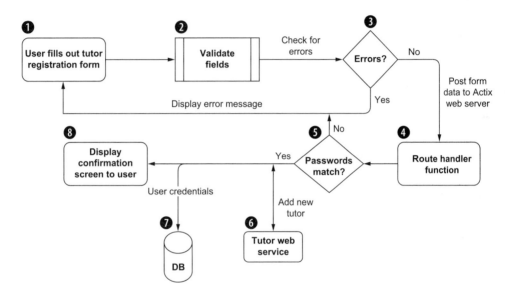

Figure 8.2   Tutor registration flow

Now that you understand what we're going to build, let's start with the static assets and templates for tutor registration.

In #PROJECT_ROOT/static/iter5/, create a register.html file, and add the following contents.

Listing 8.4   Registration template

```
<!doctype html>
<html>

<head>
    <meta charset=utf-8>
    <title>Tutor registration</title>
    <link rel="stylesheet" href="/static/tutor-styles.css">
</head>
```

The <head> section refers to an external CSS file tutor-styles.css.

```
<body>
    <div class="header">
        <h1>Welcome to EzyTutor</h1>
        <p>Start your own online tutor business in a few minutes</p>
    </div>
    <div class="center">
        <h2>
            Tutor registration
        </h2>
        <form action=/register method=POST>
            <label for="userid">Enter username</label><br>
            <input type="text" name="username" value="{{current_username}}"
            autocomplete="username" minlength="6"
                maxlength="12" required><br>
            <label for="password">Enter password</label><br>
            <input type="password" name="password"
            value="{{current_password}}" autocomplete="new-password"
                minlength="8" maxlength="12" required><br>
            <label for="confirm">Confirm password</label><br>
            <input type="password" name="confirmation"
            value="{{current_confirmation}}" autocomplete="new-password"
                minlength="8" maxlength="12" required><br>
            <label for="userid">Enter tutor name</label><br>
            <input type="text" name="name" value="{{current_name}}"
            maxlength="12" required><br>
            <label for="imageurl">Enter tutor image url</label><br>
            <input type="text" name="imageurl" value="{{current_imageurl}}"
            maxlength="30"><br>
            <label for="profile">Brief tutor profile</label><br>
            <input type="text" name="profile" value="{{current_profile}}"
            maxlength="40"><br>
            <label for="error">
                <p style="color:red">{{error}}</p>
            </label>
            <br>
            <button type=submit id="button1">Register</button>
        </form>
        <form action=/signinhome method=GET>
            <button type=submit id="button2">Sign in</button>
        </form>
    </div>
    <p>
    <div id="footer">
        (c)Photo by Author
    </div>
    </p>

</html>
```

The `<body>` section contains two `<form>` elements. The first contains five data entry fields (`<input>` elements) and a Submit button (a `<button>` element of type=submit). The second `<form>` element takes the user to the sign-in page.

The minlength and maxlength properties of the `<input>` elements enforce the field lengths. Any validation errors are handled directly within the browser with suitable messages to the user.

A `<label>` element is used to display error messages arising out of server-side validation (i.e., within the handler functions).

form action=/register method=POST> indicates that when the form is submitted, a POST HTML request is constructed with the form values. This POST request is submitted to the web server on the /register route.

The value property of the `<input>` element prepopulates the field with values. This is useful when the form is submitted to the web server and, in the case of errors, redisplayed to the user with the previously entered values. Note the use of the Tera template variable syntax with the variable name enclosed in a pair of double braces: {{ }}.

The required property of the `<input>` element specifies that the field is mandatory. This is enforced by the browser.

Let's now create a tutor-styles.css file under the $PROJECT_ROOT/static folder and add the following styling to it.

Listing 8.5   The CSS styles

```css
.header {
    padding: 20px;
    text-align: center;
    background: #fad980;
    color: rgb(48, 40, 43);
    font-size: 30px;
}

.center {
    margin: auto;
    width: 20%;
    min-width: 150px;
    border: 3px solid #ad5921;
    padding: 10px;
}

body, html {
    height: 100%;
    margin: 0;
    font-kerning: normal;
}

h1 {
    text-align: center;
}

p {
    text-align: center;
}

div {
    text-align: center;
}

div {
    background-color: rgba(241, 235, 235, 0.719);
}

body {
    background-image: url('/static/background.jpg');
    background-repeat: no-repeat;
    background-attachment: fixed;
    background-size: cover;
    height: 500px;
}

#button1, #button2 {
    display: inline-block;
}

#footer {
    position: fixed;
    padding: 10px 10px 0px 10px;
```

```
        bottom: 0;
        width: 100%;
        /* Height of the footer*/
        height: 20px;
    }
```

These are pretty standard CSS constructs, and they will provide minimal styling for the landing page that shows the tutor registration form. If you are familiar with CSS, you are encouraged to write your own styling for the page.

Note that the CSS file refers to a /static/background.jpg background image. You can find this image in the Git repo for the chapter. Download the file, and place it in the $PROJECT_ROOT/static folder. Alternatively, you can use your own background image (or none at all).

We're now ready to write the code for the show_register_form() handler function. In $PROJECT_ROOT/src/iter5/handler.rs, update the code as follows.

Listing 8.6   Handler function to show the registration form

Note the addition of the web::Data<tera::Tera> parameter to this handler function. This is injected into the handler in the main() function when the application instance is constructed.

Update the module imports to include web modules from actix_web and our custom error type.

```
use actix_web::{web, Error, HttpResponse, Result};
use crate::errors::EzyTutorError;

pub async fn show_register_form(tmpl: web::Data<tera::Tera>) ->
Result<HttpResponse, Error> {
    let mut ctx = tera::Context::new();
    ctx.insert("error", "");
    ctx.insert("current_username", "");
    ctx.insert("current_password", "");
    ctx.insert("current_confirmation", "");
    ctx.insert("current_name", "");
    ctx.insert("current_imageurl", "");
    ctx.insert("current_profile", "");
    let s = tmpl
        .render("register.html", &ctx)
        .map_err(|_| EzyTutorError::TeraError(
        "Template error".to_string()))?;

    Ok(HttpResponse::Ok().content_type("text/html").body(s))
}
```

Construct a new Tera Context object. This will be used to set values for the template variables declared in the HTML template.

Initialize the template variables.

Render the register.html template.

Return the fully constructed register.html file (with values populated for template variables) as part of the body of the HTML response.

We can do a quick test now. From $PROJECT_ROOT, run the Actix server with the following command:

```
cargo run --bin iter5-ssr
```

Visit the following URL from a browser (replace the port number with whatever you have configured in the .env file):

```
localhost:8080/
```

Assuming you have followed all the steps described, you should be able to see the landing page with the registration form. You have successfully displayed the tutor registration form. It's now time to accept user input and post the completed form back to the Actix web server. Let's see how that can be done.

8.3 Handling registration submission

You've seen how to display the registration form. Now try to fill out the values. Specifically, try the following:

- Click the Register button without entering any values. For all fields marked as required in the HTML template, you should see a message saying "Please fill in this field," or something similar, depending upon which browser you use.
- For input fields where `minlength` or `maxlength` have been specified in the HTML template, you will see error messages displayed whenever your input does not meet the criteria.

Note that these are in-browser validations enabled by the HTML specification itself. We have not written any custom code for these validations.

In-browser validations cannot be used to implement more complex validation rules. Those will have to be implemented in the server-side handler functions. One example of a validation rule in the tutor registration form is that the password and the password confirmation fields must contain the same value. To validate this, we will submit the form data to the Actix server and write validation code in the handler function. (As mentioned earlier, this password check validation could be performed within the browser using jQuery or JavaScript, but we are adopting a pure-Rust approach in this book).

As you saw in the registration workflow in figure 8.2, we also have to perform the following key steps in the handler function:

1 Verify if the password and password confirmation fields match. If not, we'll return the form to the user, along with a suitable error message. The values the user filled previously should also be returned with the form and should not be lost or discarded.

2 If the password check is successful, a POST request needs to be made on the backend tutor web service to create a new tutor. We'll be using the `awc` crate (from the Actix Web ecosystem) as the HTTP client that will talk to the tutor web service.

3 The web service will return details of the newly created tutor record, which will also include a database-generated `tutor-id`. This `tutor id` represents a unique tutor record in the tutor web service. The web application needs to remember this for future use (such as when requesting the user profile of the tutor or to retrieve a course list for the tutor). We need to store this information somewhere within the web application.

4 The username and password entered by the user in the registration form also need to be recorded within the web application so they can be used for authenticating the tutor in the future.

For storing `tutor-id`, `username`, and `password`, we will be using the Postgres database. You could use any database (or even a lighter key/value store) for this purpose, but we'll use Postgres because you already learned how to use it with Actix in earlier chapters. If you need a refresher on how to use and configure Postgres with `sqlx` and Actix, refer back to chapter 4.

Storing passwords in clear text in the database is an insecure approach and is highly discouraged for production use. We'll use a third-party crate, `argon2`, for storing hashes of passwords in the database, rather than storing them in clear text form.

Recall that we added the `sqlx`, `awc`, and `argon2` crates to Cargo.toml in the beginning of the chapter. Here is a recap of the three crates we added:

```
sqlx = {version = "0.3.5", default_features = false, features =
  ["postgres","runtime-tokio", "macros"]}
rust-argon2 = "0.8.3"
awc = "2.0.3"
```

Let's now look at the database layer. We need a database only to store registered users with their credentials. We previously defined the `User` data structure in the model.rs file as follows:

```
#[derive(Serialize, Deserialize, Debug, sqlx::FromRow)]
pub struct User {
    pub username: String,
    pub tutor_id: i32,
    pub user_password: String,
}
```

Let's create a table in the database to store user information. In $PROJECT_ROOT/ src/iter5, you've already created a dbscripts/user.sql file. Place the following code in this file:

```
drop table if exists ezyweb_user;
```
◁── **Drop the table if it already exists.**

```
create table ezyweb_user
(
    username varchar(20) primary key,
    tutor_id INT,
    user_password CHAR(100) not null
);
```
◁── **Create a database table with the name ezyweb_user. The username will be the primary key. The tutor_id will be returned from the tutor web service on the creation of a tutor record, and we will store it here. The user password will be the hash of the password entered by the user in the registration form.**

Log in to the psql shell prompt. From the project root, run the following command:

```
create database __ezytutor_web_ssr__;
create user __ssruser__ with password 'mypassword';
grant all privileges on database ezytutor_web_ssr to ssruser;
```
◁── **Create a new database.**

Create a new user. Replace the username and password with your own.

Grant privileges on the database to the newly created user. ◁──

Log out of psql, and log back in to see if the credentials are working:

```
psql -U $DATABASE_USER -d ezytutor_web_ssr -- password
\q
```

Here $DATABASE_USER refers to the username created in the database.

Lastly, quit the psql shell and, from the project root, run the following command to create the database table. Before that, ensure you have set the database user in the $DATABASE_USER environment variable so it is convenient for reuse:

```
psql -U $DATABASE_USER -d ezytutor_web_ssr < src/iter5/dbscripts/user.sql
```

Log back into the psql shell, and run the following command to check that the table has been created correctly:

```
\d+ ezyweb_user
```

You should see the metadata for the table created. If you have any trouble following these steps related to Postgres, refer back to chapter 4.

We're now ready to write the database access functions to store and read tutor data. In $PROJECT_ROOT/src/iter5/dbaccess.rs, add the following code.

Listing 8.7 Database access function to store and read tutor data

```
use crate::errors::EzyTutorError;          Import custom error type, data model
use crate::model::*;                        structs, and sqlx Postgres connection pool.
use sqlx::postgres::PgPool;

//Return result

pub async fn get_user_record(pool: &PgPool, username: String) ->
  Result<User, EzyTutorError> {           ◄──  Function to retrieve a user record from the
    // Prepare SQL statement                    database. It accepts a Postgres connection pool
    let user_row = sqlx::query_as!(            and a username (the primary key) as parameters.
        User,
        "SELECT * FROM ezyweb_user where username = $1",
        username
    )                                      Function to create a new user for user management
    .fetch_optional(pool)                  purposes. It accepts a Postgres connection pool and
    .await?;                               a new user of type User. It creates a new user with
                                             a username (the primary key), a tutor_id (which
    if let Some(user) = user_row {         is returned from the backend tutor web service),
        Ok(user)                           and a user_password (a hashed password).
    } else {
        Err(EzyTutorError::NotFound("User name not found".into()))
    }
}

pub async fn post_new_user(pool: &PgPool, new_user: User) ->
  Result<User, EzyTutorError> {           ◄─────────────────
    let user_row= sqlx::query_as!(User,"insert into ezyweb_user (
  username, tutor_id, user_password) values ($1,$2,$3)
  returning username, tutor_id, user_password",
    new_user.username, new_user.tutor_id, new_user.user_password)
    .fetch_one(pool)
    .await?;

    Ok(user_row)
}
```

Writing such database access functions should be familiar to you by now, as we have dealt with them extensively in previous chapters. Let's now move on to the handler functions to perform registration.

Which handler function should we write to handle registration form submission? You'll recall that when a form is submitted, the browser invokes an HTTP POST request on the /register route, and in the routes configuration, we specified the handler function as handle_register() for this route. Let's head into the handler.rs file under $PROJECT_ROOT/src/iter5 and update the handle_register() function as follows.

> **Listing 8.8 Function to handle registration form submission**

```
use crate::dbaccess::{get_user_record, post_new_user};     ◁──── Construct the hash of the
...                                                               password entered by the user,
use serde_json::json;    ◁───┤ Import the necessary modules.      using the argon2 library.

pub async fn handle_register(              ◁────   The handle_register() handler function
    tmpl: web::Data<tera::Tera>,                   takes three parameters—Tera templates,
    app_state: web::Data<AppState>,                application state, and form data.
    params: web::Form<TutorRegisterForm>,
) -> Result<HttpResponse, Error> {
    let mut ctx = tera::Context::new();
    let s;
    let username = params.username.clone();                      Make a call to the database access
    let user = get_user_record(&app_state.db, username.to_string()).await;  ◁──   function to check if the user is
    let user_not_found: bool = user.is_err();                              already registered in the database.
    //If user is not found in database, proceed to verification of passwords
    if user_not_found {
        if params.password != params.confirmation {     ◁────   If the user is not
            ctx.insert("error", "Passwords do not match");        registered, check if the
            ...                                                   password and password
            s = tmpl                                              confirmation entered by
                .render("register.html", &ctx)                    the user match, and
                .map_err(|_| EzyTutorError::TeraError(            process suitably.
                ⮡ "Template error".to_string())))?;
        } else {                                        ◁────   If the user is not registered, and if the
            let new_tutor = json!({                             passwords match, we construct the
                "tutor_name": ...                                parameters to send in JSON format.
            });
            let awc_client = awc::Client::default();
            let res = awc_client
                .post("http://localhost:3000/tutors/")       Multiplies a machine type's
                .send_json(&new_tutor)                       gigabytes of memory (RAM) by unit
                .await                                        price and hours in the month
                .unwrap()
                .body()                 Retrieve the body of the HTTP response sent by the tutor web
                .await?;                service (which contains the newly created tutor details).
            let tutor_response: TutorResponse = serde_json::from_str(
            ⮡ &std::str::from_utf8(&res)?)?;
            s = format!("Congratulations. ...");     ◁────   Construct a confirmation message
            // Hash the password                              that can be sent back to the user
                                                              on successful registration.
```

Annotations:
- **Return the response to the web client (the web browser or command-line HTTP client).**
- **Elided source code for concision; see the full source code on GitHub.**
- **Make the POST request to the tutor web service, and await a response.**
- **The body of the HTTP response received contains tutor data in bytes format. Convert this into string format.**

Construct the hash of the password entered by the user, using the argon2 library.

Elided source code for concision; see the full source code on GitHub.

```
let salt = b"somerandomsalt";
let config = Config::default();
let hash =
    argon2::hash_encoded(params.password.clone().as_bytes(),
    ▸salt, &config).unwrap();
let user = User {
    ...
};
let _tutor_created = post_new_user(
    ▸&app_state.db, user).await?;
    }
} else {
    ctx.insert("error", "User Id already exists");
    ...
    s = tmpl
        .render("register.html", &ctx)
        ...;    <2,14>
};

Ok(HttpResponse::Ok().content_type("text/html").body(s))
}
```

Store the username, password, and tutor-id in the Postgres database for future authentication purposes.

If the user already exists in the database, populate the template variables in the register.html template, including the error message, and render the template.

Return the response to the web client (the web browser or command-line HTTP client).

The preceding listing has been shortened a bit to keep it concise, but we import several modules that you'll recognize: the data structures from the data model to capture user input and store it in the database, AppState to store the Postgres sqlx connection pool, argon2 for password hashing and verification, and the custom error type that we defined. We're also importing the actix_web and serde modules for the web server and serialization/deserialization respectively.

One thing you haven't seen before is the hashing of the password entered by the user, using the argon2 library. You can specify any value as the salt, which is used to construct the hash. The hash is a one way-function, which means that it is not possible to reconstruct the original password from the hashed password, so it is safe to specify the salt in plain text.

We are now ready to test this. First, though, we have to ensure that the backend tutor web service is running. Go to the ezytutors/tutor-web-service folder, and run the web service as follows:

```
cargo run --bin iter5
```

Run the web application from $PROJECT_ROOT with this command:

```
cargo run --bin iter5-ssr
```

From a browser, access the URL localhost:8080/. Fill out the form and click the Register button. If all the data is entered correctly, you should see a message like the following displayed on the screen:

```
Congratulations. You have been successfully registered with EzyTutor and your
tutor id is: __xx__. To start using EzyTutor, please login with your
credentials
```

> **Improving the user interface**
>
> The interaction with the user is not ideal in this solution for at least two reasons. First, in the case of errors, we end up repeating a lot of code to rebuild the form. Second, if the user bookmarks the endpoint thinking it's the registration endpoint, they will actually get a blank page when the bookmark is used. Redirecting to / would be a better option. This modification is not trivial, but it will make a good exercise to explore.

Try registering with the same username again. You should see the registration form populated with the values you entered, along with the following error message:

```
User Id already exists
```

Register one more time, but this time ensure that the password and password confirmation fields don't match. You should once again see the registration form populated with the values you entered, along with the following error message:

```
Passwords do not match
```

These few tests conclude our section on tutor registration and the chapter. You've seen how to define a template with template variables, display the registration form to the user, perform in-browser and in-handler validations, send an HTTP request from the template, make an HTTP request to a backend web service, and store the user in a local database. We defined a custom error type to unify error handling and saw how to hash passwords before storing them in a database for security purposes.

If this were a real application intended for production, there are many improvements that could be added to the current implementation. However, that is not the goal of this book. We have just illustrated, in a fairly straightforward way, how such applications can be kickstarted using the right Rust crates.

In the next chapter, we'll conclude the server-side web application and cover topics including signing in a user and creating forms to maintain the course data.

Summary

- Architecturally, a server-rendered Rust web application consists of HTML templates (defined and rendered using a template library like Tera), routes on which HTTP requests arrive, handler functions that process the HTTP requests, and a database access layer that abstracts the details of storing and retrieving data.
- A standard HTML form can be used to capture user inputs in an Actix web application. Infusing Tera template variables into the HTML form provides a better user experience and feedback to guide the user.
- User input validations in forms can be performed either within the browser or in the server handler function. Simple validations, such as field-length checks, are usually done by the browser, and more complex validation (such as whether

the username is already registered) is done in the server handler function. When the user submits the form, a POST HTTP request, along with the form data, is sent by the browser to the Actix web server on the specified route.

- A custom error type can be defined to unify error handling in the web application. In case of errors in the form data entered by the user, the corresponding Tera form template is re-rendered by the handler function and sent to the browser, along with a suitable error message.

- Data pertaining to user management (such as username and password) is stored within the web application in a local data store (we used a Postgres database in this chapter). The passwords are stored as hashes, and not in clear text, for security purposes.

Working with forms
for course maintenance

This chapter covers

- Designing and implementing user authentication
- Routing HTTP requests
- Creating a resource with the HTTP POST method
- Updating a resource with the HTTP PUT method
- Deleting a resource with the HTTP DELETE method

In the previous chapter, we looked at registering tutors. When a user registers as a tutor, the information about the tutor is stored in two databases. The tutor's profile details, such as their name, image, and area of specialization, are maintained in a database within the backend tutor web service. The registration details for the user, such as the user ID and password, are stored locally, in a database within the web application.

In this chapter, we will build on top of the code from the previous chapter. We'll write a Rust frontend web app that allows users to sign in to the application, interact with the local database, and communicate with a backend web service.

The primary focus of this chapter will not be on writing the HTML and JavaScript user interface for the web application, as that is not the focus of this book. For this reason, we will only discuss and implement two forms in this chapter: the sign-in form and the user notification screen. Our focus will be on writing all the other components that make up a web application in Rust, including routes, request handlers, and data models, and you'll learn how to invoke APIs on the backend web service. In lieu of a user interface, we will test the web application's APIs from a command-line HTTP tool. The task of writing the rest of the HTML and JavaScript-based UI for the web application using Tera templates is left for you as an exercise.

Let's start with the tutor sign-in (authentication) functionality.

9.1 Designing user authentication

For the tutor sign-in, we'll accept two fields: `username` and `password`, and we'll use them to authenticate tutors to the web application. Figure 9.1 shows the tutor sign-in form.

Let's look at the workflow for tutor sign-in, shown in figure 9.2. The Actix web server in the figure is the frontend web application server, not the backend tutor web service:

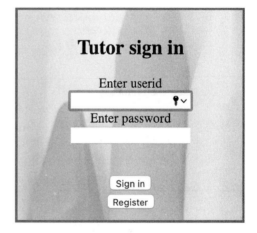

Figure 9.1 Tutor sign-in form

1 The user visits the landing page URL, and the tutor sign-in form is displayed.

2 Basic validation for the username and password is performed within the form itself, using HTML features, without requests being sent to the Actix web server.

3 If there are errors in validation, feedback is provided to the user.

4 The user submits the sign-in form. A POST request is sent to the Actix web server on the sign-in route, which then routes the request to the respective route handler.

5 The route handler function verifies the username and password by retrieving the user credentials from the local database.

6 If the authentication is not successful, the sign-in form is redisplayed to the user with an appropriate error message. Examples of error messages include incorrect username or password.

7 If the user is authenticated successfully, they are directed to the home page of the tutor web application.

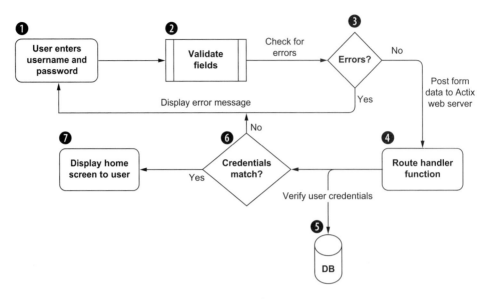

Figure 9.2   Tutor sign-in flow

Now that you know what we will be developing in this chapter, let's set up the project code structure and basic scaffolding.

9.2   *Setting up the project structure*

First, clone the ezytutors repo from chapter 8. Then set the PROJECT_ROOT environment variable to /path-to-folder/ezytutors/tutor-web-app-ssr. Henceforth, we'll refer to this folder as $PROJECT_ROOT.

Let's organize the code under the project root as follows:

1 Make a copy of the $PROJECT_ROOT/src/iter5 folder, and rename it $PROJECT_ROOT/src/iter6.
2 Make a copy of the $PROJECT_ROOT/static/iter5 folder, and rename it $PROJECT_ROOT/static/iter6. This folder will contain the HTML and Tera templates.
3 Make a copy of the $PROJECT_ROOT/src/bin/iter5-ssr.rs file, and rename it $PROJECT_ROOT/src/bin/iter6-ssr.rs. This file contains the main() function that will configure and start up the Actix web server (to serve the web application that we are building). In iter6-ssr.rs, replace all references to iter5 with iter6.

Also, make sure that the .env file in $PROJECT_ROOT is configured correctly for HOST_PORT and DATABASE_URL environment variables.

We're ready to start coding. Let's begin with the routes definition in $PROJECT_ROOT/src/iter6/routes.rs:

```
use crate::handler::{handle_register, show_register_form, show_signin_form,
➥handle_signin};
use actix_files as fs;
use actix_web::web;

pub fn app_config(config: &mut web::ServiceConfig) {
  config.service(
    web::scope("")
      .service(fs::Files::new("/static", "./static").show_files_listing())
      .service(web::resource("/").route(web::get().to(show_register_form)))
      .service(web::resource("/signinform").route(web::get().to(
      ➥show_signin_form)))
      .service(web::resource("/signin").route(web::post().to(
      ➥handle_signin)))
      .service(web::resource("/register").route(web::post().to(
      ➥handle_register)))),
    );
}
```

Add imports for show_signin_form and handle_signin. We have yet to write this handler function.

Add a /signinform route to display the sign-in form to the user when they visit the landing page. The show_signin-form handler function (yet to be written) will display the HTML form to the user.

Add a /register route to process the sign-in request from the user. A POST HTTP request will be triggered on this route when the user enters the username and password and submits the sign-in form.

With this done, we can move on to the model definition in $PROJECT_ROOT/src/ iter6/model.rs. Add the `TutorSigninForm` data structure to model.rs:

```
// Form to enable tutors to sign in
#[derive(Serialize, Deserialize, Debug)]
pub struct TutorSigninForm {
    pub username: String,
    pub password: String,
}
```

This is a Rust struct to capture the username and password entered by the user and to make it available in the handler function for processing.

With the basic structure of the project set up, we can now start to write code for signing in users.

9.3   Implementing user authentication

We have defined the routes and data model, so let's now write the handler functions for signing in users in $PROJECT_ROOT/src/iter6/handler/auth.rs.

First, make the following change to the imports:

```
use crate::model::{TutorRegisterForm, TutorResponse,
➥TutorSigninForm, User};
```

Add TutorSigninForm to the list of imports from the data model.

Add the following handler functions, and replace references to `iter5` with `iter6` in the same file:

```
pub async fn show_signin_form(tmpl: web::Data<tera::Tera>) ->
➥Result<HttpResponse, Error> {
    let mut ctx = tera::Context::new();
    ctx.insert("error", "");
    ctx.insert("current_name", "");
    ctx.insert("current_password", "");
```

This function initializes the form fields and displays the signin.html file to the user.

```
    let s = tmpl
        .render("signin.html", &ctx)
        .map_err(|_| EzyTutorError::TeraError(
        ➥"Template error".to_string()))?;

    Ok(HttpResponse::Ok().content_type("text/html").body(s))
}
pub async fn handle_signin(
    tmpl: web::Data<tera::Tera>,
    app_state: web::Data<AppState>,
    params: web::Form<TutorSigninForm>,
) -> Result<HttpResponse, Error> {

Ok(HttpResponse::Ok().finish())
}
```

> This is a placeholder for the function that will handle sign-in requests. We'll come back to it later.

Recall that the `show_signin_form` handler function is invoked in response to a request that arrives on the `/signinform` route, as defined in the routes definition.

Let's design the actual sign-in HTML form that will be displayed when the user chooses to sign in to the EzyTutors web application. Create a new signin.html file under $PROJECT_ROOT/static/iter6 folder, and add the following code to it. Note that there should already be a register.html file present in the same folder.

Listing 9.1   Tutor sign-in form

```
<!doctype html>
<html>

<head>
    <meta charset=utf-8>
    <title>Tutor registration</title>

    <style>
        ...
    </style>
</head>

<body>
    <div class="header">
        <h1>Welcome to EzyTutor</h1>
        <p>Start your own online tutor business in a few minutes</p>
    </div>

    <div class="center">
        <h2>
            Tutor sign in
        </h2>
        <form action=/signin method=POST>
            <label for="userid">Enter username</label><br>
            <input type="text" name="username" autocomplete="username"
            ➥value="{{current_name}}" minlength="6"
                maxlength="12" required><br>
            <label for="password">Enter password</label><br>
```

> This is standard CSS; the code has been elided for concision and won't be explained here (see the GitHub files for the full source code).

> When the sign-in form is submitted by the user, a POST request is made by the browser to the Tutor SSR web application on the /signin route.

Input field to enter the username

Input field to enter the password

```
<input type="password" name="password"
⮡autocomplete="new-password" value="{{current_password}}"
    minlength="8" maxlength="12" required><br>
<label for="error">
    <p style="color:red">{{error}}</p>
</label><br>
<button type=submit id="button2">Sign in</button>
```

Label to display any error messages (such as if the login is unsuccessful)

Allows the user to switch to the registration form

Button for user to submit the sign-in form after entering the sign-in credentials

```
</form>
<form action=/ method=GET>
    <button type=submit id="button2">Register</button>
</form>
</div>
<p>
<div id="footer">
    (c)Photo by Author
</div>

</p>

</html>
```

Add a user.html form to $PROJECT_ROOT/static/iter6. This will be displayed after a successful sign-in by the user.

Listing 9.2   User notification screen

```
<!DOCTYPE html>
<html>

<head>
    <meta charset=\"utf-8\" />
    <title>{{title}}</title>
</head>

<body>
    <h1>Hi, {{name}}!</h1>
    <p>{{message}}</p>
</body>

</html>
```

Lastly, let's look at the `main()` function in $PROJECT_ROOT/src/bin/iter6-ssr.rs. Here are the imports:

```
#[path = "../iter6/mod.rs"]
mod iter6;
use actix_web::{web, App, HttpServer};
use actix_web::web::Data;
use dotenv::dotenv;
use iter6::{dbaccess, errors, handler, model, routes, state};
use routes::app_config;
use sqlx::postgres::PgPool;
use std::env;
use tera::Tera;
```

The `main()` function is in the following listing.

Listing 9.3   `main()` function

```
#[actix_web::main]
async fn main() -> std::io::Result<()> {
    dotenv().ok();
    //Start HTTP server
    let host_port = env::var("HOST_PORT").expect(
        "HOST:PORT address is not set in .env file");
    println!("Listening on: {}", &host_port);
    let database_url = env::var("DATABASE_URL").expect(
        "DATABASE_URL is not set in .env file");
    let db_pool = PgPool::connect(&database_url).await.unwrap();
    // Construct App State
    let shared_data = web::Data::new(state::AppState { db: db_pool });

    HttpServer::new(move || {
        let tera = Tera::new(concat!(env!("CARGO_MANIFEST_DIR"),
            "/static/iter6/**/*")).unwrap();

        App::new()
        .app_data(Data::new(tera))
            .app_data(shared_data.clone())
            .configure(app_config)
    })
    .bind(&host_port)?
    .run()
    .await
}
```

We can test it now. Run the following command from $PROJECT_ROOT:

```
cargo run --bin iter6-ssr
```

If you get an error saying "no implementation for u32 - usize," run the following command:

```
cargo update -p lexical-core
```

This will upgrade the package dependencies in the Cargo.lock file to the latest version.

From a browser, access the following route:

```
localhost:8080/signinform
```

You should be able to see the sign-in form. You can also invoke the sign-in form by accessing the index route, /, which shows the registration form, and by clicking the Sign In button.

Once you have this working, you can implement the logic for signing in the user. Add the following code to the $PROJECT_ROOT/src/iter6/handler.rs file. Don't forget to remove the placeholder function with the same name that you created earlier.

Listing 9.4   Handler function for signing in

```
pub async fn handle_signin(
    tmpl: web::Data<tera::Tera>,
    app_state: web::Data<AppState>,
    params: web::Form<TutorSigninForm>,
) -> Result<HttpResponse, Error> {
    let mut ctx = tera::Context::new();
    let s;
    let username = params.username.clone();
    let user = get_user_record(&app_state.db,
➥ username.to_string()).await;
    if let Ok(user) = user {
        let does_password_match = argon2::verify_encoded(
            &user.user_password.trim(),
            params.password.clone().as_bytes(),
        )
        .unwrap();
        if !does_password_match {
            ctx.insert("error", "Invalid login");
            ctx.insert("current_name", &params.username);
            ctx.insert("current_password", &params.password);
            s = tmpl
                .render("signin.html", &ctx)
                .map_err(|_| EzyTutorError::TeraError(
                ➥"Template error".to_string()))?;
        } else {
            ctx.insert("name", &params.username);
            ctx.insert("title", &"Signin confirmation!".to_owned());
            ctx.insert(
                "message",
                &"You have successfully logged in to EzyTutor!".to_owned(),
            );
            s = tmpl
                .render("user.html", &ctx)
                .map_err(|_| EzyTutorError::TeraError(
                ➥"Template error".to_string()))?;
        }
    } else {
        ctx.insert("error", "User id not found");
        ctx.insert("current_name", &params.username);
        ctx.insert("current_password", &params.password);
        s = tmpl
            .render("signin.html", &ctx)
            .map_err(|_| EzyTutorError::TeraError(
            ➥"Template error".to_string()))?;
    };

    Ok(HttpResponse::Ok().content_type("text/html").body(s))
}
```

When the user submits the sign-in form, call the database access function to check if the user record is found in the database.

If the user record is found in the database but the password entered by the user does not match the one stored in the database, redisplay the sign-in form to the user with an error message.

If the user record is found in the database and the passwords match, return a confirmation message to the user.

If the username is not found in the database, return the sign-in form with an error message.

Let's test the sign-in function now. Run the following command from $PROJECT_ROOT:

```
cargo run --bin iter6-ssr
```

From a browser, access the following route:

```
localhost:8080/signinform
```

Enter the correct username and password. You should see the confirmation message.

Load the sign-in form once again, and this time enter a valid username but the wrong password. Verify that you get an error message.

Try entering the form the third time, this time with an invalid username. Again, you should see an error message.

With this, we conclude this section. You've so far seen how to define templates using the Tera template library to generate dynamic web pages and how to display the registration and sign-in forms to the user. You've also implemented the code to register and sign in a user and handle errors in user input. And you defined a custom error type to unify error handling.

Let's now move on to managing the course details. We will first implement routing and then develop the functions required for resource maintenance. From now on, we will focus on the services and won't look at the corresponding forms.

9.4   *Routing HTTP requests*

In this section, we'll add the ability for a tutor to maintain courses. We currently have all the handler functions in a single file, and we have to add handlers for course maintenance. Let's first organize the handler functions into their own module. This will give us the ability to split the handler functions across multiple source files.

Start by creating a new folder named handler in the $PROJECT_ROOT/src/iter6 folder. Then move $PROJECT_ROOT/src/iter6/handler.rs into $PROJECT_ROOT/src/iter6/handler, and rename it to auth.rs, as this file deals with the registration and login functionality.

Create new course.rs and mod.rs files under the $PROJECT_ROOT/src/iter6/handler folder. In mod.rs, add the following code to structure the files in the handler folder and export them as a Rust module:

```
pub mod auth;
pub mod course;
```

Contains the handler functions for course maintenance functionality

Contains the handler functions for user registration and sign-in functionality

Modify $PROJECT_ROOT/src/iter6/routes.rs as shown in the following listing.

Listing 9.5   Adding routes for course maintenance

```
use crate::handler::auth::{handle_register, handle_signin,
 show_register_form, show_signin_form};
use crate::handler::course::{handle_delete_course, handle_insert_course,
 handle_update_course};

use actix_files as fs;
use actix_web::web;
```

Import handler functions for course maintenance (these are yet to be created)

Import handler functions for user registration and sign-in

```
pub fn app_config(config: &mut web::ServiceConfig) {        Original route
  config.service(                                           definition
    web::scope("")
      .service(fs::Files::new("/static", "./static").show_files_listing())
      .service(web::resource("/").route(web::get().to(show_register_form)))
      .service(web::resource("/signinform").route(web::get().to(
      ➥show_signin_form)))
      .service(web::resource("/signin").route(web::post().to(
      ➥handle_signin)))
      .service(web::resource("/register").route(web::post().to(
      ➥handle_register)))),
  );
}
```

Add a new route definition for course maintenance.

```
pub fn course_config(config: &mut web::ServiceConfig) {      /courses will be the
  config.service(                                            route prefix for course
    web::scope("/courses")                                   maintenance routes.
      .service(web::resource("new/{tutor_id}").route(web::post().to(
      ➥handle_insert_course)))
      .service(
        web::resource("{tutor_id}/{course_id}").route(web::put().to(
        ➥handle_update_course)),
      )
      .service(
        web::resource("delete/{tutor_id}/{course_id}")
          .route(web::delete().to(handle_delete_course)),
      ),
  );
}
```

The POST request route for adding a new course for a tutor-id on route /courses/new/{tutor_id}

The PUT request route for updating an existing course for a tutor-id on route /courses/{tutor_id}/{course_id}

The DELETE request route to delete an existing course for a tutor-id on route /courses/delete/{tutor_id}/{course_id}

Where we have specified the {tutor_id} and {course_id} as path parameters, they can be extracted from the request's path with help of extractors provided by the Actix Web framework.

Next, we'll add the new course maintenance routes in $PROJECT_ROOT/bin/ iter6-ssr.rs. Make the following change to import the routes we defined in the previous code listing:

```
use routes::{app_config, course_config};
```

In the main() function, make the following change to add course_config routes:

```
HttpServer::new(move || {
    let tera = Tera::new(concat!(env!("CARGO_MANIFEST_DIR"),
    ➥"/static/iter6/**/*")).unwrap();

    App::new()
        .app_data(Data::new(tera))
        .app_data(shared_data.clone())
        .configure(course_config)
        .configure(app_config)
})
.bind(&host_port)?
.run()
.await
```

Add the course maintenance routes. Note that this is placed ahead of the app_config line. This matches all routes with a /courses/ prefix.

The existing route for auth (registering and signing in). This matches all routes without the /courses/ prefix.

Next, let's add placeholder handler functions for course maintenance in $PROJECT_ROOT/src/iter6/handler/course.rs. We'll write the actual logic to call the backend web service a little later.

Listing 9.6   Placeholders for course maintenance handler functions

```
use actix_web::{web, Error, HttpResponse, Result};
use crate::state::AppState;

pub async fn handle_insert_course(
    _tmpl: web::Data<tera::Tera>,
    _app_state: web::Data<AppState>,
) -> Result<HttpResponse, Error> {
    println!("Got insert request");
    Ok(HttpResponse::Ok().body("Got insert request"))
}

pub async fn handle_update_course(
    _tmpl: web::Data<tera::Tera>,
    _app_state: web::Data<AppState>,
) -> Result<HttpResponse, Error> {
    Ok(HttpResponse::Ok().body("Got update request"))
}

pub async fn handle_delete_course(
    _tmpl: web::Data<tera::Tera>,
    _app_state: web::Data<AppState>,
) -> Result<HttpResponse, Error> {
    Ok(HttpResponse::Ok().body("Got delete request"))
}
```

As you will note, the handler functions do nothing for now except return a message. We will implement the intended handler functionality later in this chapter.

Note the use of underscores (_) before the variable names. We are not going to use these parameters within the body of the handler function yet, and adding an underscore before the variable names will prevent compiler warnings.

Let's do a quick test of these four routes. Run the server with this command:

```
cargo run --bin iter6-ssr
```

To test the POST, PUT, and DELETE requests, try the following commands from the command line:

```
curl -H "Content-Type: application/json" -X POST -d '{}'
➥localhost:8080/courses/new/1
curl -H "Content-Type: application/json" -X PUT -d '{}'
➥localhost:8080/courses/1/2
curl -H "Content-Type: application/json" -X DELETE -d '{}'
➥localhost:8080/courses/delete/1/2
```

You should see the following messages returned from the server corresponding to the three HTTP preceding requests:

```
Got insert request
Got update request
Got delete request
```

We've now verified that the routes have been established correctly, and the HTTP requests are being routed to the correct handler functions. In the next section, we'll implement the logic that adds a course for a tutor in the handler function.

9.5 Creating a resource with the HTTP POST method

We'll now add a new course for a tutor by sending an API request to the backend tutor web service that we wrote in chapter 6. Go to the code repo for chapter 6 (/path-to-chapter6-folder/ezytutors/tutor-db), and start the tutor web service with the following command:

```
cargo run --bin iter5
```

The tutor web service should now be ready to receive requests from the tutor web application. Let's write the code for the course handler in the web application in $PROJECT_ROOT/src/iter6/handler/course.rs.

Modify the $PROJECT_ROOT/src/iter6/model.rs file to add the following.

Listing 9.7 Data model changes for course maintenance

```
#[derive(Deserialize, Debug, Clone)]
pub struct NewCourse {                     ◄─┐  Struct to represent user-provided
    pub course_name: String,                 │  data for creating a new course
    pub course_description: String,
    pub course_format: String,
    pub course_duration: String,
    pub course_structure: Option<String>,
    pub course_price: Option<i32>,
    pub course_language: Option<String>,
    pub course_level: Option<String>,
}

#[derive(Deserialize, Serialize, Debug, Clone)]
pub struct NewCourseResponse {             ◄─┐  Struct to represent the response
    pub course_id: i32,                      │  received from the backend tutor
    pub tutor_id: i32,                       │  web service on new course creation
    pub course_name: String,
    pub course_description: String,
    pub course_format: String,
    pub course_structure: Option<String>,
    pub course_duration: String,                  Trait implementation to convert JSON
    pub course_price: Option<i32>,                 data received from the tutor web
    pub course_language: Option<String>,        service for new course creation to the
    pub course_level: Option<String>,           NewCourseResponse struct. The fields
    pub posted_time: String,                     of data type String (heap-allocated)
}                                                are cloned, but those of integer type
                                                 (stack allocated) don't need to be.
impl From<web::Json<NewCourseResponse>> for NewCourseResponse {    ◄─┘
```

```
        fn from(new_course: web::Json<NewCourseResponse>) -> Self {
            NewCourseResponse {
                tutor_id: new_course.tutor_id,
                course_id: new_course.course_id,
                course_name: new_course.course_name.clone(),
                course_description: new_course.course_description.clone(),
                course_format: new_course.course_format.clone(),
                course_structure: new_course.course_structure.clone(),
                course_duration: new_course.course_duration.clone(),
                course_price: new_course.course_price,
                course_language: new_course.course_language.clone(),
                course_level: new_course.course_level.clone(),
                posted_time: new_course.posted_time.clone(),
            }
        }
    }
```

Also, add the following module import, which is required by the `From` trait implementation:

```
use actix_web::web;
```

Next, let's rewrite the handler function to create a new course. In $PROJECT_ROOT/src/iter6/handler/course.rs, add the following module imports:

```
use actix_web::{web, Error, HttpResponse, Result};     ◁──────  Actix Web-related imports
use crate::state::AppState;
use crate::model::{NewCourse, NewCourseResponse, UpdateCourse,
➥UpdateCourseResponse};                                 ◁──────  The Rust structs that we
use serde_json::json;                 ◁──┐                        just created to hold the
                                         │ A package containing utilities to    input and output data for
use crate::state::AppState;              │ serialize and deserialize data between    the tutor web service
                                         │ JSON format and Rust structs.
```

Next, modify the `handle_insert_course` handler function as shown in the following listing.

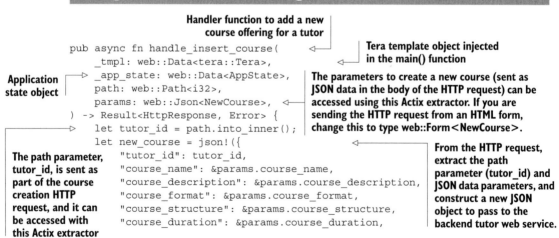

Listing 9.8   Handler function for inserting a new course

Handler function to add a new
course offering for a tutor

```
pub async fn handle_insert_course(        ◁──────  Tera template object injected
    _tmpl: web::Data<tera::Tera>,         ◁──────  in the main() function
    _app_state: web::Data<AppState>,
    path: web::Path<i32>,
    params: web::Json<NewCourse>,         ◁──────
) -> Result<HttpResponse, Error> {
    let tutor_id = path.into_inner();
    let new_course = json!({
        "tutor_id": tutor_id,
        "course_name": &params.course_name,
        "course_description": &params.course_description,
        "course_format": &params.course_format,
        "course_structure": &params.course_structure,
        "course_duration": &params.course_duration,
```

Application state object → `_app_state: web::Data<AppState>,`

The parameters to create a new course (sent as JSON data in the body of the HTTP request) can be accessed using this Actix extractor. If you are sending the HTTP request from an HTML form, change this to type web::Form<NewCourse>.

The path parameter, tutor_id, is sent as part of the course creation HTTP request, and it can be accessed with this Actix extractor

From the HTTP request, extract the path parameter (tutor_id) and JSON data parameters, and construct a new JSON object to pass to the backend tutor web service.

```
        "course_price": &params.course_price,
        "course_language": &params.course_language,
        "course_level": &params.course_level
    });
    let awc_client = awc::Client::default();
    let res = awc_client
        .post("http://localhost:3000/courses/")
        .send_json(&new_course)
        .await
.unwrap()
        .body()
        .await?;
    println!("Finished call: {:?}", res);
    let course_response: NewCourseResponse = serde_json::from_str(
    ➡&std::str::from_utf8(&res)?)?;
    Ok(HttpResponse::Ok().json(course_response))
}
```

Instantiate the Actix web client (HTTP client) to communicate with the tutor web service.

Send the HTTP POST request to the tutor web service, along with the JSON data to create a new course, and receive a response.

Convert the JSON data received (as part of the HTTP response) from the tutor web service into the Rust NewCourseResponse data struct. We implemented the From trait in the model.rs file to specify how this conversion should be done.

Return the HTTP response data received from the tutor web service to the HTTP client that made the course creation request on the tutor web app.

In the preceding listing, the Tera template object is not being used, but you are encouraged to build an HTML interface with Tera templates as an exercise. The application state object is not being used either, but it's shown to illustrate how application state can be accessed within handler functions.

Build and run the web SSR client from the $PROJECT_ROOT as follows:

```
cargo run --bin iter6-ssr
```

Let's test the new course creation with a curl request. Ensure that the tutor web service is running. Then, from another terminal, run the following command:

```
curl -X POST localhost:8080/courses/new/1 -d '{"course_name":"Rust web
➡development", "course_description":"Teaches how to write web apps in
➡Rust", "course_format":"Video", "course_duration":"3 hours",
➡"course_price":100}' -H "Content-Type: application/json"
```

Verify that the new course has been added by running a GET request on the tutor web service:

```
curl localhost:3000/courses/1
```

You should see the new course in the list of courses retrieved for the tutor-id of 1. In the next section, we'll write the handler function to update a course.

9.6   Updating a resource with the HTTP PUT method

Let's write the data structure for updating a course in the $PROJECT_ROOT/src/iter6/model.rs file.

Listing 9.9   Data model changes for updating courses

```
// Update course
#[derive(Deserialize, Serialize, Debug, Clone)]
pub struct UpdateCourse {
    pub course_name: Option<String>,
    pub course_description: Option<String>,
    pub course_format: Option<String>,
    pub course_duration: Option<String>,
    pub course_structure: Option<String>,
    pub course_price: Option<i32>,
    pub course_language: Option<String>,
    pub course_level: Option<String>,
}
```

Rust struct for capturing modified course information from the user. The Option<T> type denotes that not all course information must be sent in the course update request.

```
#[derive(Deserialize, Serialize, Debug, Clone)]
pub struct UpdateCourseResponse {
    pub course_id: i32,
    pub tutor_id: i32,
    pub course_name: String,
    pub course_description: String,
    pub course_format: String,
    pub course_structure: String,
    pub course_duration: String,
    pub course_price: i32,
    pub course_language: String,
    pub course_level: String,
    pub posted_time: String,
}
```

Rust struct to store data received from the tutor web service for the course update request

The From trait implementation to convert the JSON data received from the tutor web service into the Rust UpdateCourseResponse struct. The fields of data type String (heap-allocated) are cloned, but those of integer type (stack allocated) don't need to be.

```
impl From<web::Json<UpdateCourseResponse>> for UpdateCourseResponse {
    fn from(new_course: web::Json<UpdateCourseResponse>) -> Self {
        UpdateCourseResponse {
            tutor_id: new_course.tutor_id,
            course_id: new_course.course_id,
            course_name: new_course.course_name.clone(),
            course_description: new_course.course_description.clone(),
            course_format: new_course.course_format.clone(),
            course_structure: new_course.course_structure.clone(),
            course_duration: new_course.course_duration.clone(),
            course_price: new_course.course_price,
            course_language: new_course.course_language.clone(),
            course_level: new_course.course_level.clone(),
            posted_time: new_course.posted_time.clone(),
        }
    }
}
```

You'll notice that we have defined similar data structures for creating a course (New-Course and NewCourseResponse) and for updating a course (UpdateCourse and UpdateCourseResponse). Is it possible to optimize by reusing the same structs for both the create and update operations? Some optimization might be possible in a real-world scenario. However, for the sake of this example, we will assume that the set of mandatory fields needed to create a new course are different from those needed to update a course (where there are no mandatory fields). Also, separating the data structs for create and update operations makes the code easier to understand while learning.

Next, let's rewrite the handler function for updating course details in $PROJECT_ROOT/src/iter6/handler/course.rs.

Listing 9.10   Handler function for updating a course

```
pub async fn handle_update_course(
    _tmpl: web::Data<tera::Tera>,
    _app_state: web::Data<AppState>,
    web::Path((tutor_id, course_id)): web::Path<(i32, i32)>,
    params: web::Json<UpdateCourse>,
) -> Result<HttpResponse, Error> {            Construct JSON data to send to the tutor
    let update_course = json!({              web service in the HTTP request body.
        "course_name": &params.course_name,
        "course_description": &params.course_description,
        "course_format": &params.course_format,
        "course_duration": &params.course_duration,
        "course_structure": &params.course_structure,
        "course_price": &params.course_price,
        "course_language": &params.course_language,
        "course_level": &params.course_level,

    });                                          Create an instance of
    let awc_client = awc::Client::default();     the Actix HTTP client.
    let update_url = format!("http://localhost:3000/courses/{}/{}",
    tutor_id, course_id);                             Construct the URL
    let res = awc_client                    Send the HTTP request to    with path parameters.
        .put(update_url)                    the tutor web service to
        .send_json(&update_course)          update course details,
        .await                              and receive a response.
    .unwrap()
        .body()
        .await?;
    let course_response: UpdateCourseResponse = serde_json::from_str(
    &std::str::from_utf8(&res)?)?;                      Convert the JSON response data
                                                        received from the tutor web
    Ok(HttpResponse::Ok().json(course_response))        service into a Rust struct.

}
```

Make sure to import the update-related structs as follows:

```
use crate::model::{NewCourse, NewCourseResponse, UpdateCourse,
    UpdateCourseResponse};
```

Build and run the web SSR client from the $PROJECT_ROOT:

```
cargo run --bin iter6-ssr
```

Let's test this with a curl request that updates the course we previously created. Ensure that the tutor web service is running. Then, from a new terminal, run the following command. Replace the tutor-id and course-id with those for the course that you previously created:

```
curl  -X PUT -d '{"course_name":"Rust advanced web development",
➡"course_description":"Teaches how to write advanced web apps in Rust",
➡"course_format":"Video", "course_duration":"4 hours",
➡"course_price":100}' localhost:8080/courses/1/27 -H
➡"Content-Type: application/json"
```

Verify that the course details have been updated by running a GET request on the tutor web service (replace the course_id of 1 with the correct value for the course you updated):

```
curl localhost:3000/courses/1
```

You should see the updated course details in the output. Let's move on to deleting a course.

9.7   *Deleting a resource with the HTTP DELETE method*

Let's update the handler function to delete a course in $PROJECT_ROOT/src/iter6/handler/course.rs.

Listing 9.11   Handler function for deleting a course

```
pub async fn handle_delete_course(            Actix extractor for path
    _tmpl: web::Data<tera::Tera>,             parameters tutor_id and
    _app_state: web::Data<AppState>,          course_id, which uniquely
    path: web::Path<(i32, i32)>,      ◀────── identify the course to delete      Instantiate the Actix
) -> Result<HttpResponse, Error> {                                                HTTP client to
    let (tutor_id, course_id) = path.into_inner();                                communicate with
    let awc_client = awc::Client::default();  ◀───────────────────────────────── the tutor web service.
    let delete_url = format!("http://localhost:3000/courses/{}/{}",
➡tutor_id, course_id);
    let _res = awc_client.delete(delete_url).send().await.unwrap();  ◀──────────┐
    Ok(HttpResponse::Ok().body("Course deleted"))  ◀────────┐
}                                                           │         Send the DELETE
                                          Return a confirmation     HTTP request to the
                                               to the caller.       tutor web service.
```

Construct a URL with path parameters.

Build and run the tutor web app from the $PROJECT_ROOT:

```
cargo run --bin iter6-ssr
```

Now run the delete request, replacing the tutor_id and course_id values with your own:

```
curl -X DELETE localhost:8080/courses/delete/1/19
```

Verify that the course has been deleted by running a query on the tutor web service (replace the tutor_id with your own):

```
curl localhost:3000/courses/1
```

You should see that the course has been deleted in the tutor web service.

You have now seen how to add, update, and delete a course from the web client frontend written in Rust. As an exercise, you can try the following additional tasks:

- Implement a new route to retrieve the list of courses for a tutor.
- Create HTML and Tera templates for creating, updating, and deleting a course.
- Add additional error handling for cases with invalid user input.

Once all these elements are in place, our application will be on the path to completion. We can congratulate ourselves: the hardest part of our project is done!

We have come to the conclusion of this chapter and also this part of the book on Rust web application development. In the next chapter, we'll take a look at an advanced topic relating to asynchronous servers in Rust.

Summary

- You structured and wrote a web application project in Rust that talks to a backend web service.
- You designed and implemented user authentication functionality that allows the user to enter their credentials in an HTML form and then stores them in a local database. The handling of errors in user input was also covered.
- You saw how to structure the project and modularize the code for a web frontend application that includes HTTP request handlers, database interaction logic, a data model, and web UI and HTML templates.
- You wrote code to create, update, and delete specific data in the database in response to HTTP POST, PUT, and DELETE method requests. You also learned how to extract parameters sent as part of the HTTP requests.
- You learned how to construct HTTP requests to invoke APIs on a backend web service and to interpret the responses received, including serializing and deserializing data.
- In summary, you have learned how to build a web application in Rust that can communicate with a backend web service, interact with a local database, and perform basic create, update, and delete operations on data in response to incoming HTTP requests.

Advanced topic: Async Rust

The third part of this book covers three advanced topics that are not directly related to the tutor web service and web app that we have built so far, but that are important topics for anyone interested in building complex Rust servers and preparing them for production deployment.

Chapter 10 is devoted to asynchronous programming. Although not new, asynchronous (or async) programming remains a hot topic today because it is of the utmost importance in modern systems. Async programming allows developers to make the best possible use of computing resources when data processing activities vary widely in time or when there is latency in the system. Async programming is all the more significant for distributed systems. We'll start with a brief overview of concurrent programming and then look at examples of how to write multithreaded versus async programs in Rust. We'll delve deep into Rust's async primitives, such as futures, and see how to write async programs in Rust from first principles.

In chapter 11, we'll move on to the more complex world of peer-to-peer (P2P) architectures, which further build on async programming. P2P is not required for simple, low-traffic web applications, like the examples in this book, but you should be aware of Rust's vast potential in advanced distributed architectures. P2P servers are different from the web services that we saw in the first part of the book, and this section shows how it can be advantageous to use P2P architectures for certain classes of applications.

In chapter 12, we will look at the deployment of Rust-based web applications. Containers are a mature and widely accepted technology, both in the cloud and in corporate data centers. This is no surprise given the flexibility and other benefits offered by containers (isolation, security, startup times, etc.). In complex environments, with large distributed applications, containers need to be orchestrated with solutions like Kubernetes or, beyond pure Kubernetes, OpenShift. In this chapter, you'll learn how to use Docker in a simple context while still reaping its benefits. We will build and deploy EzyTutors using Docker Compose, a basic orchestration tool for Docker.

Having read this part, you will be able to apply what you have learned to develop different types of async applications in Rust and deploy any type of Rust server or application using Docker.

Understanding async Rust

10

This chapter covers

- Introducing async programming concepts
- Writing concurrent programs
- Diving deeper into async Rust
- Understanding futures
- Implementing a custom future

In the previous chapters, we built a web service and a web application using Rust. We've used the Actix Web framework to handle the network communications, mostly submitting HTTP requests to the Actix web server from a single browser window or a command-line terminal. But have you thought about what happens when tens or hundreds of users send requests concurrently to register tutors or courses? Or, more broadly, how modern web servers handle tens of thousands of concurrent requests? Read on to find out.

In this part of the book, we will put our EzyTutors web application aside for a while so we can focus on the fascinating aspects of Rust that allow us to implement efficient, state-of-the-art services. We will come back to EzyTutors at the end of the book, where you'll see how to deploy it in an efficient and flexible way.

229

In this chapter, we will thus take a detour from our web application and look under the hood to understand what asynchronous Rust is, why we might need to use it, and how it works in practice. By the end of this chapter, you'll have a better understanding of the magic that Actix (and other modern web frameworks) perform to handle heavy concurrent loads while delivering swift responses to user requests.

> **NOTE** This chapter and the next are intended as advanced topics, aimed at those who want to get into the details of asynchronous programming in Rust. It is not necessary to master these skills, or even read these chapters, to do web programming in Rust. You can skip these chapters now and come back to them later when you are ready for an async deep-dive.

Let's get started with a few basic concepts involved in concurrent programming.

10.1 *Introducing async programming concepts*

In computer science, *concurrency* is the ability of different parts of a program to be executed out of order, or at the same time simultaneously, without affecting the final outcome.

Strictly speaking, executing parts of a program out of order is *concurrency*, whereas executing multiple tasks simultaneously is *parallelism*. Figure 10.1 illustrates this difference, but for this chapter, let's use the term *concurrency* to broadly refer to both of these aspects. In practice, both concurrency and parallelism are used in conjunction to achieve the overall outcome of processing multiple requests that arrive at the same time in an efficient and safe manner.

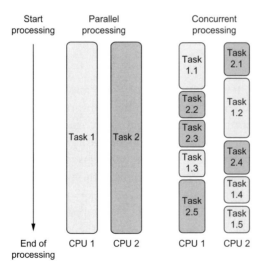

In concurrent processing, each available CPU/core allocates fractional time to execute a portion of the scheduled tasks. In this figure

- There are two tasks to be scheduled: task 1 and task 2.
- There are two available CPUs: CPU 1 and CPU 2.
- Tasks 1.1 to 1.5 and tasks 2.1 to 2.5 represent smaller chunks of tasks 1 and 2.
- CPU 1 and CPU 2 load each of these code chunks, one at a time, and execute them.

Figure 10.1   Concurrency vs. parallelism

You may wonder why one would want to execute parts of a program out of order. After all, programs are supposed to execute from top to bottom, statement by statement, right?

There are two primary drivers for using concurrent programming—one from the demand side and another from the supply side:

- *Demand side*—On the user demand side, the expectation for programs to run faster drives software developers to consider concurrent programming techniques.
- *Supply side*—On the hardware supply side, the availability of multiple CPUs, and multiple cores in CPUs, on computers (both at the consumer level and in high-end servers) creates an opportunity for software developers to write programs that can take advantage of multiple cores and processors to make the overall execution faster and efficient.

But designing and coding concurrent programs is complex. It starts with determining what tasks can be performed concurrently. How do developers determine this? Let's go back to figure 10.1. It shows two tasks, task 1 and task 2, to be executed. Let's assume that these tasks are two functions in a Rust program. The easiest way to visualize this is to schedule task 1 on CPU 1 and task 2 on CPU 2. This is what the parallel processing example shows. But is this the most efficient model for utilizing the available CPU time?

It may not be. To understand this better, let's classify all processing performed by software programs broadly into two categories: *CPU-intensive* tasks and *I/O-intensive* tasks, although most code in the real world involves a mix of both. Examples of CPU-intensive tasks include genome sequencing, video encoding, graphics processing, and computing cryptographic proofs in a blockchain. I/O-intensive tasks include accessing data from file systems or databases and processing network TCP/HTTP requests.

In CPU-intensive tasks, most of the work involves accessing data in memory, loading program instructions and data on the stack, and executing them. What kind of concurrency is possible here? Let's consider a simple program that takes a list of numbers and computes the square root of each number. The programmer could write a single function that does the following:

- Takes a reference to a list of numbers loaded into memory
- Iterates through the list in a sequence
- Computes the square root for each number
- Writes the result back to memory

This is an example of sequential processing. In a computer where there are multiple processors or cores, the programmer also has the opportunity to structure the program in such a way that each number is read from memory and sent to the next available CPU or core for square-root processing because each number can be processed independently of the others. This is a trivial example, but it illustrates the type of opportunity where programmers can utilize multiple processors or cores in complex CPU-intensive tasks.

Let's next look at where concurrency can be used in I/O-intensive tasks. Let's take the familiar example of HTTP request processing in web services and applications, which is generally more I/O-intensive than CPU-intensive.

In web applications, data is stored in databases, and all create, read, update, and delete operations, corresponding to HTTP POST, GET, PUT, and DELETE requests respectively, require the web application to transfer data to and from the database. This requires the processor (CPU) to wait for the data to be read or written to disk. In spite of advances in disk technologies, disk access is slow (in the range of milliseconds, as opposed to memory access, which is in nanoseconds). So, if the application is trying to retrieve 10,000 user records from a Postgres database, it makes calls to the operating system for disk access, and the CPU waits during this time. What options does the programmer have when a part of their code makes the processor wait? The answer is that the processor could perform another task in this time. This is an example of an opportunity where programmers can design concurrent programs.

Another source of "delays," or "waiting," in web applications is network request handling. The HTTP model is quite simple: The client establishes a connection to the remote server and issues a request (sent as an HTTP request message). The server then processes the request, issues a response, and closes the connection. The challenge arises when a new request arrives while the processor is still serving the previous request. For example, suppose a GET request arrives to retrieve a set of courses for tutor 1, and while this is being processed, a new request arrives to POST a new course from tutor 2. Should the second request wait in a queue until the first request is fully processed? Or can we schedule the second request on the next available core or processor? This is when we start to appreciate the need for concurrent programming.

> **NOTE** HTTP/2 has introduced some improvements that minimize the number of request-response cycles and handshakes. For more details on HTTP/2, see Barry Pollard's *HTTP/2 in Action* (Manning, 2019).

We have so far looked at examples of opportunities where programmers can use concurrent programming techniques, both in CPU-intensive and I/O-intensive tasks. Let's now look at the tools available to programmers for writing concurrent programs.

Figure 10.2 shows the various options programmers have to structure their code for execution on CPUs. Specifically, it highlights the differences between *synchronous* processing and the two modes of *concurrent* processing: *multithreading* and *async* processing. It illustrates the differences with an example where three tasks need to be executed: task 1, task 2, and task 3.

Let's also assume task 1 contains three parts:

- *Part 1*—Processing input data
- *Part 2*—A blocking operation
- *Part 3*—Packaging the data to be returned

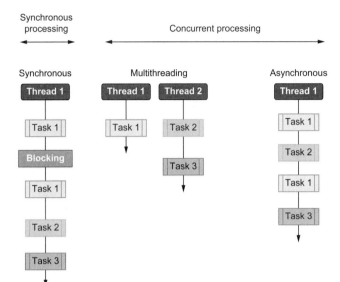

Figure 10.2 Synchronous, asynchronous, and multithreading processing

Note the blocking operation. This means that the current thread of execution is blocked, waiting for some external operation to complete, such as reading from a large file or database. Let's look at how we could handle these tasks in three different programming modes: synchronous processing, multithreaded processing, and async processing.

In the case of synchronous processing, the processor completes part 1, waits for the result of the blocking operation, and then proceeds to execute part 3 of the task.

If the same task were to be executed in multithreaded mode, task 1, which contains the blocking operation, could be spawned off on a separate operating system thread and the processor could execute other tasks on another thread.

If async processing is used, an async runtime (such as Tokio) would manage the scheduling of tasks on the processor. In this case, it would execute task 1 until it blocked, waiting for I/O. At this point, the async runtime would schedule task 2. When the blocking operation in task 1 completed, task 1 would again be scheduled for execution on the processor.

At a high level, this is how synchronous processing differs from the two modes of concurrent processing. Programmers need to determine the best approach for the use case and computation involved.

Let's now look at a second example of a web server receiving multiple simultaneous network requests and see how the two concurrent processing techniques can be applied.

The multithreading approach to concurrency involves using native operating system threads, as shown in figure 10.3. In this case, a new thread is started within the web server process to handle each incoming request. The Rust standard library provides good built-in support for multithreading with the std::thread module.

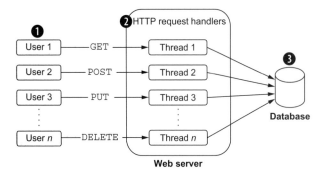

① A number of simultaneous HTTP requests are sent from the users to the web server.

② For each incoming request, a separate operating system thread is created to handle the incoming request.

③ The operating system schedules the threads for execution on the processor/core, which make database requests and send back responses to the users.

Figure 10.3   Multithreading in HTTP request processing

In this model, we are distributing the program (web server) computation on multiple threads. This can improve performance because the threads can run simultaneously, but it's not as simple as that. Multithreading adds a new layer of complexity:

- The order of execution of threads is unpredictable.
- There can be deadlocks when multiple threads are trying to access the same piece of data in memory.
- There can be race conditions, where one thread may have read a piece of data from memory and be performing some computation with it, and another thread updates the value in the meantime.

Writing multithreaded programs requires careful design compared to single-threaded programs.

Another challenge in multithreading has to do with the type of threading model implemented by the programming language. There are two types of threading models: a *1:1 thread model*, where there is a single operating system thread per language thread, and an *M:N model*, where there are M green (quasi) threads per N operating system threads. The Rust standard library implements the 1:1 thread model, but this does not mean that we can create an endless number of threads corresponding to new network requests. Each operating system has a limit on the number of threads, and this is also influenced by the stack size and amount of virtual memory available in the server. In addition, there is a context-switching cost associated with multiple threads—when a CPU switches from one thread to another, it needs to save the local data, program pointer, etc., of the current thread, and load the program pointer and data for the next thread. Overall, using operating system threads incurs these context-switching costs along with some operating system resource costs for managing the threads.

Thus, multithreading, while suitable for certain scenarios, is not the perfect solution for all situations that require concurrent processing. The second approach to concurrent programming (which has become increasingly popular over the last several years) is asynchronous programming (or *async* for short). In web applications, async programming can be used on both the client side and server side. Async web request processing on the server side is illustrated in figure 10.4.

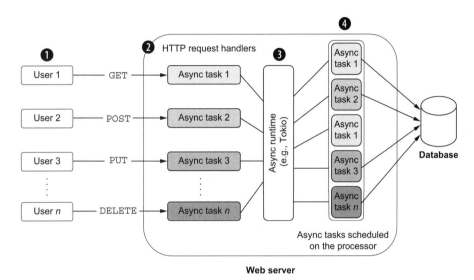

❶ Users send HTTP requests to the web server simultaneously.

❷ A new async task is spawned to process each incoming request.

❸ The async tasks are managed by the async runtime (e.g., Tokio).

❹ The async runtime schedules the async tasks for execution on the processor/core. When task 1 waits for a database operation to complete, the async runtime schedules the next task for execution. When the blocking operation in task 1 completes, the async runtime is notified, which then reschedules task 1 on the processor for completion.

Figure 10.4 Async programming in HTTP request processing

Figure 10.4 shows how async processing can be used by an API server or web service to handle multiple incoming requests concurrently on the server side. Here, as each HTTP request is received by the async web server, the server spawns a new async task to handle it. The scheduling of various async tasks on the available CPUs is handled by the async runtime.

Figure 10.5 shows what async looks like on the client side. Let's consider the example of a JavaScript application running within a browser trying to upload a file to the server. Without concurrency, the screen would freeze for the user until the file was uploaded and a response was received from the server. The user wouldn't be able to do anything else during this period. With async on the client side, the browser-based UI can continue to process user inputs while waiting for the server to respond to the previous request.

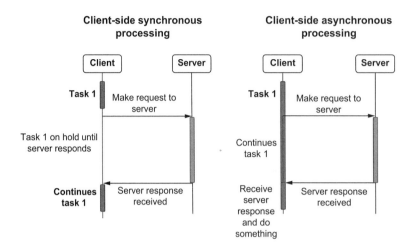

Figure 10.5   Client-side async processing

You've now seen the differences between synchronous, multithreaded, and async programming in several examples. Let's implement these different techniques in code.

10.2   *Writing concurrent programs*

In this section, we'll write synchronous, multithreaded, and async programs in Rust. We're going to dive into some beginner code straight away, showing synchronous processing.

Start a new project with these commands:

```
cargo new --bin async-hello
cd async-hello
```

Add the following code to src/main.rs:

```
fn main() {
    println!("Hello before reading file!");
    let file_contents = read_from_file();
    println!("{:?}", file_contents);
    println!("Hello after reading file!");
}

fn read_from_file() -> String {
    String::from("Hello, there")
}
```

This is a simple Rust program. It has a `read_from_file()` function that simulates reading a file and returning the contents. This function is invoked from the `main()` function. Note that the call from the `main()` function to the `read_from_file()` function is synchronous, meaning that the `main()` function waits for the called function to finish executing and return before continuing with the rest of the `main()` program.

   Run the program:

```
cargo run
```

You should see the following printed out to your terminal:

```
Hello before reading file!
"Hello, there"
Hello after reading file!
```

There's nothing special about this program. Next, let's simulate a delay in reading the file by adding a timer. Modify src/main.rs to look like this:

```
use std::thread::sleep;                                              Import the sleep function
use std::time::Duration;        Import the Duration data type,       from the standard library.
                                which represents a span of time.
fn main() {
    println!("Hello before reading file!");
    let file_contents = read_from_file();
    println!("{:?}", file_contents);
    println!("Hello after reading file!");
}

// function that simulates reading from a file          Put the current thread to
fn read_from_file() -> String {                          sleep for 2 seconds before
    sleep(Duration::new(2, 0));                           returning from the function.
    String::from("Hello, there")
}
```

In this code, we import the sleep function from the standard library. The `sleep()` function puts the current thread to sleep for a specified amount of time, and in the Rust standard library, it's a blocking function, meaning that it blocks the current thread of execution for the duration specified. This is a poor way to simulate delays in reading a file, but it serves our purposes here.

   Note that the `main()` function still only synchronously calls the `read_from_file()` function, meaning that it waits until the called function is complete (including the added delay) before printing out the file contents.

   Run the program:

```
cargo run
```

You can now see the final print statement on your terminal after the specified delay period.

   Let's add another computation to the mix. Modify the program in src/main.rs as follows:

```
use std::thread::sleep;
use std::time::Duration;

fn main() {
    println!("Hello before reading file!");
    let file1_contents = read_from_file1();        Call the function that simulates
    println!("{:?}", file1_contents);              a delay in reading from file 1.
    println!("Hello after reading file1!");
    let file2_contents = read_from_file2();        Call the function that simulates
    println!("{:?}", file2_contents);              a delay in reading from file 2.
    println!("Hello after reading file2!");
}

// function that simulates reading from a file
fn read_from_file1() -> String {
    sleep(Duration::new(4, 0));
    String::from("Hello, there from file 1")
}

// function that simulates reading from a file
fn read_from_file2() -> String {
    sleep(Duration::new(2, 0));
    String::from("Hello, there from file 2")
}
```

Run the program again, and you'll see that there is a 4-second delay in the execution of the first function and a 2-second delay for the second function, amounting to a total delay of 6 seconds. Can we not do better?

Since the two files are distinct, why can't we read the two files at the same time? Can we use a concurrent programming technique here? Sure, we can use the native operating system threads to achieve this. Modify the code in src/main.rs as shown:

```
use std::thread;
use std::thread::sleep;
use std::time::Duration;

fn main() {
    println!("Hello before reading file!");
    let handle1 = thread::spawn(|| {             Spawn a new thread
        let file1_contents = read_from_file1();  to read file 1.
        println!("{:?}", file1_contents);
    });
    let handle2 = thread::spawn(|| {             Spawn a new thread
        let file2_contents = read_from_file2();  to read file 2.
        println!("{:?}", file2_contents);
    });
    handle1.join().unwrap();                      Prevents the main thread from exiting
    handle2.join().unwrap();                      until the first thread completes execution
}
                                                  Prevents the main thread from exiting until
                                                  the second thread completes execution
// function that simulates reading from a file
fn read_from_file1() -> String {
    sleep(Duration::new(4, 0));
    String::from("Hello, there from file 1")
}
```

```
// function that simulates reading from a file
fn read_from_file2() -> String {
    sleep(Duration::new(2, 0));
    String::from("Hello, there from file 2")
}
```

Run the program again. This time, you'll see that it does not take 6 seconds for the two functions to complete execution, but much less, because both files are being read concurrently in two separate operating system threads of execution. You've just seen concurrency in action using multithreading.

What if there were another way to process the two files concurrently on a single thread? Let's explore this further using asynchronous programming techniques.

For writing basic multithreaded programs, the Rust standard library contains the needed primitives (even though external libraries, such as Rayon, are available that have additional features). However, when writing and executing async programs, only the bare essentials are provided by the Rust standard library, which is not adequate. This necessitates the use of external async libraries. In this chapter, we will make use of the Tokio async runtime to illustrate how asynchronous programs can be written in Rust.

Add the following to cargo.toml:

```
[dependencies]
tokio = { version = "1", features = ["full"] }
```

Modify the src/main.rs file as follows:

```
use std::thread::sleep;
use std::time::Duration;

#[tokio::main]
async fn main() {
    println!("Hello before reading file!");

    let h1 = tokio::spawn(async {
        let _file1_contents = read_from_file1();
    });

    let h2 = tokio::spawn(async {
        let _file2_contents = read_from_file2();
    });
    let _ = tokio::join!(h1, h2);
}
// function that simulates reading from a file
async fn read_from_file1() -> String {
    sleep(Duration::new(4, 0));
    println!("{:?}", "Processing file 1");
    String::from("Hello, there from file 1")
}

// function that simulates reading from a file
async fn read_from_file2() -> String {
    sleep(Duration::new(2, 0));
```

Instruct the compiler to add Tokio as the async runtime.

Declare the main function as async.

Spawn a new asynchronous task managed by the Tokio runtime. The task may execute on the current thread or on a different thread, depending on the Tokio runtime configuration.

The main() function waits on multiple concurrent branches, and it returns when all the branches complete. This is similar to the join statement in the previous multithreading example.

The functions now have an async prefix to denote that they can be scheduled as async tasks by the Tokio runtime and executed concurrently.

```
        println!("{:?}", "Processing file 2");
        String::from("Hello, there from file 2")
}
```

You'll see many similarities between this example and the previous multithreaded example. New async tasks are spawned much like new threads are spawned. The `join!` macro waits for all the async tasks to complete before completing execution of the `main()` function.

However, you'll also notice a few key differences. All the functions, including `main()`, have been prefixed with the `async` keyword. Another key difference is the annotation `#[tokio::main]`. We'll delve deeper into these concepts shortly, but let's first try to execute the program.

Run the program with `cargo run`, and you'll see the following message printed to the terminal:

```
Hello before reading file!
```

The statement is printed from the `main()` function. However, you will notice that the print statements from the two functions `read_from_file_1()` and `read_from_file_2()` are not printed. This means the functions were not even executed. The reason for this is that, in Rust, asynchronous functions are lazy, in that they are executed only when activated with the `.await` keyword.

Let's try this one more time and add the `.await` keyword in the call to the two functions. Change the code in src/main.rs as shown here:

```
use std::thread::sleep;
use std::time::Duration;

#[tokio::main]
async fn main() {
    println!("Hello before reading file!");

    let h1 = tokio::spawn(async {
        let file1_contents = read_from_file1().await;      Add the .await
        println!("{:?}", file1_contents);                  keyword while
    });                                                    invoking the
                                                           function.
    let h2 = tokio::spawn(async {
        let file2_contents = read_from_file2().await;
        println!("{:?}", file2_contents);
    });
    let _ = tokio::join!(h1, h2);
}

// function that simulates reading from a file
async fn read_from_file1() -> String {
    sleep(Duration::new(4, 0));
    println!("{:?}", "Processing file 1");
    String::from("Hello, there from file 1")
}
```

```
// function that simulates reading from a file
async fn read_from_file2() -> String {
    sleep(Duration::new(2, 0));
    println!("{:?}", "Processing file 2");
    String::from("Hello, there from file 2")
}
```

Run the program again. You should see the following output on your terminal:

```
Hello before reading file!
"Processing file 2"
"Hello, there from file 2"
"Processing file 1"
"Hello, there from file 1"
```

Let's see what just happened. Both of the functions called from `main()` are spawned as separate asynchronous tasks on the Tokio runtime, which schedules the execution of both functions concurrently (analogous to running the two functions on two separate threads). The difference is that these two tasks can be scheduled either on the current thread or on different threads, depending on how we configure the Tokio runtime. You'll also notice that the `read_from_file2()` function completes executing before `read_from_file1()`. This is because the sleep time interval for the former is 2 seconds, while for the latter it's 4 seconds. So even though `read_from_file1()` was spawned before `read_from_file2()` in the `main()` function, the async runtime executed `read_from_file2()` first because it woke up from the sleep interval earlier than `read_from_file1()`.

In this section, you've seen simple examples of how to write synchronous, multi-threaded, and async programs in Rust. In the next section, let's go down the async Rust rabbit hole.

10.3   Diving deeper into async Rust

As you've seen, asynchronous programming allows us to process multiple tasks at the same time on a single operating system thread. But how is this possible? A CPU can only process one set of instructions at a time, right?

The trick to achieving this is to exploit situations in code execution where the CPU is waiting for some external event or action to complete. Examples could be waiting to read or write a file to disk, waiting for bytes to arrive on a network connection, or waiting for timers to complete (like you saw in the previous example). While a piece of code or a function is waiting on a disk subsystem or network socket for data, the async runtime (such as Tokio) can schedule other async tasks on the processor that can continue execution. When the system interrupts arrive from the disk or I/O subsystems, the async runtime recognizes this and schedules the original task to continue processing.

As a general guideline, programs that are I/O bound (programs where the rate of progress generally depends on the speed of the I/O subsystem) may be good candidates for asynchronous task execution, as opposed to CPU-bound programs (programs where the rate of progress is dependent on the speed of the CPU, as in the case of complex number-crunching). This is a broad and general guideline, and, as always, there are exceptions.

Since web development deals with a lot of network, file, and database I/O, asynchronous programming, if done right, can speed up overall program execution and improve response times for end users. Imagine a case where your web server has to handle 10,000 or more concurrent connections. Using multithreading to spawn a separate OS thread per connection would be prohibitively expensive from the perspective of system resource consumption. Early web servers used this model but then hit limitations when it came to web-scale systems. This is the reason the Actix Web framework (and many other Rust frameworks) have an async runtime built into the framework. As a matter of fact, Actix Web uses the Tokio library underneath for asynchronous task execution (with some modifications and enhancements).

The `async` and `.await` keywords represent the core built-in set of primitives in the Rust standard library for asynchronous programming. They are just special parts of Rust syntax that make it easier for Rust developers to write asynchronous code that looks like synchronous code.

However, at the core of Rust async is a concept called *futures*. Futures are single eventual values produced by an asynchronous computation (or function). Futures basically represent deferred computations. Async functions in Rust return a future.

Promises in JavaScript

In JavaScript, the analogous concept to a Rust *future* is a *promise*. When JavaScript code is executed within a browser, and when a user makes a request to fetch a URL or load an image, it does not block the current thread. The user can continue to interact with the web page. This is achieved by the JavaScript engine using asynchronous processing for network fetch requests.

Note that a Rust future is a lower-level concept than a promise in JavaScript. A Rust future is something that can be polled for readiness, whereas a JavaScript promise has higher semantics (e.g., a promise can be rejected). However, this is a useful analogy in the context of this discussion.

Does this mean our previous program actually used *futures*? The short answer is yes. Let's rewrite the program to show the use of futures:

```
use std::thread::sleep;
use std::time::Duration;
use std::future::Future;

#[tokio::main]
async fn main() {
    println!("Hello before reading file!");

    let h1 = tokio::spawn(async {
        let file1_contents = read_from_file1().await;
```

```
            println!("{:?}", file1_contents);
    });

    let h2 = tokio::spawn(async {
        let file2_contents = read_from_file2().await;
        println!("{:?}", file2_contents);
    });
    let _ = tokio::join!(h1, h2);
}

// function that simulates reading from a file
fn read_from_file1() -> impl Future<Output=String> {
 async {    sleep(Duration::new(4, 0));
    println!("{:?}", "Processing file 1");
    String::from("Hello, there from file 1")
 }
}

// function that simulates reading from a file
fn read_from_file2() -> impl Future<Output=String> {
    async {
    sleep(Duration::new(3, 0));
    println!("{:?}", "Processing file 2");
    String::from("Hello, there from file 2")
    }
}
```

The body of the function is enclosed within an async block.

The return value of the function implements the Future trait.

Run the program. You should see the same result as earlier.

```
Hello before reading file!
"Processing file 2"
"Hello, there from file 2"
"Processing file 1"
"Hello, there from file 1"
```

The main change we've made to the program is within the two functions, read_from_file1() and read_from_file2(). The first difference you'll notice is that the return value of the function has changed from String to impl Future<Output=String>. This is a way of saying that the function returns a future, or more specifically, something that implements the Future trait.

The async keyword defines an async block or function. Specifying this keyword on a function or a code block instructs the compiler to transform the code into something that generates a future. This is why the following function signature

```
async fn read_from_file1() -> String {
    sleep(Duration::new(4, 0));
    println!("{:?}", "Processing file 1");
    String::from("Hello, there from file 1")
}
```

is analogous to the following one:

```
fn read_from_file1() -> impl Future<Output=String> {
 async {    sleep(Duration::new(4, 0));
```

```
        println!("{:?}", "Processing file 1");
        String::from("Hello, there from file 1")
    }
}
```

The `async` keyword in the first of these two examples is just syntactic sugar for writing the code shown in the second example.

Let's see what the `Future` trait looks like:

```
pub trait Future {
    type Output;
    fn poll(self: Pin<&mut Self>, cx: &mut Context<'_>) -> Poll<Self::Output>;
}
```

A future represents an asynchronous computation. The `Output` type represents the data type returned when a future successfully completes. In our example, we are returning a `String` data type from the function, so we specified the function return value as `impl Future<Output=String>`.

The `poll` method is critical to the functioning of the asynchronous program. This method is called by the async runtime to check if the asynchronous computation has completed. The `poll` function returns a data type that is of `enum` type, which can have one of two possible values:

```
Poll::Pending
Poll::Ready(val)
```

The poll function returns this, along with the value of this future, if it finished successfully.

The poll function returns this value if the future is not ready yet.

The next question is, who calls the `poll` function? Rust futures are lazy, as we saw earlier when the following statement did not execute:

```
let h1 = tokio::spawn(async {
    let _file1_contents = read_from_file1();
});
```

Rust futures need someone to constantly follow up with them for completion, like a project manager who micromanages! This role is performed by an *async executor*, which is part of the async runtime. The future executors take a set of futures and follow them to completion by calling `poll` on them.

In our case, the Tokio library has a future executor that performs this function. This is the reason we annotate the function with the `async` keyword:

```
async fn read_from_file1() -> String {
    sleep(Duration::new(4, 0));
    println!("{:?}", "Processing file 1");
    String::from("Hello, there from file 1")
}
```

Or we can write an `async` code block within a function to achieve the same effect:

```
fn read_from_file1() -> String {
```

```
async {
    sleep(Duration::new(4, 0));
    println!("{:?}", "Processing file 1");
    String::from("Hello, there from file 1")
    }
}
```

The `async` keyword in front of a function or a code block tells the Tokio executor that a future is returned, and it needs to be driven to completion. But how does the Tokio executor know when the async function is ready to yield a value? Does it keep pooling the async function repeatedly? To understand how the Tokio executor does this, let's take a closer look at futures.

10.4   Understanding futures

To understand futures better, let's use the concrete example of the Tokio async library. Figure 10.6 shows the relationship between the Tokio runtime, a spawned task, and a future.

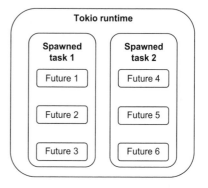

Figure 10.6   The Tokio executor

The Tokio runtime is the component that manages the async tasks and schedules them on the processor for execution. Several async tasks can be spawned in a given program, and each async task may contain one or more futures that return a `Poll::Ready` when the future is ready to be executed, or a `Poll:::Pending` when it is waiting for an external event (such as a network packet to arrive or a database to return a value).

In the previous section, we wrote a `main()` program that spawned two async tasks, which simulated futures. In this section and the next, we'll write code that will help us better understand how futures work. In this section, we'll look at the structure of a future, and in the next section, we'll write a custom async timer as a future. The program structure is illustrated in figure 10.7.

Writing a custom future is the best way to understand how a future works, so let's write one. Modify src/main.rs as follows:

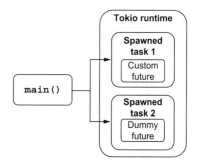

Figure 10.7   Implementing a custom future

```
use std::future::Future;
use std::pin::Pin;
use std::task::{Context, Poll};
use std::thread::sleep;
use std::time::Duration;
```

To poll futures, they should be pinned using a special type called Pin<T>.

Context contains the context of an async task, which can be used to wake the current task. Poll is an enum type that indicates whether a value is available or not.

Create a custom struct which will implement the Future trait.

```
struct ReadFileFuture {}
```
←

Implement the Future trait on the custom struct.

```
impl Future for ReadFileFuture {
    type Output = String;
```
←

Specify the data type of the return value from the future, when the future value becomes available.

```
    fn poll(self: Pin<&mut Self>, _cx: &mut Context<'_>) ->
      Poll<Self::Output> {
```
←

```
        println!("Tokio! Stop polling me");
        Poll::Pending
    }
}
```

Implement the poll() function that's part of the Future trait.

```
#[tokio::main]
async fn main() {
    println!("Hello before reading file!");

    let h1 = tokio::spawn(async {
        let future1 = ReadFileFuture {};
        future1.await
    });
```
←

Call the custom implementation of the future in the main() function.

```
    let h2 = tokio::spawn(async {
        let file2_contents = read_from_file2().await;
        println!("{:?}", file2_contents);
    });
    let _ = tokio::join!(h1, h2);
}

// function that simulates reading from a file
fn read_from_file2() -> impl Future<Output = String> {
    async {
        sleep(Duration::new(2, 0));
        println!("{:?}", "Processing file 2");
        String::from("Hello, there from file 2")
    }
}
```

We've introduced a new concept here: a `Pin`. Futures have to be polled repeatedly by the async runtime, so pinning futures to a particular spot in memory is necessary for the safe functioning of the code within the async block. This is an advanced concept, so for now it will suffice to treat it as a technical requirement in Rust for writing futures, even if you do not understand it fully.

The `poll()` function is called by the Tokio executor in its attempt to resolve the future into a final value (of type `String`, in our example). If the future value is not available, the current task is registered with the Waker component, so that when the value from the future becomes available, the Waker component can tell the Tokio runtime to call the `poll()` function again in the future. The `poll()` function returns one of two values: `Poll::Pending` if the future is not ready yet, or `Poll::Ready (future_value)` if the `future_value` is available from the function. Figure 10.8 illustrates the sequence of steps in program execution:

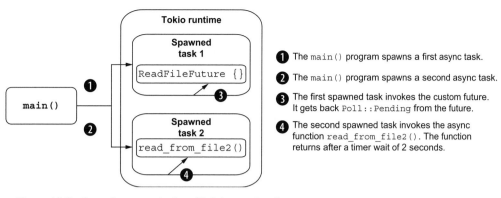

Figure 10.8   Spawning async tasks with futures, step 1

> **future vs. `Future`**
> If you are confused about the difference between a future and a `Future`, recall that a future is an asynchronous computation that can return a value at a future point of time. It returns a `Future` type (or something that implements the `Future` trait). But to return a value, the future has to be polled by the async runtime executor.

Notice the changes we've made to the `main()` function compared to the code in the previous section. The main (pun intended) change is that we've replaced the call to the `read_from_file1()` async function, which returns a future of type `impl Future <Output=String>`, with a custom implementation that returns a future with the same return type, `impl Future<Output=String>`.

Run the program, and you should see the following output on your terminal:

```
Hello before reading file!
Tokio! Stop polling me
"Processing file 2"
"Hello, there from file 2"
```

You'll also notice that the program does not terminate and continues to hang as though it's waiting for something.

Referring back to figure 10.8, let's look at what just happened here. The `main()` function calls two asynchronous computations (code that returns a `Future`): `Read-FileFuture {}` and `read_from_file2()`. It spawns each of these as an asynchronous task on the Tokio runtime. The Tokio executor (part of the Tokio runtime) polls the first future, which returns `Poll::Pending`. It then polls the second future, which yields a value of `Poll::Ready` after the sleep timer expires, and the corresponding statements are printed to the terminal. The Tokio runtime continues to wait for the first future to be ready to be scheduled for execution, But this will never happen because we are unconditionally returning `Poll::Pending` from the `poll` function.

Also note that once a future has finished, the Tokio runtime will not call it again. That's why the second function is executed only once.

How does the Tokio executor know when to poll the first future again? Does it keep polling repeatedly? The answer is no, as otherwise we would have seen the print statement within the poll function several times on the terminal, but we saw that the poll function was executed only once.

Tokio (and Rust async design) handle this by using a `Waker` component. When a task that's polled by the async executor is not ready to yield a value, the task is registered with a `Waker`, and a handle to the `Waker` is stored in the `Context` object associated with the task. The `Waker` has a `wake()` method that can be used to tell the async executor that the associated task should be awoken. When the `wake()` method is called, the Tokio executor is informed that it's time to poll the async task again by invoking the `poll()` function on the task.

Let's see this in action. Modify the `poll()` function in src/main.rs as follows:

```
impl Future for ReadFileFuture {
    type Output = String;

    fn poll(self: Pin<&mut Self>, cx: &mut Context<'_>) ->
      Poll<Self::Output> {
        println!("Tokio! Stop polling me");
        cx.waker().wake_by_ref();
        Poll::Pending
    }
}
```

The Context object associated with the task is made available to the poll function.

The wake_by_ref() function on the Waker instance is invoked, which in turn informs the Tokio runtime that the async task is now ready to be scheduled for execution again.

Figure 10.9 illustrates this flow.

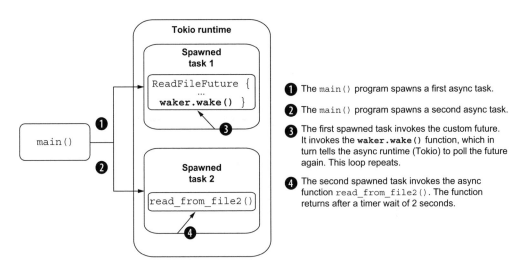

① The main() program spawns a first async task.

② The main() program spawns a second async task.

③ The first spawned task invokes the custom future. It invokes the **waker.wake()** function, which in turn tells the async runtime (Tokio) to poll the future again. This loop repeats.

④ The second spawned task invokes the async function read_from_file2(). The function returns after a timer wait of 2 seconds.

Figure 10.9 Writing a future with a waker component, step 2

Run the program again, and you should see the `poll()` function being invoked continually. This is because in the poll function we are calling the `wake_by_ref()` function on the `Waker` instance, which in turn tells the async executor to poll the function again, and the cycle repeats. The `wake_by_ref()` function wakes up the task associated with the `Waker`.

When you run the program, you should see the print statements continually being printed to the terminal until the program is terminated:

```
Tokio! Stop polling me
Tokio! Stop polling me
Tokio! Stop polling me
Tokio! Stop polling me
Tokio! Stop polling me
Tokio! Stop polling me
Tokio! Stop polling me
Tokio! Stop polling me
...
```

Now, you may wonder, what is the `Waker` component, and how does it fit into the Tokio ecosystem? Figure 10.10 shows the various components of Tokio in the context of the underlying hardware and operating system.

The Tokio runtime needs to understand operating system (kernel) methods such as `epoll` to start I/O operations, such as reading from a network or writing to a file.

The Tokio runtime registers the async handler to be called when an event happens as part of the I/O operation. The component of the Tokio

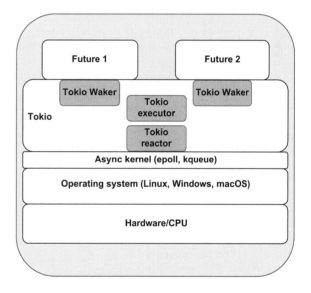

Figure 10.10   Tokio components

runtime that listens to these events from the kernel and communicates to the rest of the Tokio runtime is the *reactor*.

The Tokio executor is the component that takes a future and drives it to completion by calling the `poll()` function of the future whenever the future can make progress.

How do the futures indicate to the executor that they are ready to make progress? They call the `wake()` function of the `Waker` component. The `Waker` component informs the executor, which then places the future back on the queue and invokes the `poll()` function again, until the future has completed.

Here is a simplified flow that shows how the various Tokio components work together to read from a file:

1 The main function of a program spawns async task 1 on the Tokio runtime.
2 Async task 1 has a future that reads data from a large file.
3 The request to read from the file is handed over to the kernel's file subsystem.
4 In the meantime, async task 2 is scheduled for processing by the Tokio runtime.
5 When the file operation associated with async task 1 is complete, the file subsystem triggers an operating system interrupt, which is translated into an event that is recognized by the Tokio reactor.
6 The Tokio reactor informs async task 1 that the data from the file operation is ready.
7 Async task 1 informs the `Waker` component registered with it that it is ready to yield a value.
8 The `Waker` component informs the Tokio executor to call the `poll()` function associated with async task 1.
9 The Tokio executor schedules async task 1 for processing and invokes the `poll()` function.
10 Async task 1 yields a value.

In summary, the future, which performs an I/O operation in an async fashion, is informed by the Tokio reactor about an I/O event. On receipt of the I/O event, the future becomes ready to make progress and invokes the Tokio `Waker` component. The `Waker` component then tells the Tokio executor that the future is ready to make progress, which triggers the Tokio executor to schedule the future for execution and invoke the `poll()` function on the future.

With this background, let's continue with our coding exercise. Let's modify the previous program to return a valid value from the `poll()` function and see what happens. Modify the `poll()` function in src/main.rs as follows, and rerun the program:

```
use std::future::Future;
use std::pin::Pin;
use std::task::{Context, Poll};
use std::thread::sleep;
use std::time::Duration;

struct ReadFileFuture {}

impl Future for ReadFileFuture {
    type Output = String;

    fn poll(self: Pin<&mut Self>, cx: &mut Context<'_>) ->
      Poll<Self::Output> {
        println!("Tokio! Stop polling me");
        cx.waker().wake_by_ref();
        Poll::Ready(String::from("Hello, there from file 1"))
    }
}
```

Instead of returning Poll::Pending, return Poll::Ready with a valid string value from the poll() function.

```
#[tokio::main]
async fn main() {
    println!("Hello before reading file!");

    let h1 = tokio::spawn(async {
        let future1 = ReadFileFuture {};
        println!("{:?}", future1.await);
    });

    let h2 = tokio::spawn(async {
        let file2_contents = read_from_file2().await;
        println!("{:?}", file2_contents);
    });
    let _ = tokio::join!(h1, h2);
}

// function that simulates reading from a file
fn read_from_file2() -> impl Future<Output = String> {
    async {
        sleep(Duration::new(2, 0));
        String::from("Hello, there from file 2")
    }
}
```

Figure 10.11 illustrates the preceding code.

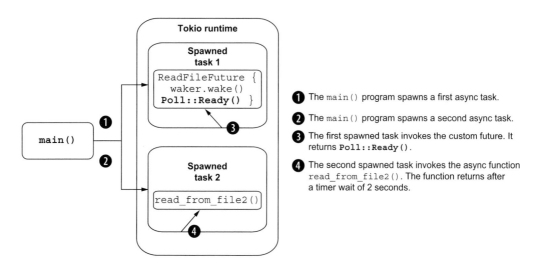

Figure 10.11   Custom future with `Poll::Ready`, step 3

① The `main()` program spawns a first async task.

② The `main()` program spawns a second async task.

③ The first spawned task invokes the custom future. It returns `Poll::Ready()`.

④ The second spawned task invokes the async function `read_from_file2()`. The function returns after a timer wait of 2 seconds.

You should now see the following output on your terminal:

```
Hello before reading file!
Tokio! Stop polling me
"Hello, there from file 1"
"Hello, there from file 2"
```

The program now does not hang; it completes successfully after executing the two async tasks to completion.

In the next section, we'll take this program one step further and enhance the future to implement an asynchronous timer. When the time elapses, the Waker will inform the Tokio runtime that the task associated with it is ready to be polled again. When the Tokio runtime polls the function for the second time, it will receive a value from the function. This should help us understand even better how futures work.

10.5   *Implementing a custom future*

Let's create a new future representing an async timer that does the following:

1   The timer accepts an expiration time.
2   Whenever it is polled by the runtime executor, it will do the following checks:

   – If the current time is greater than the expiration time, it will return `Poll::Ready` with a `String` value.
   – If the current time is less than the expiration time, it will go to sleep until the expiration time and then trigger the `wake()` call on the `Waker`, which will then inform the async runtime executor to schedule and execute the task again.

Figure 10.12 illustrates the logic of this custom future.

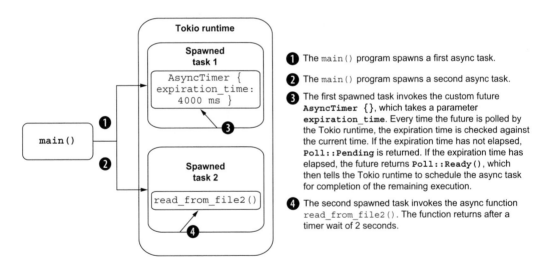

Figure 10.12   Custom future with expiration time, step 4

Modify src/main.rs as follows:

```
use std::future::Future;
use std::pin::Pin;
use std::task::{Context, Poll};
```

```
use std::thread::sleep;
use std::time::{Duration, Instant};
```

Define the future type AsyncTimer with a variable to store the expiration time.

```
struct AsyncTimer {
    expiration_time: Instant,
}
```

Implement the Future trait on the AsyncTimer.   **Specify the future's output value as a String type.**

```
impl Future for AsyncTimer {
    type Output = String;

    fn poll(self: Pin<&mut Self>, cx: &mut Context<'_>) ->
        Poll<Self::Output> {
        if Instant::now() >= self.expiration_time {
            println!("Hello, it's time for Future 1");
            Poll::Ready(String::from("Future 1 has completed"))
        } else {
            println!("Hello, it's not yet time for Future 1. Going to sleep");
            let waker = cx.waker().clone();
            let expiration_time = self.expiration_time;
            std::thread::spawn(move || {
                let current_time = Instant::now();
                if current_time < expiration_time {
                    std::thread::sleep(expiration_time - current_time);
                }
                waker.wake();
            });
            Poll::Pending
        }
    }
}
```

Implement the poll() function.

If current_time < expiration_time, initiate thread sleep for the required duration.

Invoke the wake() function, which will tell the async executor to schedule the task for execution again.

Within the poll() function, first check if current_time >= expiration_time. If so, return Poll::Ready from the function with the String value.

```
#[tokio::main]
async fn main() {
    let h1 = tokio::spawn(async {
        let future1 = AsyncTimer {
            expiration_time: Instant::now() + Duration::from_millis(4000),
        };
        println!("{:?}", future1.await);
    });

    let h2 = tokio::spawn(async {
        let file2_contents = read_from_file2().await;
        println!("{:?}", file2_contents);
    });
    let _ = tokio::join!(h1, h2);
}

// function that simulates reading from a file
fn read_from_file2() -> impl Future<Output = String> {
    async {
        sleep(Duration::new(2, 0));
        String::from("Future 2 has completed")
    }
}
```

In the main() function, initialize the future type with the expiration time for the timer.

We've now implemented a custom future and invoked it within the main function. We've also retained the call to the second future `read_from_file2()` from the main function, which we implemented earlier. Note that both futures eventually implement a timer, but the first future is a fully async way of implementing the timer functionality, while the second future simulates an async timer (but uses a synchronous call to the `std::thread::sleep()` internally).

Run the program, and you should see the following output on your terminal:

```
Hello, it's not yet time for Future 1. Going to sleep
"Future 2 has completed"
Hello, it's time for Future 1
"Future 1 has completed"
```

Let's analyze what just happened here. Figure 10.13 illustrates the sequence of events:

1 In the `main()` function, the first async computation to be scheduled on the async runtime is the call to the future `AsyncTimer`, which is our custom future implementation. Let's call this future 1.

2 The async executor calls the `poll()` function on future 1. Since the expiration time has not yet been reached, the statement "Hello, it's not yet time for Future 1. Going to sleep" is printed to the terminal. The `poll()` function then spawns a new thread and initiates a thread sleep. The `poll()` function returns `Poll::Pending__`, which indicates to the executor that other tasks can be scheduled for execution, as this async function is not yet ready to yield a value.

3 The async runtime, in the meantime, schedules the task `read_from_file2()` for execution. This function pauses the current thread for 2 seconds and then returns `Poll::Ready` with a `String` value. The "Future 2 has completed" statement from this future is printed to the terminal.

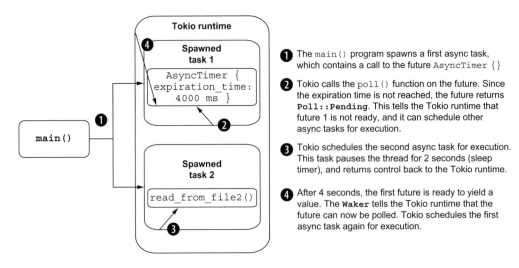

Figure 10.13 Custom future with expiration timer and waker component, step 5

4 In the meantime, the first future becomes ready to yield a value. It calls the `wake()` function on the `Waker` associated with this async task, which in turn informs the async executor that future 1 is ready to be scheduled for execution again. The executor calls the `poll()` function on future 1, which now returns `Poll::Ready` with a string value. The following two print statements are printed to the terminal: "Hello, it's time for Future 1" and "Future 1 has completed."

That concludes this section on writing a custom future. I hope the exercises in this chapter have given you a better understanding of how async functions work and how they are implemented in Rust. In many cases, you may not even implement your own futures, but instead use the developer-friendly APIs provided by async runtimes such as Tokio or by higher level frameworks such as Actix Web. But it helps to understand how async and futures work under the hood.

Futures and async programming are key mechanisms for implementing efficient and robust distributed applications. You now have a very good foundation on which you can build a variety of asynchronous applications or components in a standard and very readable (and therefore maintainable) way!

In the next chapter, we'll implement a networking project in async Rust.

Summary

- Concurrency is the ability of different parts of a program to be executed out of order, or at the same time, without affecting the final outcome. On the other hand, executing multiple tasks simultaneously is parallelism.

- Multithreading and async are two concurrency programming models. The former uses native operating system threads, and the scheduling of the tasks on the CPU is handled by the operating system. The latter uses an async runtime (we used Tokio in this chapter), which takes care of scheduling multiple tasks on an operating system thread. Tokio does this using its own implementation of threads (a.k.a. green threads), which are lightweight compared to operating system threads.

- A future is an asynchronous computation that can return a value at a future point in time. A `Future` is a type that is returned by a future, and it can take either of these two values: `Poll:Pending` or `Poll::Ready(future_value)`.

- When a task that's polled by the Tokio async executor (the Tokio runtime) is not ready to yield a value, the task is registered with a `Waker`. The `Waker` has a `wake()` method that can be used to tell the async executor that the associated task should be awoken. When the `wake()` method is called, the Tokio executor is informed that it's time to poll the async task again by invoking the `poll()` function on the task.

Building a P2P node
with async Rust

This chapter covers

- Introducing peer-to-peer networks
- Understanding the core architecture of libp2p networking
- Exchanging ping commands between peer nodes
- Discovering peers in a P2P network

In the previous chapter, we covered the basics of async programming and how to write async code with Rust. In this chapter, we'll build a few simple examples of peer-to-peer (P2P) applications using a low-level P2P networking library and asynchronous programming using Rust.

Why learn about P2P? P2P is a networking technology that enables the sharing of various computing resources, such as CPU, network bandwidth, and storage, across different computers. P2P is a very commonly used method for sharing files (such as music, images, and other digital media) between users online. BitTorrent and Gnutella are examples of popular file-sharing P2P apps. They do not rely on a central server or an intermediary to connect multiple clients. And most importantly, they make use of users' computers as both clients and servers, thus offloading computations from a central server.

How do P2P networks operate, and how are they different? Let's delve into the foundational concepts behind peer-to-peer networks.

NOTE This chapter draws heavily on material from the libp2p documentation at https://libp2p.io/. The code examples use the Rust implementation of the libp2p protocol, which can be found on GitHub: https://github.com/libp2p/rust-libp2p.

11.1 Introducing peer-to-peer networks

Traditional distributed systems deployed within enterprises or the web use the *client/server* paradigm. A web browser and a web server together serve as a good example of a client/server system, where the web browser (the client) requests information (such as with a GET request) or a computation (POST, PUT, and DELETE requests) on a particular resource hosted on the web server (the server). The web server then checks that the client is authorized to receive that information or perform that computation, and if so, it fulfills the request.

P2P networks are another type of distributed system. In P2P, a set of nodes (or *peers*) interact directly with one another to collectively provide a common service, without having a central coordinator or administrator. Examples of peer-to-peer systems include file-sharing networks such as IPFS and BitTorrent and blockchain networks such as Bitcoin and Ethereum. Each node (or peer) in a P2P system can act as both a client (requesting information from other nodes) and a server (storing and retrieving data and performing necessary computations in response to client requests). While the nodes in a P2P network need not be identical, one key characteristic that differentiates client/server networks from P2P networks is the absence of dedicated servers that have unique privileges. In open, permissionless P2P networks, any node can decide to offer a full or partial set of services associated with a P2P node.

Compared to client/server networks, P2P networks enable a different class of applications to be built over them that are permissionless, fault-tolerant, and censorship-resistant.

- *Permissionless*—No server can cut off a client's access to information, as the data and state are replicated across multiple nodes.
- *Fault-tolerant*—There is no single point of failure, such as a central server.
- *Censorship-resistant*—Because data in a P2P network is replicated across nodes, it is difficult to censor (compared to data stored on a centralized server).

P2P computing also enables better utilization of resources. Imagine all the network bandwidth, storage, and processing power that's available from clients at the edge of the network. These resources are not fully utilized in client/server computing.

Figure 11.1 illustrates the differences between client/server and P2P networks. Note that we will use the terms *node* and *peer* interchangeably in the context of a P2P network.

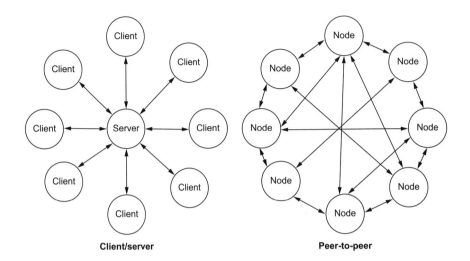

Figure 11.1   Client/server vs. peer-to-peer computing

Building P2P systems can be more complex than building traditional client/server systems. There are several technical requirements associated with building P2P systems:

- *Transport*—Each peer in a P2P network can speak a different protocol, such as HTTP(s), TCP, UDP, etc.
- *Peer identity*—Each peer needs to know the identity of the peer to which it wants to connect and send a message.
- *Security*—Each peer should be able to communicate with other peers in a secure manner without the risk of a third party intercepting or modifying messages.
- *Peer routing*—Each peer can receive a message from other peers through a variety of routes (like how data packets are distributed in the IP protocol), which means that each peer should have the ability to route the message to other peers if the message is not intended for itself.
- *Messaging*—P2P networks should be able to send point-to-point messages or group messages (in a publish/subscribe pattern).
- *Stream multiplexing*—P2P networks should support multiple streams of information over a common communication link. This enables concurrent communications with multiple nodes.

Let's take a closer look at each of these requirements.

11.1.1 Transport

The TCP/IP and UDP protocols are ubiquitous and are popular for writing networked applications. However, there are other higher-level protocols, such as HTTP (layered over TCP) and QUIC (layered over UDP). Each peer in a P2P network should have the ability to initiate a connection to another node and be able to listen to incoming connections over multiple protocols because of the diversity of peers in the network.

11.1.2 Peer identity

Unlike the web development domain, where a server is identified by a unique domain name (such as www.rust-lang.org, which is then resolved to the IP address of the server via a domain name service), nodes in a peer-to-peer network need a unique identity so that the other nodes can reach them. Nodes in a peer-to-peer network use a public and private key pair (asymmetric public key cryptography) to establish secure communications with other nodes. The identity of a node in a peer-to-peer network is called the `PeerId`, which is a cryptographic hash of the node's public key.

11.1.3 Security

The cryptographic key pair and `PeerId` enable a node to establish secure, authenticated communication channels with its peers. But that's only one aspect of security. Nodes also need to implement frameworks for authorization, which establish rules for what kinds of operations can be performed by which node. There are also network-level security threats to be addressed, such as Sybil attacks (where one of the node operators spins up a large number of nodes with distinct identities to gain an advantageous position in the network) or eclipse attacks (where a group of malicious nodes collude to target a specific node, such that the latter cannot reach any legitimate nodes).

11.1.4 Peer routing

A node in a P2P network first needs to find other peers in order to communicate. This is achieved by maintaining a peer routing table, which contains references to other peers in the network. But in a P2P network that has thousands of nodes or more that are changing dynamically (i.e., nodes frequently join and leave the network), it is difficult for any single node to maintain a complete and accurate routing table for all nodes in the network. Peer routing enables nodes to route messages that are not meant for them to the destination nodes.

11.1.5 Messaging

Nodes in a P2P network can send messages to specific nodes, and they can also participate in *broadcast* messaging protocols. An example is publish/subscribe where nodes register interest in a particular topic (they subscribe), and any node can send messages (publish) on that topic that are received by all nodes that subscribe to that topic. This technique is commonly used to transmit the contents of a message to the entire network. Publish/subscribe is a well-known architectural pattern for messaging in a distributed system between a sender and a receiver.

11.1.6 Stream multiplexing

You previously saw (in section 11.1.1) how a node in a P2P network can support multiple transports. Stream multiplexing is a way to send multiple streams of information over a common communication link. In the case of P2P, it allows multiple independent "logical" streams to share a common P2P transport layer. This becomes important when a node may have multiple streams of communication with different peers or when there can be many concurrent connections between two remote nodes. Stream multiplexing helps us optimize the overhead of establishing connections between peers. Multiplexing is common in backend services development, where a client can establish an underlying network connection with a server, and then multiplex different streams (each with unique port numbers) over the underlying network connection.

In this section, we have looked at a few foundational concepts that are involved in the design of peer-to-peer systems. Next, we'll take a closer look at a popular Rust library that is used for P2P networking, as we will use this library to write some async Rust code in later sections.

11.2 Understanding the core architecture of libp2p networking

Writing your own networking layer for P2P applications is a mammoth task. If someone has already done the hard work, why reinvent the wheel? We will use a low-level P2P networking library called `libp2p`, which makes it a lot easier to build P2P applications.

The `libp2p` library is a modular system of protocols, specifications, and libraries that enable the development of peer-to-peer applications. `libp2p` supports three programming languages at the time of writing: Go, JavaScript, and Rust. `libp2p` is used by many popular projects such as IPFS, Filecoin, and Polkadot.

Figure 11.2 highlights the key modules of libp2p that are used to build a robust peer-to-peer network:

- *Transport*—Responsible for the actual transmission and receipt of data from one peer node to another.
- *Identity*—`libp2p` uses public key cryptography (PKI) as the basis of peer node identity. A unique peer ID is generated for each node using a cryptographic algorithm.
- *Security*—Nodes sign messages using their private key. Also, the transport connections between nodes can be upgraded to secure encrypted channels so that the remote peers can mutually trust one another, and no third party can intercept communications between them.
- *Peer discovery*—Enables peers to find and communicate with one another in the libp2p network.

- *Peer routing*—Enables communication with a peer node using the knowledge of other peers.
- *Content discovery*—Enables peer nodes to get a piece of content from other peers without knowing which peer has it.
- *Messaging*—Enables sending messages to a group of peers that are interested in a topic.

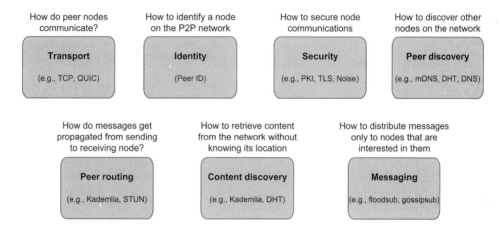

Figure 11.2   Components of libp2p

In this chapter, you will learn how to leverage a subset of the features of the libp2p protocol to build P2P applications using Rust. Let's start by taking a look at a few core primitives of the Rust `libp2p` library using code examples.

11.2.1 Peer IDs and key pairs

Let's start with generating peer IDs and key pairs for a P2P node. Cryptographic key pairs are used by P2P nodes to sign messages, and peer IDs represent unique peer identities that uniquely identify nodes on the P2P network, as shown in figure 11.3.

Peer ID: 12D3KooWBu3fmjZgSMLkQ2p1DG35UmEayYBrhsk6WEe1xco1JFbV

A p2p node is identified by a unique peer ID that is cryptographically generated.

Figure 11.3   Identity of a P2P node

Start a new project with `cargo new p2p-learn`. Then, in Cargo.toml, add the following entry:

Use the latest version of the library at the time you are reading this.

```
libp2p = "0.42.2"
tokio = { version = "1.16.1", features = ["full"] }
```

Create a bin folder under the src folder. Create a new src/bin/iter1.rs file, and add the following code to it:

The identity module contains functions to generate a new random key pair for the node. The PeerId struct contains the methods to generate a peer ID from the public key of the node.

This compiler annotation specifies Tokio as the async runtime.

```
use libp2p::{identity, PeerId};      ⟵

#[tokio::main]
async fn main() {
    let new_key = identity::Keypair::generate_ed25519();
    let new_peer_id = PeerId::from(new_key.public());      ⟵
    println!("New peer id: {:?}", new_peer_id);
}
```

The async keyword denotes that the main() function has async code to be executed by Tokio.

Generates a key pair of type ED25519. A key pair consists of a private key and a public key. The private key is never shared.

Generates a peer ID from the public key of the key pair. In libp2p, the public key is not directly used to identify a peer, but a hashed version of it is used as the peer ID.

NOTE The ED25519 key pair type is an elliptic curve-based public key system that is commonly used in SSH authentication to connect to a server without a password.

What are public and private keys?

Cryptographic identity uses Public Key Infrastructure (PKI), which is widely used to provide unique identities for users, devices, and applications, and to secure end-to-end communications. It works by creating two different cryptographic keys, also known as a *key pair* comprising a private key and a public key, which have a mathematical relationship between them. Key pairs have many applications, but in a P2P network, nodes identify and authenticate themselves to each other using key pairs. The public key can be shared with others in a network, but the private key of a node must never be revealed.

A good example of using a key pair is in traditional server access. For example, if you want to connect to a remote server (using SSH) hosted in a data center or a cloud, a key pair can be configured for access instead of using a password. In this example, a user can generate a key pair and configure the public key on the remote server, which grants access to the user. But how does the remote server know which user is the owner of that public key? To enable this, when connecting (over SSH) to the remote server, the user must specify the private key that is associated with the public key stored on the server. The private key is never sent to the remote server, but the

SSH client (running on the local server) uses the user's private key to authenticate itself to the remote SSH server.

Private and public keys have many other uses, such as for encryption, decryption, and digital signatures, but that is out of scope for this chapter.

Run the program with `cargo run --bin iter1`, and you should see something similar to this printed to your terminal:

```
New peer id: PeerId("12D3KooWBu3fmjZgSMLkQ2p1DG35UmEayYBrhsk6WEe1xco1JFbV")
```

In libp2p, a peer's identity is stable and verifiable for the entire lifetime of the peer. However, libp2p makes a distinction between a peer's *identity* and its *location*. As discussed before, the identity of a peer is the peer ID. The location of a peer is the network address at which the peer can be reached. For example, a peer can be reached over TCP, websockets, QUIC, or any other protocol. libp2p encodes these network addresses in a self-describing format called *multiaddresses* (`multiaddr`). So, in libp2p, the multiaddress represents the location of a peer. We'll look at using multiaddresses next.

11.2.2 Multiaddresses

When humans share contact information, they use their phone numbers, social media profiles, or physical location addresses (when receiving delivery of goods). When nodes on a P2P network share their contact information, they send a multiaddress containing both the network address and their peer ID.

The peer ID component of a multiaddress for a node is represented like this:

```
/p2p/12D3KooWBu3fmjZgSMLkQ2p1DG35UmEayYBrhsk6WEe1xco1JFbV
```

The string `12D3KooWBu3fmjZgSMLkQ2p1DG35UmEayYBrhsk6WEe1xco1JFbV` represents the peer ID of the node. You learned how to generate the peer ID for a node in the previous section.

The network address component of a multiaddress (also known as the transport address) looks like this:

```
/ip4/192.158.1.23/tcp/1234
```

This says that IPv4 is the transport protocol used, the IP address is 192.158.1.23, and the TCP port on which it listens is 1234.

The complete multiaddress of a node is just a combination of the peer ID and network address, and it looks like this:

```
/ip4/192.158.1.23/tcp/1234/p2p/
    12D3KooWBu3fmjZgSMLkQ2p1DG35UmEayYBrhsk6WEe1xco1JFbV
```

Peers exchange this multiaddress with other peers in this format.

The `libp2p` library internally converts this "name-based" address, /ip4/ 192.158.1.23, into a regular IP address using the DNS protocol, as shown in figure 11.4.

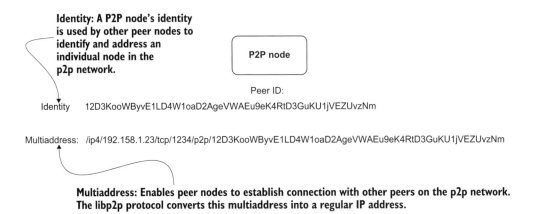

Identity: A P2P node's identity is used by other peer nodes to identify and address an individual node in the p2p network.

P2P node

Peer ID:

Identity   12D3KooWByvE1LD4W1oaD2AgeVWAEu9eK4RtD3GuKU1jVEZUvzNm

Multiaddress: /ip4/192.158.1.23/tcp/1234/p2p/12D3KooWByvE1LD4W1oaD2AgeVWAEu9eK4RtD3GuKU1jVEZUvzNm

Multiaddress: Enables peer nodes to establish connection with other peers on the p2p network. The libp2p protocol converts this multiaddress into a regular IP address.

Figure 11.4   Multiaddress of a P2P node

We'll use the multiaddress in code in the next section.

11.2.3 *Swarm and network behavior*

Swarm is the network manager module within a given P2P node in libp2p. It maintains all active and pending connections to remote nodes from a given node, and it manages the state of all the substreams that have been opened.

The structure and context of Swarm is depicted in figure 11.5 and is explained in detail later in this section.

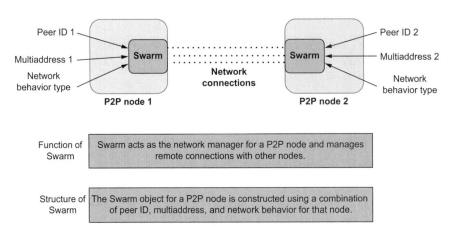

Figure 11.5   Network management for a P2P node

Let's now extend the previous example. Create a new src/bin/iter2.rs file, and add the following code:

```
use libp2p::swarm::{DummyBehaviour, Swarm, SwarmEvent};
use libp2p::futures::StreamExt;
use libp2p::{identity, PeerId};
use std::error::Error;

#[tokio::main]
async fn main() -> Result<(), Box<dyn Error>> {
    let new_key = identity::Keypair::generate_ed25519();
    let new_peer_id = PeerId::from(new_key.public());
    println!("local peer id is: {:?}", new_peer_id);
    let behaviour = DummyBehaviour::default();
    let transport = libp2p::development_transport(new_key).await?;
    let mut swarm = Swarm::new(transport, behaviour, new_peer_id);
    swarm.listen_on("/ip4/0.0.0.0/tcp/0".parse()?)?;

    loop {
        match swarm.select_next_some().await {
            SwarmEvent::NewListenAddr { address, .. } => {
                println!("Listening on local address {:?}", address)
            }
            _ => {}
        }
    }
}
```

Annotations:
- **Swarm is the network manager component associated with a node in libp2p.** (→ `use libp2p::swarm::{DummyBehaviour, Swarm, SwarmEvent};`)
- **Used to exchange streams of data between nodes** (→ `use libp2p::futures::StreamExt;`)
- **Create a new Swarm using transport, network behavior, and peer ID.** (→ `let mut swarm = Swarm::new(...)`)
- **Construct a dummy network behavior to associate with the swarm.** (→ `let behaviour = DummyBehaviour::default();`)
- **Construct a transport with the new key pair.** (→ `let transport = libp2p::development_transport(new_key).await?;`)
- **Listen on a multiaddress for incoming connections.** (→ `swarm.listen_on(...)`)
- **The swarm needs to be continuously polled to check for events.** (→ `match swarm.select_next_some().await {`)
- **Listen for an event that creates a new listen address.** (→ `println!("Listening on local address {:?}", address)`)

We need to construct a Swarm network manager before we can communicate with other nodes. Swarm represents a low-level interface, and it provides fine-grained control over the libp2p network. Swarm is constructed using a combination of the transport, network behavior, and peer ID for the node. You've previously seen what a transport and a peer ID are. Let's now look at what network behavior is.

While the transport specifies how to send bytes over the network, the network behavior specifies what bytes to send and to whom. Examples of network behaviors in libp2p include ping (where nodes send and respond to ping messages), mDNS, which is used to discover other peer nodes on the network, and Kademlia, used for peer routing and content routing functionality. To keep this example simple, we are using a dummy network behavior. Multiple network behaviors can be associated with a single running node.

Toward the end of the preceding code, we have swarm.select_next_some() .await. The await keyword is used to schedule the asynchronous task to poll the protocols and connections, and when it's ready, swarm events are received. When there is nothing to process, the task will be idle, and the swarm will output Poll::Pending. This is another example of async Rust in action.

Note that the same code runs on all nodes of a libp2p network, unlike a client/server model where the client and the server have different codebases.

Let's run the code. Create two terminal sessions on your computer. From the first terminal, from the project root directory, run this command:

```
cargo run  --bin iter2
```

You should see output similar to the following printed to your terminal for the first node:

```
local peer id is: PeerId("12D3KooWByvE1LD4W1oaD2AgeVWAEu9eK4RtD3GuKU1jVEZUvzNm")
Listening on local address "/ip4/127.0.0.1/tcp/
    55436"
Listening on local address "/ip4/192.168.1.74/tcp/55436"
```

Prints the local address on which this node is listening for incoming connections and streams

Prints the new peer ID generated for the node

From the second terminal, from the project root directory, run the following:

```
cargo run --bin iter2
```

You should see terminal output similar to this for the second node:

```
local peer id is: PeerId("12D3KooWQiQZA5zcLzhF86kuRoq9f6yAgiLtGqD5bDG516kVzW46")
Listening on local address "/ip4/127.0.0.1/tcp/55501"
Listening on local address "/ip4/192.168.1.74/tcp/55501"
```

Again, you can see the local address on which node2 is listening (printed out to the terminal).

If you got this far, it's a good start. However, there isn't anything interesting happening in this code. We were able to start two nodes and ask them to connect to each other, but we don't know whether the connection has been established correctly or if the two can communicate. Let's enhance this code to exchange ping commands between nodes.

11.3 *Exchanging ping commands between peer nodes*

Create a new src/bin/iter3.rs file, and add the following code:

```
use libp2p::swarm::{Swarm, SwarmEvent};
use libp2p::futures::StreamExt;
use libp2p::ping::{Ping, PingConfig};
use libp2p::{identity, Multiaddr, PeerId};
use std::error::Error;

#[tokio::main]
async fn main() -> Result<(), Box<dyn Error>> {
    let new_key = identity::Keypair::generate_ed25519();
    let new_peer_id = PeerId::from(new_key.public());
    println!("local peer id is: {:?}", new_peer_id);

    let transport = libp2p::development_transport(new_key).await?;
    let behaviour = Ping::new(PingConfig::new().with_keep_alive(true));
    let mut swarm = Swarm::new(transport, behaviour, new_peer_id);
    swarm.listen_on("/ip4/0.0.0.0/tcp/0".parse()?)?;

    if let Some(remote_peer) = std::env::args().nth(1) {
        let remote_peer_multiaddr: Multiaddr = remote_peer.parse()?;
        swarm.dial(remote_peer_multiaddr)?;
        println!("Dialed remote peer: {:?}", remote_peer);
    }
```

Instantiate a new network behavior that enables ping messages between nodes. Ping is a built-in network behavior of libp2p.

/ip4/0.0.0.0/tcp/0 is the address that the configured transport (TCP) should listen on.

This code block shows the outgoing connection from the local node to the remote node.

The swarm is polled in a loop to trigger the network behavior configured.

```
loop {
    match swarm.select_next_some().await {
        SwarmEvent::NewListenAddr { address, .. } => {
            println!("Listening on local address {:?}", address)
        }
        SwarmEvent::Behaviour(event) => println!
        ("Event received from peer is {:?}", event),
        _ => {}
    }
}
}
```

When a local node sends a ping message, the remote node responds with a pong message. This event is received and printed out to the terminal.

In the listen_on() method, 0.0.0.0 means it will listen on all IPv4 addresses on the local machine. For example, if a host has two IP addresses, 192.168.1.2 and 10.0.0.1, and a server running on the host listens on 0.0.0.0, it will be reachable at both IPs. The 0 port means that it will choose a random available port.

Note also that the remote node multiaddress is parsed from the command-line parameter. The local node then establishes a connection to the remote node on this multiaddress.

Let's now build and test this P2P example with two nodes. Create two terminal sessions on your computer. From the first terminal, from the project root directory, run this command:

```
cargo run  --bin iter3
```

You should see output similar to the following printed to your terminal for the first node, which we'll call node 1:

```
local peer id is: PeerId("12D3KooWByvE1LD4W1oaD2AgeVWAEu9eK4RtD3GuKU1jVEZUvzNm")
Listening on local address "/ip4/127.0.0.1/tcp/55872"
Listening on local address "/ip4/192.168.1.74/tcp/55872"
```

At this point, there is no remote node to connect to, so the local node just prints out the listen event along with the multiaddress at which it is listening for new connections. The ping network behavior, even though it has been configured in the local node, is not active yet. For this, we need to start the second node.

From the second terminal, from the project root directory, run the following command. Make sure you specify the multiaddress of the first node in the command-line parameter:

```
cargo run --bin iter3 /ip4/127.0.0.1/tcp/55872
```

Let's call this node 2, and at this point it has started. It will similarly print out the local address on which it is listening. Since the remote node multiaddress has been specified, node 2 establishes a connection with node 1 and starts to listen to events. On receipt of the incoming connection from node 2, node 1 sends the ping message to node 2, and node 2 responds with a pong message. These messages should start to appear on the terminals of both node 1 and node 2, and they'll continue in a loop after a time interval (approximately every 15 seconds or so). Note also that the P2P node uses async Rust with the Tokio runtime to execute concurrent tasks to process multiple data streams and events coming from remote nodes.

In this section, you have seen how you can have two P2P nodes exchange ping messages with each other. In this example, we connected node 2 to node 1 by specifying the multiaddress node 1 is listening on. However, in a P2P network, nodes join and leave dynamically. In the next section, you'll see how peer nodes can discover each other on a P2P network.

11.4 Discovering peers

Let's code a P2P node to automatically detect other nodes on the network on startup. Place the following code in src/bin/iter4.rs:

```
use libp2p::{
    futures::StreamExt,
    identity,
    mdns::{Mdns, MdnsConfig, MdnsEvent},
    swarm::{Swarm, SwarmEvent},
    PeerId,
};
use std::error::Error;

#[tokio::main]
async fn main() -> Result<(), Box<dyn Error>> {
    let id_keys = identity::Keypair::generate_ed25519();      Generate a PeerId
    let peer_id = PeerId::from(id_keys.public());          ◁  for the node.
    println!("Local peer id: {:?}", peer_id);

    let transport = libp2p::development_transport(id_keys).await?;
                                                        Create an mDNS
    let behaviour = Mdns::new(MdnsConfig::default()).await?;  ◁  network behavior.

    let mut swarm = Swarm::new(transport, behaviour, peer_id);   ◁
    swarm.listen_on("/ip4/0.0.0.0/tcp/0".parse()?)?;

    loop {
        match swarm.select_next_some().await {
            SwarmEvent::NewListenAddr { address, .. } => {
                println!("Listening on local address {:?}", address)
            }
            SwarmEvent::Behaviour(MdnsEvent::Discovered(peers)) => {
                for (peer, addr) in peers {
                    println!("discovered {} {}", peer, addr);
                }
            }
            SwarmEvent::Behaviour(MdnsEvent::Expired(expired)) => {
                for (peer, addr) in expired {
                    println!("expired {} {}", peer, addr);
                }
            }
            _ => {}
        }
    }
}
```

Create a transport. (label pointing to `let transport` line)

Create a Swarm that establishes connections through the given transport. Note that the mDNS behavior itself will not initiate any connections, as it only uses UDP.

Multicast DNS (mDNS) is a protocol defined by RFC 6762 (https://datatracker.ietf .org/doc/html/rfc6762), and it resolves host names to IP addresses. The mDNS network behavior implemented in libp2p will automatically discover other libp2p nodes on the local network.

Let's see this working by building and running the code:

```
cargo run --bin iter4
```

Let's call this node 1, and you'll see something like the following printed to node 1's terminal window:

```
Local peer id: PeerId("12D3KooWNgYbVg8ZyJ4ict2N1hdJLKoydB5sTqwiWN2SHtC3HwWt")
Listening on local address "/ip4/127.0.0.1/tcp/50960"
Listening on local address "/ip4/192.168.1.74/tcp/50960"
```

Note that in this example, node 1 is listening on TCP port 50960.

From terminal 2, run the program with the same command. Note that, unlike before, we are not specifying the multiaddress of node 1:

```
cargo run --bin iter4
```

We'll call this node 2, and you should be able to see similar messages printed to its terminal:

```
Local peer id: PeerId("12D3KooWCVVb2EyxB1WdAcLeMuyaJ7nnfUCq45YNNuFYcZPGBY1f")
Listening on local address "/ip4/127.0.0.1/tcp/50967"
Listening on local address "/ip4/192.168.1.74/tcp/50967"
discovered 12D3KooWNgYbVg8ZyJ4ict2N1hdJLKoydB5sTqwiWN2SHtC3HwWt /ip4/
    192.168.1.74/tcp/50960
discovered 12D3KooWNgYbVg8ZyJ4ict2N1hdJLKoydB5sTqwiWN2SHtC3HwWt /ip4/
    127.0.0.1/tcp/50960
```

Notice that node 2 was able to discover node 1 listening on port 50960, while node 2 is listening to new events and messages on port 50967.

Start a third node (node 3) from another terminal:

```
cargo run --bin iter4
```

You'll see the following messages on the terminal of node 3:

```
Local peer id: PeerId("12D3KooWC95ziPjTXvKPNgoz3CSe2yp6SBtKh785eTdY5L2YK7Tc")
Listening on local address "/ip4/127.0.0.1/tcp/50996"
Listening on local address "/ip4/192.168.1.74/tcp/50996"
discovered 12D3KooWCVVb2EyxB1WdAcLeMuyaJ7nnfUCq45YNNuFYcZPGBY1f /ip4/
    192.168.1.74/tcp/50967
discovered 12D3KooWCVVb2EyxB1WdAcLeMuyaJ7nnfUCq45YNNuFYcZPGBY1f /ip4/
    127.0.0.1/tcp/50967
discovered 12D3KooWNgYbVg8ZyJ4ict2N1hdJLKoydB5sTqwiWN2SHtC3HwWt /ip4/
    192.168.1.74/tcp/50960
discovered 12D3KooWNgYbVg8ZyJ4ict2N1hdJLKoydB5sTqwiWN2SHtC3HwWt /ip4/
    127.0.0.1/tcp/50960
```

Notice that node 3 has discovered both node 1 listening on port 50960 and node 2 listening on port 50967.

This looks trivial until you realize that we have not told node 3 where the other two nodes are running. Using the mDNS protocol, node 3 was able to detect and connect to other libp2p nodes on the local network.

Exercises

If you are looking for additional code challenges, here are a suggestions of P2P applications that can be built using libp2p:

- Implement a simple P2P chat application.
- Implement a distributed P2P key/value store.
- Implement a distributed file storing network (like IPFS).

The `libp2p` library has several prebuilt code examples that can be referred to in order to implement these exercises. The libp2p code repository can be found here: https://libp2p.io/.

We have come to the end of this chapter. In the next (and last) chapter, we'll look at preparing Rust servers and apps for production deployment.

Summary

- In the client/server model of computation, the client and server represent two distinct pieces of software: the server is the custodian of data and associated computation, and the client requests the server to send data or perform a computation on a resource managed by the server. In P2P networks, communication occurs between peer nodes, each of which can perform the role of both the client and the server. One key characteristic that differentiates client/server networks from P2P networks is the absence of dedicated servers that have unique privileges
- libp2p is a modular system of protocols, specifications, and libraries that enable the development of peer-to-peer applications. It is used in many prominent P2P projects. Key architectural components of libp2p include transport, identity, security, peer discovery, peer routing, content routing, and messaging.
- Using code examples, you learned how to generate a unique peer ID for a node that other nodes can use to uniquely identify it.
- We also delved into the basics of multiaddresses and how they represent the complete path for communicating with a node over the P2P network. The peer ID of a node is a part of the overall multiaddress of the node.
- You wrote a Rust program where nodes exchange simple ping-pong messages among themselves. This example demonstrated configuring the Swarm network management object for a node to listen and act on specific events on the P2P network.
- We concluded the chapter by writing another Rust program with the `libp2p` library that shows how peer nodes can use the mDNS protocol to discover each other on a P2P network.

Deploying web services with Docker

In the previous chapters, you learned how to build a web service and a web application using Rust. We also looked into async programming and even addressed the P2P architecture. We tested our applications in a local development environment. But these are only the first steps. The ultimate goal is usually to deploy in a production environment.

In this last chapter, we will focus on packaging the software using a popular method of production deployment called *containerization*. It involves packaging the application's components and its dependencies in a container. This container can then be deployed on multiple environments, including the cloud. One of the advantages of using containers is that the application remains cleanly separated from other containers, avoiding the risks of incompatible libraries.

We'll take a detailed look at the steps needed to containerize our Rust web service. Once the web service is available as a Docker container, it is no different from any web service or application written in any other programming language from a production deployment standpoint. All the standard guidelines and options for deploying Docker containers will apply.

> **NOTE** Production deployment involves many aspects that are outside the scope of this book, such as selecting an infrastructure provider, packaging the software, configuring secrets, adding configurable logs for monitoring and debugging, adding application-level security to the web service API endpoints, adding server-level security (with TLS and CORS), protecting secrets such as access credentials and keys, configuring monitoring tools and alerts, adding database backups, and a lot more. This book cannot address all the considerations involved in preparing and deploying an application or service into production because this is not a Rust-specific topic. There is a lot of publicly available material (and other books) that cover this topic very well.

Packaging software in containers is a subject in itself, so we can only scratch the surface here. For a deeper dive into the fascinating world of containers, take a look at *Docker in Action, 2nd ed.* by Jeff Nickoloff and Stephen Kuenzli (Manning, 2019) and *Learn Docker in a Month of Lunches* by Elton Stoneman (Manning, 2020).

Containers are increasingly not deployed in isolation but in clusters that need to be very well orchestrated, and Kubernetes is probably the most popular container orchestrator nowadays. Several Manning titles will quickly bring you up to date on Kubernetes, such as *Kubernetes in Action, 2nd ed.* by Marko Lukša or *Kubernetes for Developers* by William Denniss (both available from Manning).

In this chapter, we won't go as far as using Kubernetes (which would require much explanation and is beyond our needs in this case). We will resort to a simpler (but less powerful) solution called Docker Compose. Docker Compose is an interesting solution for development environments that don't require all the power of a true container orchestrator.

Let's get started with an overview of the production deployment lifecycle.

12.1 Introducing production deployment of servers and apps

In this section, we will cover two introductory topics that will outline where production deployment fits in the software lifecycle and Docker's role as a container technology for deployment.

12.1.1 Software deployment cycle

The software deployment cycle involves multiple levels of developer unit and integration testing, followed by the preparation and deployment of the release. Once the release is deployed and running, the system is monitored, key parameters are measured, and optimization is performed.

While the specific steps in the production deployment lifecycle vary by team and DevOps technologies, figure 12.1 shows a representative set of steps that are typically performed.

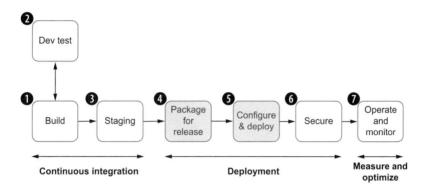

Figure 12.1 The production deployment lifecycle

The actual development steps and terminology used by various organizations differ widely, but let's look at these stages to gain an understanding in broad strokes:

1 *Build*—Software is written (or modified), and the binary is locally built by the developers. In most cases, this would be a development build (which facilitates debugging and takes less time to build), as opposed to a production build (which optimizes the binary size but typically takes longer to build in most programming languages).

2 *Dev test*—The developers perform unit tests in a local development environment.

3 *Staging*—The code is merged with the other branches that are planned as part of a software release, and it is deployed in a staging environment. Here, integration tests involving code and modules written by other developers are performed.

4 *Package for release*—After successful integration tests, the final production build is constructed. The method of packaging will depend on how the binary will be deployed (e.g., as a standalone binary or in a container or a public cloud service).

In this chapter, we will focus on how to create a Docker build for the Rust web service.

5 *Configure and deploy*—The production binary file is then deployed to the target environment (e.g., a virtual machine), and the necessary configuration and environmental parameters are set up. This is also the stage where any connection to additional components in the production infrastructure is performed. For example, the binary may be required to work with load balancers or reverse proxies.

In this chapter, we will use Docker Compose to streamline the process of configuring, automating builds, and starting and stopping the set of Docker containers needed to run the web service.

6 *Secure*—This is where that additional security requirements are configured, such as authentication (e.g., for user and API authentication), authorization (setting up user and group permissions), and network and server security (e.g., firewalls, encryption, secrets storage, TLS termination, certificates, CORS, IP port enabling, etc.).

7 *Operate and monitor*—This is where the server is started in order to receive network requests, and the performance of the server is monitored using network, server, application, and cloud-monitoring tools. Examples of such tools include Nagios, Prometheus, Kibana, and Grafana, to name a few.

In organizations where DevOps tools are deployed, *continuous integration, continuous delivery*, and *continuous deployment* practices and tools are used to automate many of these steps. There is a plethora of publicly available information if you want to explore these terms in more detail.

In this chapter, we will focus only on a subset of these topics and show you how to perform them in the context of the Rust programming language. We will specifically cover steps 4 and 5: the *package for release* and *configure and deploy* steps. For the latter, we will only focus on deploying the Docker containers on a Linux Ubuntu virtual machine (VM), but Docker containers can be deployed to any cloud provider (though there may be provider-specific steps needed for the deployment).

You will specifically learn the following:

- *Building the release binary and packaging*—You'll learn how to build the Rust server as a Docker image that can be deployed to any host with a container runtime. You'll learn how to write Dockerfiles, create Docker volumes and networks, configure environment variables, do multistep Docker builds, and reduce the size of final Docker images.
- *Configuring and deploying the web service*—You'll learn how to use Docker Compose to define the runtime configuration of the web service and Postgres database containers, define the dependencies between them, configure runtime environment variables, initiate Docker builds, and start and stop the Docker containers through simple commands.

Let's start with a brief introduction to Docker.

12.1.2 *Docker container basics*

Container technology has changed the way software is built, deployed, and managed, enabling DevOps automation by bridging the gap between development and IT operation teams. *Docker* is both the name of the company that played a major role in popularizing container technology and the name of the software product (www.docker .com).

Docker containers are completely isolated environments with their own processes, networking interfaces, and volume mounts. One important aspect of Docker containers is that they all ultimately share the same operating system kernel. Traditional VMs are an abstraction of physical hardware, turning one physical server into multiple "logical" servers. The hypervisor allows multiple VMs to run on a single machine, and each VM includes a full copy of the operating system. Containers, on the other hand, are an abstraction at the application layer that packages code and dependencies together. Multiple containers run on the same physical machine and share the OS kernel with other containers. (See the Docker site for more information: www.docker .com/resources/what-container/.)

Figure 12.2 shows a simple layered view of how Docker containers fit on the hardware infrastructure. Docker containers can contain any software application—a web service, a web application, a database, or a messaging system, to name a few. Docker containers are lightweight (compared to VMs), can start up and shut down very quickly, and are self-contained in terms of the software application and all associated dependencies, such as third-party crates and other libraries.

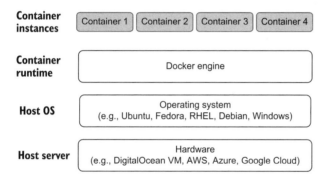

Figure 12.2   Docker overview

One interesting aspect of Docker containers is that although the Docker host might be running the Ubuntu operating system, the Docker container can encapsulate a web service process running on the Debian OS. This gives us tremendous flexibility during development and deployment.

How does this facilitate the handshake between software developers and the operations teams? In traditional software deployment, the development team hands over the software components and associated configuration (in our case, the web service code repo, build instructions, instructions on prerequisites to be set up, Postgres database scripts, environment files with secrets, etc.). The operations team then has to follow the instructions to build and deploy the web service in the production environment. Developers are likely to build and test code in an environment different from the production environment. The operations team, unfamiliar with the software, may run into issues that will require the presence of the development teams to resolve.

Docker containers solve this problem. Developers specify the infrastructure configuration and instructions to set up the environment, download and link the dependencies, and build the binary in a Dockerfile. The Dockerfile is a text file in YAML syntax. It allows you to specify parameters such as the base Docker image, environment variables to use, filesystem volumes to mount, ports to expose, and so on.

The Dockerfile is then built into a customized Docker image based on the rules specified in the Dockerfile. The Docker image is the template from which multiple container runtimes can be instantiated. (The relationship between a Docker *image* and a Docker *container* is similar to the relationship between a class and an object in object-oriented programming languages.).

The developers instantiate the Docker image into Docker containers and test their software application. They then hand over the Docker image to the software operations team for a production deployment. Given that the Docker image is guaranteed to run the same way in any Docker host, regardless of the hardware infrastructure, it is a lot easier for the operations teams to deploy and instantiate the software application in the production environment. Docker thus dramatically reduces the friction and human error in production deployments of software applications. However, one requirement for using Docker is that it requires skilled Docker engineers to configure the build rules for an application.

To follow along with the code in this chapter, you'll need to install the Docker development environment on your development machine or server (macOS, Windows, or Linux). See Docker's instructions here: https://docs.docker.com/get-docker/. More information about Docker can be found here: https://docs.docker .com/get-started/overview/.

In the next section, we will write our first Docker container, and we'll optimize its size.

12.2   *Writing the Docker container*

In this section, we will check the installation of Docker, write the Dockerfile and build it into a Docker image, and optimize the size of the final Docker image using a multi-stage build.

Let's start with checking the Docker installation.

12.2.1   *Checking the Docker installation*

You can create a project folder in your development server to follow along with the code in this section.

From the terminal, check your Docker installation with this command:

```
docker --version
```

You should get a response similar to the following on your terminal:

```
Docker version 20.10.16, build aa7e414
```

Let's test the official Docker image:

```
docker pull hello-world
```

You should see similar output to this:

```
Using default tag: latest
latest: Pulling from library/hello-world
2db29710123e: Pull complete
Digest: sha256:80f31da1ac7b312ba29d65080fddf797dd76acfb870e677f390d5
➡acba9741b17
Status: Downloaded newer image for hello-world:latest
docker.io/library/hello-world:latest
```

Now check if the Docker image is available on your local dev server:

```
docker images
```

You should see the following:

```
REPOSITORY       TAG        IMAGE ID        CREATED        SIZE
hello-world      latest     feb5d9fea6a5    8 months ago   13.3kB
```

You will see a `hello-world` Docker image available in your local dev server with a Docker image ID specified. Note also the size of the Docker image. We'll talk later in the chapter about optimizing the size of Docker images.

As mentioned earlier, a Docker image is a template for creating a Docker container instance. Let's instantiate the Docker image and see what happens:

```
docker run hello-world
```

If you see the following message, your Docker environment is good to go:

```
Hello from Docker!
This message shows that your installation appears to be working correctly.

To generate this message, Docker took the following steps:

1. The Docker client contacted the Docker daemon.
2. The Docker daemon pulled the "hello-world" image from the Docker Hub.
   (amd64)
3. The Docker daemon created a new container from that image which runs the
   executable that produces the output you are currently reading.
4. The Docker daemon streamed that output to the Docker client, which sent
   it to your terminal.

To try something more ambitious, you can run an Ubuntu container with:
 $ docker run -it ubuntu bash

Share images, automate workflows, and more with a free Docker ID:
 https://hub.docker.com/

For more examples and ideas, visit:
 https://docs.docker.com/get-started/
```

This official Docker image prints out the "Hello from Docker!" message. That's all it does.

Using a Docker image created by someone else is useful, but it is more interesting to create your own Docker image. Let's do that next.

12.2.2 Writing a simple Docker container

Start a new project with these commands:

```
cargo new --bin docker-rust
cd docker-rust
```

This docker-rust folder will be the project root folder. Add Actix Web to the Cargo.toml dependencies:

```
[dependencies]
actix-web = "4.2.1"
```

Add the following to src/main.rs:

```
use actix_web::{get, web, App, HttpResponse, HttpServer, Responder};

#[get("/")]
async fn gm() -> impl Responder {
    HttpResponse::Ok().body("Hello, Good morning!")
}

async fn hello() -> impl Responder {
    HttpResponse::Ok().body("Hello there!")
}

#[actix_web::main]
async fn main() -> std::io::Result<()> {
    HttpServer::new(|| {
        App::new()
            .service(gm)
            .route("/hello", web::get().to(hello))
    })
    .bind(("0.0.0.0", 8080))?
    .run()
    .await
}
```

Let's now build and run the server in the regular manner (without Docker):

```
cargo run
```

From the browser window, test the following:

```
localhost:8080
localhost:8080/hello
```

You should see the following messages (corresponding to the previous two GET requests) in the browser window:

```
Hello, Good morning!
Hello there!
```

Now that we've confirmed that the web service is working, let's *containerize* this web service with Docker. Figure 12.3 shows what we will be building.

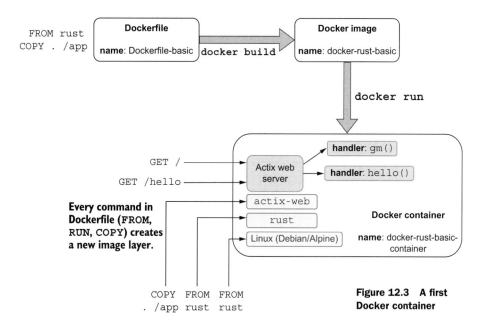

Figure 12.3   A first Docker container

Create a new Dockerfile-basic file in the project root, and add the following:

```
# Use the main rust Docker image
FROM rust

# copy app into docker image
COPY . /app

# Set the workdirectory
WORKDIR /app

# build the app
RUN cargo build --release

# start the application
CMD ["./target/release/docker-rust"]
```

Run the following command to build the Docker image:

```
docker build -f Dockerfile-basic . -t docker-rust-basic
```

You will see a series of messages ending with these:

```
=> => exporting layers                                                   0.8s
 => => writing image
➡sha256:
➡20fe6699b10e9945a1f0072607da46f726476f82b15f9fbe3102a68becb7e1a3   0.1s
 => => naming to docker.io/library/docker-rust-basic
```

To check the Docker image that has been built, run the following command:

```
docker images
```

You should see output on your terminal similar to this:

```
REPOSITORY            TAG        IMAGE ID       CREATED          SIZE
docker-rust-basic     latest     20fe6699b10e   9 seconds ago    1.32GB
```

You will notice that a Docker image with the name `docker-rust-basic` has been created with a specific Docker image ID. The Docker image has a size of 1.32 GB; this is because Docker images include all the layers along with all their dependencies. For example, in this case, the Rust Docker image contains the Rust compiler and all the intermediate build artifacts, which are not necessary to run the final application.

Getting a large Docker image size in the first iteration is normal, as our initial priority is to get the Docker image defined and constructed the right way. We'll look later at how to reduce the size of the Docker image.

Let's run the web server within this Docker container as follows:

```
docker run -p 8080:8080 -t docker-rust-basic
```

From the browser window, test the following:

```
localhost:8080
localhost:8080/hello
```

You should see the respective messages displayed in the browser window.

We have now tested the web service in two versions: the basic version with `cargo run` and the Dockerized version. But we're not done yet. The problem we still have is that the Docker image of the web service has a size of 1.32 GB. Not exactly small. Docker binaries are expected to have a small footprint, but the Dockerized version of this very simple (and trivial) Rust web service is large. Can we fix it? We'll look at that in the next section.

12.2.3 *Multistage Docker build*

In this section, let's try to reduce the size of the Docker image. Figure 12.4 shows what we will be doing in this section.

Create a new Dockerfile, Dockerfile-lite, in the project root, and add the following:

```
# Use the main rust Docker image
FROM rust as build

# copy app into Docker image
COPY . /app

# Set the workdirectory
WORKDIR /app

# build the app
RUN cargo build --release
```

```
# use google distroless as runtime image
FROM gcr.io/distroless/cc-debian11

# copy app from builder
COPY --from=build /app/target/release/docker-rust /app/docker-rust
WORKDIR /app

# start the application
CMD ["./docker-rust"]
```

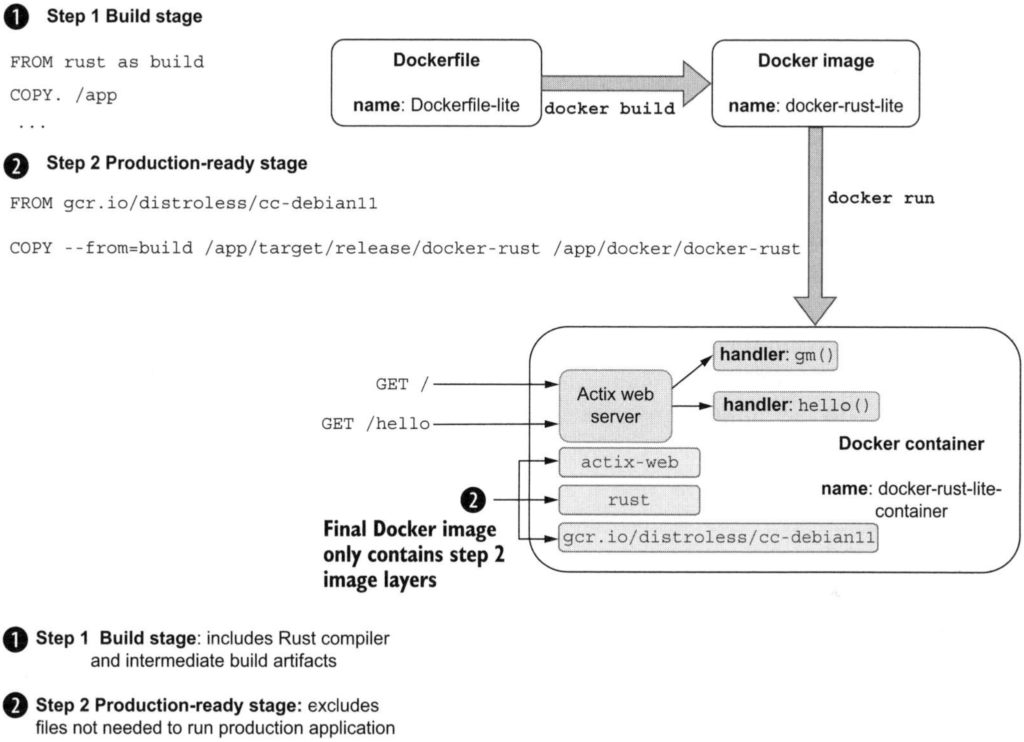

1 **Step 1 Build stage**

```
FROM rust as build
COPY. /app
...
```

2 **Step 2 Production-ready stage**

```
FROM gcr.io/distroless/cc-debian11

COPY --from=build /app/target/release/docker-rust /app/docker/docker-rust
```

Figure 12.4 A lite Docker container

Run the following command to build the Docker image:

```
docker build -f Dockerfile-lite . -t docker-rust-lite
```

To check the Docker image that has been built, run the following command:

```
docker images
```

You should see output on your terminal similar to this:

```
REPOSITORY          TAG       IMAGE ID        CREATED          SIZE
docker-rust-lite    latest    40103591baaf    12 seconds ago   31.8MB
```

You'll now notice that the size of the Docker image has been reduced to 31.8 MB. Before we analyze it, let's first confirm that this Docker image works. Run the Docker image with the following command:

```
docker run -p 8080:8080 -t docker-rust-lite
```

Check the running container:

```
docker ps
```

You should see the `docker-rust-lite` container shown in the list.

From the browser window, test the following:

```
localhost:8080
localhost:8080/hello
```

You should see the respective greeting messages displayed in the browser window.

So, how did this work? We used what is called a *multistage* build. A multistage Docker build is a series of steps that create a Docker image. The main benefit of a multistage build is that you can clean up after a development build and reduce the size of the final binary by removing extraneous files in the final Docker image. It lets developers automate the process of creating several versions of a binary, aimed at different target OS environments, and it also offers security and caching benefits.

A Docker multistage build uses several `FROM` statements to reference a specific image for a particular stage. Each stage can be named using the `AS` keyword. In the Dockerfile-lite example shown previously, we have two stages. The first stage builds a release binary. The second build stage uses `google distroless` as a runtime image and copies over the release binary previously created, which results in a smaller Docker image size.

Figure 12.5 shows an example of a Docker multistage build with a single Dockerfile defining two build steps. The first step creates a developer build Docker image that contains development-related artifacts. The second build step builds a production-ready Docker image, which achieves a smaller size by excluding unwanted files. You'll find more details on multistage Docker builds in the documentation: https://docs.docker.com/develop/develop-images/multistage-build/.

To summarize, the main difference between what's shown in figures 12.3 and 12.4 is that in the latter we built the Docker image in two steps, with the second (final) step excluding all the development tools and artifacts in the final Docker image.

Now that you understand how to build and optimize a basic Rust Actix program with Docker, let's shift our focus to the EzyTutors web service.

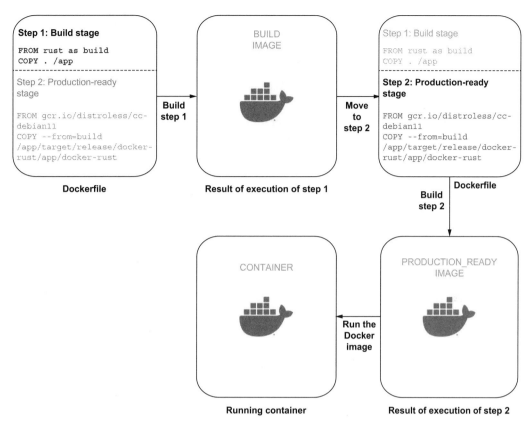

Figure 12.5   Multistage Docker builds

12.3   *Building the database container*

The EzyTutors web backend has two distinct components: the web service serving the APIs and the Postgres database. Figure 12.6 shows how we want to package the two components as Docker containers and then have mobile and web clients send requests.

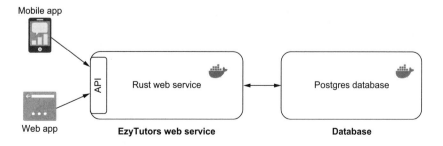

Figure 12.6   Multicontainer configuration

Let's first Dockerize the Postgres database. We'll package the EzyTutors web service as a container in the next section.

Is there any real benefit to packaging the database as a Docker container? Yes, because we want the database to be easily portable across machines and not be tied to a specific hardware environment. We also eventually want to be able to operate (start, stop, etc.) the database and web service together as one unit, and that is easier if the database is also packaged as a container.

Let's get started.

12.3.1 *Packaging the Postgres database*

First, clone the Git repo for the book. Navigate to chapter6/ezytutors/tutor-db—this is the project root folder for the web service.

Install Docker Compose on an Ubuntu server (or any other preferred configuration of virtual machine). You can refer to the Docker documentation here: https://docs.docker.com/compose/install/.

The command to verify your Docker Compose installation on Ubuntu is `docker compose version`. You should see output similar to this:

```
Docker Compose version v2.5.0
```

Create a new Docker network to interconnect the tutor web service and the Postgres database containers:

```
docker network create tutor-network
docker ls
```

You should see something similar to this:

```
6fc670fb70ba    bridge            bridge    local
75d560b02bbe    host              host      local
7d2c59b2f3a5    none              null      local
e230e1a9c55d    tutor-network     bridge    local
```

Docker volumes are the preferred way to persist data generated by and used by Docker containers. They are completely managed by Docker, they are easy to back up, and you can use volume drivers to store data on remote hosts or cloud providers. A volume's contents exist outside the lifecycle of a Docker container. More details can be found here in the Docker documentation: https://docs.docker.com/storage/volumes/.

Let's create a Docker volume as follows:

```
docker volume create tutor-data
docker volume ls
```

You should see output like this:

```
DRIVER     VOLUME NAME
local      tutor-data
```

Stop the Postgresql database instance, if it's running, on the Docker host:

```
systemctl status postgresql
systemctl stop postgresql
```

Create a new Docker Compose file with the name docker-compose.yml. Add the following code:

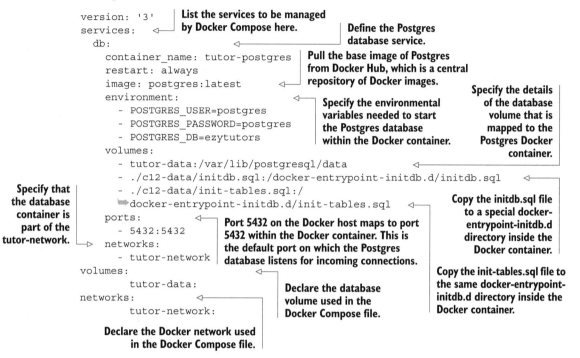

In the preceding code, the `services:` keyword represents a separate Docker container. In this case, we're telling Docker Compose that `db` is the name of the service and that a separate Docker container should be spun up for the `db` service.

Under the `volumes:` keyword, the `tutor-data` volume on the Docker host is mapped to /var/lib/postgresql/data (the default database folder of Postgres) within the Docker container. The initdb.sql file contains the database scripts to create the database and users, along with the grant permissions. The init-tables.sql file contains the database scripts to create the database tables and load initial test data.

Now build and run the Postgres Docker image:

```
docker compose up -d
docker ps
```

You should see output similar to this:

```
CONTAINER ID    IMAGE             COMMAND               CREATED            |
d43b6ae99846    postgres:latest   "docker-entrypoint.s…"   4 seconds ago      |
```

```
|  STATUS          PORTS                                      NAMES
|  Up 1 second     0.0.0.0:5432->5432/tcp,  :::5432->5432/tcp   tutor-postgres
```

The `tutor-postgres` Docker container has been instantiated from the `postgres`
`:latest` Docker image. Let's check if the database and tables have been created and if
the test data has been loaded. To do so, connect to the Docker container:

```
                                              ┌── Connect to the Docker
                                              │   container shell.
docker exec -it d43b6ae99846 /bin/bash  ◁────┘
psql postgres://postgres:postgres@localhost:5432/ezytutors            ◁──────────┐
\list   ◁──┐ Once in the psql shell,                                             │
           │ list all the databases.              Log in to the psql shell within │
                                                  the Postgres Docker container.  │
```

You should see terminal output similar to this:

```
psql (12.11 (Ubuntu 12.11-0ubuntu0.20.04.1), server 14.3 (Debian 14.3-
    1.pgdg110+1))
WARNING: psql major version 12, server major version 14.
        Some psql features might not work.
Type "help" for help.

ezytutors=# \list
                          List of databases
    Name   |  Owner  | Encoding|  Collate   |  Ctype   |  Access privileges
---------+---------+---------+-----------+-----------+--------------------
ezytutors| postgres| UTF8    | en_US.utf8| en_US.utf8|
postgres | postgres| UTF8    | en_US.utf8| en_US.utf8|
template0| postgres| UTF8    | en_US.utf8| en_US.utf8| =c/postgres         +
         |         |         |           |           | postgres=CTc/postgres
template1| postgres| UTF8    | en_US.utf8| en_US.utf8| =c/postgres         +
         |         |         |           |           | postgres=CTc/postgres
(4 rows)
```

You should see the `ezytutors` database listed. This is because we placed the initdb.sql
file within the Docker container in the /docker-entrypoint-initdb.d folder. Any script
placed within this folder should automatically be executed when the container starts.

Enter \q and exit the psql shell, followed by `exit` in the Docker bash shell to exit
the Docker container.

There is another way to access the database, which is to connect to the Docker container and execute psql from within it:

```
docker ps
docker exec -it 0027d5c1cfaf /bin/bash
psql -U postgres
\list
```

You should see output like this:

```
bash-5.1# psql -U postgres
psql (11.16)
Type "help" for help.
```

```
postgres=# \list
                              List of databases
    Name   |  Owner  | Encoding|  Collate   |   Ctype    |  Access privileges
 ---------+---------+---------+-----------+-----------+----------------------
 ezytutors| postgres| UTF8    | en_US.utf8| en_US.utf8| =Tc/postgres          +
          |         |         |           |           | postgres=CTc/postgres+
          |         |         |           |           | truuser=CTc/postgres
 postgres | postgres| UTF8    | en_US.utf8| en_US.utf8|
 template0| postgres| UTF8    | en_US.utf8| en_US.utf8| =c/postgres           +
          |         |         |           |           | postgres=CTc/postgres
 template1| postgres| UTF8    | en_US.utf8| en_US.utf8| =c/postgres           +
          |         |         |           |           | postgres=CTc/postgres
 (4 rows)
```

Both of these approaches are acceptable ways to access the Postgres database within the `tutor-postgres` container. As you can see, the `ezytutors` database has been created.

Let's check if the user `truuser` has been created and ensure privileges have been assigned to the user. From within the Docker container, execute the following command at the command prompt:

```
psql -U truuser ezytutors
 ezytutors=>\list
```

If you are able to see the `ezytutors` database listed, it's good. Otherwise, execute the following steps within the psql shell:

```
postgres=# drop database ezytutors
postgres=# \list
```

You should see output similar to this:

```
postgres=# drop database ezytutors;
DROP DATABASE
postgres=# \list
                              List of databases
    Name   |  Owner  | Encoding|  Collate   |   Ctype    |  Access privileges
 ---------+---------+---------+-----------+-----------+----------------------
 postgres | postgres| UTF8    | en_US.utf8| en_US.utf8|
 template0| postgres| UTF8    | en_US.utf8| en_US.utf8| =c/postgres           +
          |         |         |           |           | postgres=CTc/postgres
 template1| postgres| UTF8    | en_US.utf8| en_US.utf8| =c/postgres           +
          |         |         |           |           | postgres=CTc/postgres
 (3 rows)
```

We have deleted the `ezytutors` database because we want to execute the initdb.sql script in its entirety once again.

Now let's run the two initialization scripts that we stored within the Postgres Docker container under docker-entrypoint-initdb.d. Go back to the Docker container bash shell (not the psql shell), and execute the following commands:

```
postgres=#  \i /docker-entrypoint-initdb.d/initdb.sql
```

You should see output like this in your terminal:

```
postgres=# \i /docker-entrypoint-initdb.d/initdb.sql
CREATE DATABASE
CREATE ROLE
GRANT
ALTER ROLE
ALTER ROLE
```

The initdb.sql script creates the database, creates a new `truuser` user, and grants all permissions to this new user on the `ezytutors` database.

Now quit the psql shell with \q, and log back in from the Docker container bash shell with the `truuser` ID:

```
psql -U truuser ezytutors
 ezytutors=>\list
```

You should see the following on your terminal:

```
ezytutors=> \list
                             List of databases
   Name    |  Owner   |Encoding| Collate   |  Ctype    |Access privileges
-----------+----------+--------+-----------+-----------+------------------
 ezytutors |postgres  |UTF8    |en_US.utf8 |en_US.utf8 |=Tc/postgres     +
           |          |        |           |           |postgres=CTc/postgres+
           |          |        |           |           |truuser=CTc/postgres
 postgres  |postgres  |UTF8    |en_US.utf8 |en_US.utf8 |
 template0 |postgres  |UTF8    |en_US.utf8 |en_US.utf8 |=c/postgres      +
           |          |        |           |           |postgres=CTc/postgres
 template1 |postgres  |UTF8    |en_US.utf8 |en_US.utf8 |=c/postgres      +
           |          |        |           |           |postgres=CTc/postgres
(4 rows)
```

The `ezytutors` database can now be accessed by `truuser`. In the next section, we'll look at how to create database tables within the Docker container.

12.3.2 Creating database tables

From the command prompt of the Postgres Docker container, check if the database tables have been created:

```
ezytutors=> \d
Did not find any relations.
```

If you see the list of tables, it's all good. But if you see the preceding error message, "Did not find any relations," then you'll need to manually run the script to create the tables and load the test data.

Let's create the tutor- and course-related tables in the `ezytutors` database and then list the database tables (called *relations* in Postgres terms). We'll do this by executing the init-tables.sql script. You should see this:

```
ezytutors=> \i /docker-entrypoint-initdb.d/init-tables.sql
psql:/docker-entrypoint-initdb.d/init-tables.sql:4: NOTICE:
```

```
↳table "ezy_course_c6" does not exist, skipping
DROP TABLE
psql:/docker-entrypoint-initdb.d/init-tables.sql:5: NOTICE:
↳table "ezy_tutor_c6" does not exist, skipping
DROP TABLE
CREATE TABLE
CREATE TABLE
GRANT
GRANT
INSERT 0 1
INSERT 0 1
INSERT 0 1
INSERT 0 1
ezytutors=> \d
                     List of relations
  Schema  |              Name               |   Type   |  Owner
----------+---------------------------------+----------+----------
 public | ezy_course_c6                  | table    | truuser
 public | ezy_course_c6_course_id_seq    | sequence | truuser
 public | ezy_tutor_c6                   | table    | truuser
 public | ezy_tutor_c6_tutor_id_seq      | sequence | truuser
(4 rows)
```

The tables have been created. Let's also check if the initial test data has been loaded into the tutor and course tables:

```
ezytutors=> select tutor_id, tutor_name, tutor_pic_url from ezy_tutor_c6;

 tutor_id | tutor_name |         tutor_pic_url
----------+------------+----------------------------
        1 | Merlene    | http://s3.amazon.aws.com/pic1
        2 | Frank      | http://s3.amazon.aws.com/pic2
(2 rows)

ezytutors=> select course_id, tutor_id, course_name, course_format,
course_level, from ezy_course_c6;

 course_id | tutor_id |  course_name  |   course_format    | course_level
-----------+----------+---------------+--------------------+----------+
         1 |        1 | First course  |                    | Beginner
         2 |        2 | Second course | ebook              |
(2 rows)
```

All good so far. It is now time to conduct a test. What happens when we stop the container? Will the data persist between container restarts? To check this, let's add a new record to the tutor table, shut down the container, and restart it to check if the data has persisted:

```
ezytutors=> insert into ezy_tutor_c6 values(
↳3,'Johnny','http://s3.amazon.aws.com/pic2',
↳'Johnny is an expert marriage counselor');
 ezytutors=> \q
 exit
 root@1dfd3bd87e2c:/# exit
```

Exit the psql shell with q, and then issue the exit command on the bash shell of the Docker Postgres container. This should take you to your project home folder.

Now shut down the Docker container:

```
docker compose down
docker ps
```

Your Postgres container should no longer be running. Now restart the container, and get into the running container shell:

```
docker compose up -d
docker ps
docker exec -it 7e7c11273911 /bin/bash
```

Then, in the container, log in to the database with the psql client, and check that the tutor table has the additional entry that you added previously:

```
root@7e7c11273911:/# psql -U truuser ezytutors
psql (14.3 (Debian 14.3-1.pgdg110+1))
Type "help" for help.

ezytutors=> \d
                    List of relations
  Schema |             Name             |   Type   |  Owner
 --------+------------------------------+----------+---------
  public | ezy_course_c6                | table    | truuser
  public | ezy_course_c6_course_id_seq  | sequence | truuser
  public | ezy_tutor_c6                 | table    | truuser
  public | ezy_tutor_c6_tutor_id_seq    | sequence | truuser
 (4 rows)

ezytutors=> select * from ezy_tutor_c6;
  tutor_id | tutor_name |         tutor_pic_url          |   tutor_profile
 ----------+------------+--------------------------------+-------------------
         1 | Merlene    | http://s3.amazon.aws.com/pic1  | Merlene is an ..
         2 | Frank      | http://s3.amazon.aws.com/pic2  | Frank is an ..
         3 | Johnny     | http://s3.amazon.aws.com/pic2  | Johnny is an ..
 (3 rows)
```

The data has indeed been persisted.

We have now completed the task of creating a Postgres database container, initializing the database, and loading test data. This concludes the setup of the Docker Postgres container.

We can now move on to Dockerizing the tutor web service.

12.4 *Packaging the web service with Docker*

In the previous section, we packaged the EzyTutors Postgres database as a Docker container. In this section, let's turn our attention to packaging the tutor web service as a Docker container.

We will first create a Dockerfile because we want to create a custom Docker image for the tutor web service (as opposed to using the standard Postgres image in the previous section). The custom Dockerfile is required for two reasons:

- There is no standard Docker image available in Docker Hub for our tutor web service. This is our custom code, and we need to give instructions in the Dockerfile to package it as a container.

- We want to specify instructions to create a static self-contained binary, without the use of shared libraries. By default, the Rust standard library dynamically links to the system libc implementation. Since we want a 100% static binary for the web service, we will use musl libc on the Linux distribution we use within the web service Docker container.

Why use Rust with musl?

By default, Rust statically links all Rust code. But if you use the standard library (which we do in this book), it will dynamically link to the system libc implementation. Unfortunately, operating system differences can cause Rust binaries to break when run in a different environment compared to what they were compiled in. For example, if the binary was built using a newer version of Glibc compared to the target system (where the Rust program is deployed and run), it will fail to run. One way to avoid this problem is to statically compile musl into the binaries.

musl is a lightweight replacement for Glibc used in Alpine Linux. When musl is statically compiled into your Rust program, you can create a self-contained executable that will run without dependencies on Glibc. This is the approach we will use in this book to package Rust in Docker containers. (See William Saar's "Shipping Linux binaries that don't break with Rust" article for more information: http://mng.bz/44ra.)

Let's first create the Dockerfile for the tutor web service. Create a Dockerfile named Dockerfile-tutor-webservice, and add the following:

```
# Use the main rust docker image        Pull the official rust Docker
FROM rust as build                ◁──   image from Docker Hub.
RUN apt-get update && apt-get -y upgrade              Install the prerequisites
RUN apt-get install libssl-dev                        to build a static binary
RUN apt-get -y install pkg-config musl musl-dev musl-tools   using musl libc.
RUN rustup target add x86_64-unknown-linux-musl   ◁──┐  Set the Rust binary
                                                      │  build target.
# copy app into Docker image    Copy the ezytutors project
COPY . /app                ◁──  folder to the Docker container.
                           Set the working directory within the Docker
# Set the workdirectory    container. Subsequent commands are
WORKDIR /app          ◁──  executed by Docker from this directory.       Make the release
                                                                      build of the EzyTutors
# build the app                                                             web service.
RUN cargo build --target x86_64-unknown-linux-musl --release --bin iter5  ◁──┘

CMD ["./target/x86_64-unknown-linux-musl/release/iter5"]            ◁──────┐

                               Run the binary. This will start up the Actix web
                               server and listen for incoming HTTP requests.
```

We have created the Dockerfile. We can run the `Docker build` command directly on this Dockerfile. But we will do it in a different way. You'll see how in the next section.

12.5   *Orchestrating Docker containers with Docker Compose*

In this section, we will use Docker Compose to create a multicontainer configuration
for the EzyTutors application.

> ### Why use Docker Compose?
>
> Docker Compose is a client-side tool that lets you run an application stack with multiple containers. Docker has made it easy to create local development environments for individual services, but when there are multiple Docker containers to manage for an application (as we have in our EzyTutors example), it becomes cumbersome. Docker Compose solves this problem by specifying the configuration of one or more Docker containers within a single YAML configuration file.
>
> Using Docker Compose, you can specify the build instructions, storage configuration, environment variables, and network parameters for each Docker container that is part of your application. Once those are defined, Docker Compose allows you to build, start, and stop all the containers using a single set of commands.

Let's add the tutor web service as a service within the Docker Compose file that we created in the previous section for the Postgres database container. In this way, we will have a single Docker Compose file that has details for both the Docker containers needed to build and run the tutor web service. Also, we can specify the dependencies between the two containers and connect them through a common Docker network. And we can specify the Docker volume to which Postgres data should be persisted between Docker container runs.

Figure 12.7 illustrates the key elements of the final Docker Compose file for our application.

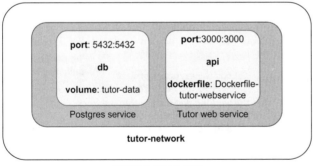

docker-compose.yml

Figure 12.7   Docker Compose configuration

In docker-compose.yml, add `tutor-webservice` as a service. The complete docker-compose.yml file should look like this:

```
version: '3'
services:
```

```
db:                              ◁──────   Specifies the Postgres database
  container_name: tutor-postgres           as a service (this was defined in
  restart: always                          the previous section).
  image: postgres:latest
  environment:
   - POSTGRES_USER=postgres
   - POSTGRES_PASSWORD=postgres
   - POSTGRES_DB=ezytutors
  volumes:
   - tutor-data:/var/lib/postgresql/data
   - ./c12-data/initdb.sql:/docker-entrypoint-initdb.d/initdb.sql
   - ./c12-data/init-tables.sql:/docker-entrypoint-initdb.d/init-tables.sql
  ports:
   - 5432:5432
  networks:                    A new service, api, is
   - tutor-network             defined to refer to the
 api:                   ◁──┘   tutor web service.      Instructions to build the api service
  restart: on-failure                                  are defined, including the name of the
  container_name: tutor-webservice                     Dockerfile to build the Docker image.
  build:
    context: ./            ◁──
    dockerfile: Dockerfile-tutor-webservice            Environment variables will be passed
    network: host                                      from the Docker host shell environment
  environment:                        ◁──              into the Docker Compose file when
   - DATABASE_URL=${DATABASE_URL}                      building and running the api service.
   - HOST_PORT=${HOST_PORT}
  depends_on:            The Postgres database is defined as a
   - db          ◁────   dependency for the tutor web service.
  ports:
   - ":3000:3000"          ◁──                         Port 3000 on the Docker
  networks:                                            host is mapped to port 3000
   - tutor-network   ◁──┐  The api service (Docker     on the Docker container.
volumes:                 │  container) is specified to be
      tutor-data:        │  a part of the tutor-network.
networks:
      tutor-network:
```

We can now start the Postgres database container:

```
docker compose up db -d
```

This will start the database container alone as a background process. Before we build and run the tutor web service container, let's first check the environment variable settings:

```
cat .env
```

You should see this:

```
DATABASE_URL=postgres://truuser:trupwd@localhost:5432/ezytutors
HOST_PORT=0.0.0.0:3000
```

Next, set the DATABASE_URL environment variable in the current terminal shell:

```
source .env
echo $DATABASE_URL
```

You should see the value of DATABASE_URL correctly set as the environment variable. This step is important because sqlx does compile-time checking of the database while building the tutor web service:

```
postgres://truuser:trupwd@localhost:5432/ezytutors
```

Let's double-check that the Postgres URL is accessible from the Docker host shell (to avoid unwanted delays in the compilation process):

```
psql postgres://truuser:trupwd@localhost:5432/ezytutors
\q
```

If this takes you to the Postgres shell, you are ready to build the tutor web service container, as follows:

```
docker compose build api
```

It will take a while, depending on the configuration of your machine. So go grab a coffee (or another drink of your choice).

Once the process is complete, check the built image with this command:

```
docker images
```

You should see this:

```
REPOSITORY      TAG       IMAGE ID        CREATED         SIZE
tutor-db_api    latest    23bee1bda139    52 seconds ago  2.87GB
postgres        latest    5b21e2e86aab    7 days ago      376MB
```

Now that you have built the web service container, you can start it up. But before that, you will have to shut down the running Postgres container because the Docker Compose file will start both the api (web service container) and db (Postgres container) services together.

Get the Docker image ID, and remove the running Postgres container:

```
docker ps
docker stop <image id>
docker rm <image id>
```

Before you start the containers, there is one more step to be done. Recall that the tutor web service uses the DATABASE_URL environment variable to connect to the Postgres database. While building the web service container, we set the following value to DATABASE_URL:

```
DATABASE_URL=postgres://truuser:trupwd@localhost:5432/ezytutors
```

Note that the value after the @ symbol represents the host on which the Postgres database runs. During the build phase, we set it to localhost, but for the tutor webservice container (named api in the Docker Compose file), localhost refers to itself. So how did it connect to the Postgres container at build time? The answer is that we made a small hack at build time. If you look back at the Docker Compose file for building the tutor web service, you will notice the network parameter is set to host:

```
api:
    restart: on-failure
    container_name: tutor-webservice
    build:
      context: ./
      dockerfile: Dockerfile-tutor-webservice
    network: host
```

This parameter enabled the build process of the tutor web service container to proceed by connecting to the localhost port of the Docker host from which the Docker container build happened. This is not suitable for a production environment, and it's why we have created a separate Docker network called tutor-network and specified that both containers are to be connected to this network. You can verify that now:

```
docker network ls
docker inspect tutor-network
```

If you do not see any reference to the tutor web service or Postgres containers, add them manually as follows:

```
docker network connect tutor-network tutor-webservice
docker network connect tutor-network tutor-postgres
docker inspect tutor-network
```

You should see output like this:

```
"Containers": {
  "26a5fc9ac00d815cb933bf66755d1fd04f6dca1efe1ffbc96f28da50e65238ba": {
    "Name": "tutor-postgres",
    "EndpointID":
    ➡ "e870c365731463198fbdf46ea4a7d22b3f9f497727b410852b86fe1567c8a3e6",
    "MacAddress": "02:42:ac:1b:00:03",
    "IPv4Address": "172.27.0.3/16",
    "IPv6Address": ""
  },
  "af6e823821b36d13bf1b381b2b427efc6f5048386b4132925ebd1ea3ecfa5eaa": {
    "Name": "tutor-webservice",
    "EndpointID":
    ➡ "015e1dbc36ae8e454dc4377ad9168b6a01cae978eac4e0ec8e14be98d08b4f1c",
    "MacAddress": "02:42:ac:1b:00:02",
    "IPv4Address": "172.27.0.2/16",
    "IPv6Address": ""
  }
},
```

The two containers, tutor-postgres and tutor-webservice, have been added to the tutor-network.

Within a network, the containers can access each other by their container names. So, the tutor-webservice can access the Postgres container using the name tutor-postgres. Let's now modify the database URL as follows in the .env file:

```
DATABASE_URL=postgres://truuser:trupwd@tutor-postgres:5432/ezytutors
```

Note that the host value is now set to `tutor-postgres` instead of `localhost`. Let's set the environment variable in the shell and restart the containers.

```
source .env
echo $DATABASE_URL
echo $HOST_PORT                    Shut down the two
docker compose down       ⊲───┘   Docker containers.          Restart the two
docker compose up -d                              ⊲───────┘   Docker containers.
docker network connect tutor-network tutor-webservice
docker network connect tutor-network tutor-postgres           Since the containers have
docker inspect tutor-network    ⊲─────────────┐               been restarted, they have
                                                              to be added again to the
          Inspect the tutor-network, and                     tutor-network.
          verify that the two containers
           are a part of the network.
```

Now, from your server terminal (not inside Docker), run the following command to check the web service endpoint:

```
curl localhost:3000/tutors/
```

You should see the following result:

```
[{"tutor_id":1,"tutor_name":"Merlene",
"tutor_pic_url":"http://s3.amazon.aws.com/pic1",
"tutor_profile":"Merlene is an experienced finance professional"},
{"tutor_id":2,
"tutor_name":"Frank",
"tutor_pic_url":"http://s3.amazon.aws.com/pic2",
"tutor_profile":"Frank is an expert nuclear engineer"},
{"tutor_id":3,
"tutor_name":"Johnny",
"tutor_pic_url":"http://s3.amazon.aws.com/pic2",
"tutor_profile":"Johnny is an expert marriage counselor"}]
```

Note that the entry you added to the list of tutors is also shown, confirming that the database changes are persisted to the local volume across container restarts. You can also run tests on the other endpoints as an exercise.

Congrats if you have come this far. You have successfully Dockerized the tutor web service and the Postgres database. You have also made the task greatly simpler by using Docker Compose to build, start, and stop all the containers together with simple commands.

With this, we have come to the end of this chapter, and also of this book. This book was designed to get you started on your journey to writing web services and applications in Rust, but this is where I get off. You can now explore and enjoy the world of Rust web development on your own. I wish you the best in your continued exploration of Rust servers, services, and app development.

Suggested exercises

If you are looking for additional code challenges, here are a few:

- Docker `build` commands can take a long time to create a Docker image. Explore the use of cargo-chef (https://github.com/LukeMathWalker/cargo -chef) to speed up container builds.
- Add middleware to the Actix web server to add additional functionality such as CORS, JWT authentication of API endpoints, and logging levels. For more details, see the Actix documentation's discussion of middleware: https:// actix.rs/docs/middleware/.
- The size of the tutor web service's container image in the previous section is large—2.87 GB. As an exercise, enhance the `Dockerfile-tutor -webservice` Dockerfile to include a multistage build and reduce the size of the Docker image. More details on multistage builds can be found here in the Docker documentation: https://docs.docker.com/develop/develop-images/ multistage-build/.

Summary

- Rust web services, applications, and databases can be packaged into Docker containers. Docker is a popular way to build and run lightweight containers that removes friction between the software developers and operations teams.
- Docker files contain the instructions to build the Docker image. From the image, containers can be instantiated and can then service requests. For containerizing Rust programs, building static Rust binaries with musl helps avoid issues with libc versions on different target environments.
- Multistage Docker builds can be used to reduce the size of final Docker images. In the case of Rust, the first stage involves installing the Rust development environment and associated dependencies to build the static Rust binary. The second stage involves removing the Rust compiler and intermediate build artifacts by creating a new base image and copying only the final (self-contained) Rust static binary.
- Docker containers can be grouped together using Docker Compose, a tool to build, run, and manage the life cycle of a set of Docker containers.
- Docker containers can be interconnected using a custom Docker network.
- Docker volumes can be used to persist data to disk between Docker container runs.
- Docker Compose greatly simplifies the life cycle management of a group of containers.
- Dockerfiles and Docker Compose files for a project can be used to deploy an application or service on various virtual infrastructure and cloud providers.

appendix
Postgres installation

You can choose to install Postgres in one of the following ways:

- Install locally on a macOS, Windows, or Linux/Unix development environment.
- Run a Postgres database in a Docker container.
- Connect to a hosted and managed Postgres database on the cloud, such as AWS, Azure, Google Cloud, Heroku, or DigitalOcean.

The instructions for installing Postgres on a Linux Ubuntu server are given in this appendix. For other configurations, there are good sources of information available publicly.

Refresh the local package index:

```
sudo apt update
```

Install the `postgres` package along with a `contrib` package that has additional utilities:

```
sudo apt install postgresql postgresql-contrib
```

The Postgres software is now installed. The installation also automatically starts the postgresql server as a systemd process in Linux. To verify this, type the following:

```
ps aux | grep postgres
```

You should see the Postgres processes running in the background.

Let's now interact with the Postgres database management system. By default, Postgres uses the concept of a *role* (which is similar to a *user* in Linux/Unix) to handle authentication and authorization. The installation process creates a user account called `postgres`. Log into the account as follows:

```
sudo -i -u postgres
```

You should now see the shell corresponding to the `postgres` user. From here, you can access the Postgres shell prompt, which allows you to interact with the Postgres database management system to perform tasks such as creating a database, creating users, etc. Simply type the following:

```
psql
```

This will log you into a psql prompt. You can exit from the prompt at any time using this command:

```
\q
```

Now exit the Postgres user prompt:

```
exit
```

Next, we need to make a change to the Postgres configuration to allow peer authentication. Look for the pg_hba.conf file under /etc/postgres. For example, in a Postgres version 12 installation, this file can be found at /etc/postgresql/12/main/pg_hba .conf.

Open the file in a text editor, such as vim or nano, and look for the following entry:

```
# "local" is for Unix domain socket connections only
local   all             all                                     peer
```

Replace `peer` with `md5` as follows:

```
local   all             all                                     md5
```

Save the file, and restart the Postgres server as follows:

```
sudo systemctl restart postgresql
```

This configuration change allows you to log in to a Postgres database with a password once you are logged in to the server.

The following steps also need to be performed:

1 Create a database.
2 Create a user and associate a password.
3 Assign privileges for the user to the database.

Once these steps have been completed, you will be able to log in to the Postgres database from the command line using this command:

```
psql -U <database-user> -d <database-name> --password
```

The `database-user` and `database-name` will need to be replaced with your own. The `--password` flag will prompt you for a password.

For more details, refer to the official Postgres documentation at www.postgresql .org/docs/.

index